CRISIS OF CATHOLIC AUTHORITY

Faith and Power in the Diocese of Lincoln, Nebraska

CRISIS OF CATHOLIC AUTHORITY

Faith and Power in the Diocese of Lincoln, Nebraska

Rachel Pokora

Paragon House

First Edition 2013

Published in the United States by

Paragon House
1925 Oakcrest Ave, Suite 7
St. Paul, MN 55113
www.ParagonHouse.com

Library of Congress Cataloging-in-Publication Data

Pokora, Rachel M., 1968-
  Crisis of Catholic authority : faith and power in the Diocese of Lincoln, Nebraska / by Rachel M. Pokora. -- First Edition.
      pages cm
  Summary: "The story of the struggle and excommunication of members of Catholics for Active Liturgical Life (CALL) and Call To Action Nebraska (CTAN) when they sought reform in the Lincoln Diocese and to engage in social action moved by their faith as they confronted the Roman Catholic authorities and organizational structure"--Provided by publisher.
  Includes bibliographical references and index.
  ISBN 978-1-55778-906-8 (pbk.)
  1. Authority--Religious aspects--Catholic Church--History. 2. Church--Authority. 3. Excommunication--Catholic Church. 4. Catholic Church--Discipline. 5. Church renewal--Catholic Church--History--21st century. 6. Catholic Church. Diocese of Lincoln (Neb.)--History--21st century. I. Title.
  BX1746.P55 2013
  282'.7822--dc23
                        2013019171

The paper used in this publication meets the minimum requirements of American National Standard for Information Sciences— Permanence of Paper for Printed Library Materials, ANSIZ39.48-1984.

Manufactured in the United States of America
10 9 8 7 6 5 4 3 2 1

For current information about all releases from Paragon House, visit the website at http://www.ParagonHouse.com

For my parents, Dan and Marie Pokora

Contents

Acknowledgements   *viii*

Chapter 1
A Matter of Voice   1

Chapter 2
Early Organized Reform Efforts: Catholics for Active Liturgical Life   23

Chapter 3
Working Within Church Structure: CALL   59

Chapter 4
CALL Disbands   93

Chapter 5
The Founding of Call To Action Nebraska   113

Chapter 6
Reaction to the Extra-Synodal Legislation   137

Chapter 7
Appeal   183

Chapter 8
The Exercise of Power   237

Chapter 9
Power and Authority in Church Structure   265

Selected Bibliography   *293*

Index   *295*

Acknowledgements

Thank you to the members of Catholics for Active Liturgical Life and Call To Action Nebraska who generously shared their thoughts, experiences, and archival materials with me. I hope this work honors their many years of faith, hope, and love.

I am grateful for the support I received from Nebraska Wesleyan University in the form of sabbatical leave as well as grants to pay for equipment and transcription. NWU colleagues, Lindsey Brownfield and Theresa Lassek, offered technical support.

My department colleagues at Nebraska Wesleyan far exceed what a reasonable person could hope for. Rachel Droogsma, Karla Jensen, Patty Hawk, and David Whitt, I treasure what we are creating together.

Several people read this manuscript and offered essential feedback and advice: Marie Pokora (who carefully poured over every word not once, but twice), Kevin Bower, Joan Johnson, Betty Peterson, Dan Pokora, and Lloyd Vermaat.

I have been blessed with wonderful friends and colleagues who have offered support throughout this endeavor, each in his/her own way. Some of these include: Dan Daley, Rod Diercks, Sara Jane Dietzman, Christine Drewel, Alice Jaswal, Travis Jensen, Jerry Johnson, Joan Johnson, Rebecca Johnson, Elaine Kruse, Sandra Mathews, Robert McClory, Paula Rossi, and Nicole Sotelo.

Mary and Patty Hawk, professional colleagues, fellow Call To Action members, and dear friends have offered insight and support from the beginning to the end of this project.

My family cheered me on through two international sabbaticals and supported me on the journey of writing. In particular I am grateful to Valerie, Jim, Colin and Dylan McCloskey, Shirley and Ted Host, Denise Host, Joe and Diane Pokora, and Robbie and Gerry Gedris.

Kevin Bower listened, supported, advised, and made me laugh. A lot.

Thank you to my parents, Dan and Marie Pokora, my first and best teachers. My life is built on their words and example.

CHAPTER 1

A Matter of Voice

Over the pope as the expression of the binding claim of ecclesiastical authority, there still stands one's own conscience, which must be obeyed above all else, if necessary even against the requirement of ecclesiastical authority.[1]—Cardinal Joseph Ratzinger/Pope Benedict XVI, 1968

WHEN I MOVED TO LINCOLN, Nebraska in August 1996, I began to have a recurring dream. In my dream I was somewhere in Italy trying to get to the Vatican. Something always prevented me from reaching my destination. I didn't need an expert to explain this dream to me; the meaning was clear. I had just moved to the most conservative Roman Catholic diocese in the United States and after living twenty-eight years as a committed and highly involved Catholic, I found myself confronted with a church I did not recognize. The Lincoln diocese bore a resemblance to the church I knew, but its heart and spirit were unfamiliar to me. I missed my church.

I interviewed for a job in Lincoln at Nebraska Wesleyan University in the spring of 1996 shortly after the then-Bishop of Lincoln, Fabian Bruskewitz, issued extra-synodal legislation that excommunicated members of twelve different organizations, an extraordinarily unusual action. The media covered the legislation widely, so I had learned of it where I was living in Lafayette, Indiana. Two of the organizations targeted by Bishop Bruskewitz were Call To Action (CTA-USA) and Call To Action

Nebraska (CTAN). Bishop Bruskewitz promulgated this legislation shortly after receiving a letter from the founding co-presidents of CTAN informing him that a group of Nebraska Catholics was forming a chapter. Though not then a member of this organization, I supported the Call To Action platform of social justice, increased role for women in the church, married priesthood, meaningful involvement of lay people, and dialogue.

The reputation of the Lincoln diocese gave me pause but I happily accepted a job at a university that was an excellent fit for me. I knew that the climate in the Lincoln diocese would be different from any I had experienced before. I was even warned by one priest, "You have no idea what it's like." Yet I held on to hope that I would find a parish that would nurture and respect me and happily make use of my gifts.

I was naïve.

Before I moved to Lincoln, I had worshipped with people from across the Catholic ideological spectrum. We had served side-by-side in ministries united by our love for the church and the people who make up that church. In my experience, everyone had a place at God's table. As I went about the business of growing up and becoming educated, I was unaware of the true extent of the tensions that exist in some parts of the Church. I was highly involved in my parish but I did not know much of the powerful conflicts that played themselves out in arenas beyond my parish and how these conflicts affected my spiritual and religious life.

I considered myself an educated Catholic, which is why I was so bewildered by what I encountered in the Lincoln diocese. At that time I had no idea how much power and control an individual bishop has in his diocese. The diocese of Lincoln, due to the efforts of the current and former bishops, is unlike any other diocese in the United States. For example, there are no Eucharistic Ministers; rather, acolytes who are, by definition, male, help the priest distribute communion during Mass. The Eucharist is offered to the people under only the species of bread, not wine. Also, girls are not permitted to be altar servers.

My experience of the Roman Catholic Church has changed in profound ways over my lifetime. Born two and a half years after the close of the Second Vatican Council, my life unfolded in the wake of that significant event. Sweeping changes in the larger culture, such as an expansion of personal and professional options for women, impacted the Church in the United States and my experience of it as well.

US Catholics have responded to recent changes in the church in a variety of ways.[2] Some Catholics reject the Vatican II council. Others feel a loss for at least some parts of the liturgy they knew and loved. I asked my maternal grandmother, Agatha Gedris, about her reaction thirty years after Vatican II and she told me she still mourned the loss of the Latin liturgy. Others believe the reforms that came after Vatican II have gone too far. They believe the documents have been misinterpreted which has led to a variety of liturgical abuses; these persons are sometimes said to desire a "reform of the reform." For example, former Lincoln bishop, Fabian Bruskewitz, believes there is a great deal of misunderstanding regarding Vatican II because of what he refers to as a "para-council" which he described as "the group of hangers-on, lobbyists, experts, journalists and general commentators who frequently gave an impression of that council and the impression that continues sometimes even today that is exceptionally erroneous."[3] Finally, many Catholics fear the backlash of returning to old practices in the church; they celebrate the reforms implemented since Vatican II and desire continual renewal of the Church.

A number of years ago I read Mary Jo Weaver and R. Scott Appleby's edited volume *Being Right*.[4] That book helped me better to understand Bishop Bruskewitz than had many years of living and worshipping in his diocese. Weaver explained that conservative Catholics believe Catholic identity can be "measured in obedience to the teaching church."[5] With that basic piece of information, I finally understood something that had baffled me: How could Bishop Bruskewitz declare practicing, committed Catholics to be non-Catholics? The answer was that the Catholics in question did not submit in all ways to Bishop Bruskewitz's teaching authority. The unit of measure was complete obedience.

As a graduate student I had studied the significance of organizational power and authority, but those issues took on so much more personal importance when I encountered the Lincoln diocese. When I moved about 600 miles west, I was poised to learn a powerful and disturbing lesson. I went from being a practicing and valued member of a church community to being virtually voiceless and disposable.

The Lincoln diocese is the canary in the coalmine of the United States Catholic Church. The diocese was at one time so unusual that perhaps it could be dismissed as an outlier. In recent years, however, more and more conservative Catholics have been named bishops and they have increasingly emphasized Church authority. U.S. Catholics would do well to be educated about this shift. Sociologists who study religion conclude, "Clearly, commitment to the Church enhances compliance with its teachings, but it does not preclude dissent."[6] How will the U.S. bishop deal with the dissent of the faithful? The answer to that question will tell us something about the condition of U.S. Roman Catholicism today and where it is headed in the future. If the Lincoln diocese becomes the model, more and more practicing Catholics will find themselves unwelcome in their own churches.

At a news conference after his election as President of the United States Conference of Catholic Bishops (USCCB), Archbishop Timothy Dolan of New York reportedly said the bishops' role is to act as "pastors and teachers, not just one set of teachers in the Catholic community, but *the* teachers" [emphasis in original].[7] Outgoing USCCB President, Cardinal Francis George addressed this issue as well in his final presidential address, "The bishops ... speak for the church in matters of faith and in moral issues and the laws surrounding them. . . All the rest is opinion, often well-considered opinion and important opinion that deserves a careful and respectful hearing, but still opinion."[8]

The bishops' role is to shepherd and teach. I am also a teacher. My understanding of teaching has changed as I have grown in age and experience, but I have always understood that, because of their life experiences, students in my classes know more about some things than I know. Because my students have first-hand experience, they can help me understand and learn new things. In addition, a student who looks at a theory with fresh eyes might offer new insights. Openness to my students' knowledge, experience and ideas does not compromise my authority in the classroom. Of course, I do not believe I have received my teaching authority directly from God. My authority comes from my knowledge and my professional position. In contrast, the bishops teach that they are the arbiters of the work of the Holy Spirit. Roman Catholics receive the gifts of the Spirit in the sacraments of baptism and confirmation. However, some bishops act as if they alone have the authority to decide if the Spirit is actually working in a person.

A consequence of claiming to have the only authentic teaching authority, along with the requirement of obedience to that authority, is that those who have discerned that the Holy Spirit has led them to believe something different from their bishops can be called not truly Catholic and turned away from full participation in the church. Claiming that those who are led to question certain church teachings or disciplines are not authentically Catholic may be one way of creating a smaller but purer Catholic Church. The phrase, "smaller but purer," is often attributed to Pope Benedict XVI. Scholars who have searched for this specific reference have come up empty handed. Priest and theology professor, Joseph Komonchak, writes in an online blog that he has found no evidence that Pope Benedict used those specific words.[9] Still, Cardinal Ratzinger, before he became Pope Benedict, suggested that if Christianity wished to remain true to itself, it may, indeed, become less culturally significant.[10] In contrast to the metaphor of bishop as shepherd, rather than seeking out the sheep the shepherd considers lost, the bishops define that sheep as not really a part of their flock. Charles Morris points out that the "risk of the conservative vision is that the church will dwindle to a narrow sect of true believers, too small to sustain the world symbolism of the church."[11]

Though labels can gloss over real and significant ways a person differs from a larger group, they can help us understand how actors might be situated in a broader context. Avery Dulles offers a typology of United States Catholics based on how they interact with culture. Dulles' analysis offers insight into the conflict playing out in the Lincoln diocese. The four types include: traditionalism, neo-conservatism, liberalism and prophetic radicalism.[12] Those who adopt traditionalism heavily critique American culture and advocate for the "the more centralized and authoritarian Catholicism of the years before World War II."[13] Neo-conservatives argue that God has "sovereignty over the nation" and "Human rights are inalienable because they have their source in God's eternal law."[14] Neo-conservatives advocate a democracy in which passions are "curbed by moral values."[15] Catholic liberals highlight ways "Americanism can help to modernize the church,"[16] including reform of the church through participatory democracy. Prophetic radicalism is counter-cultural and includes Catholic pacifists and creationists. People such as Dorothy Day and Fr. Daniel Berrigan fall into this group.

Dulles explains that according to this typology based on Catholicism's relationship with American culture, neo-conservatives and radicals are diametrically opposed while traditionalists and liberals are diametrically opposed. Dulles asserts that both American Catholicism and American culture are complex and none of these strategies is wrong. Each of the strategies has strengths and something to offer. Each, also, has weaknesses. Yet, Dulles argues

> Each group should respect the intentions of the others and humbly recognize its own limitations. The internecine struggles between opposed factions are a scandal and a waste of energies that could more profitably be devoted to the common mission of the church as a whole to minister to the salvation of the world. By generously recognizing the diverse gifts of the Holy Spirit, all can help build up the body of Christ in unity and strength.[17]

Crisis of Catholic Authority tells the story of a group of people who could be characterized by Dulles' Catholic liberal or prophetic radicalism who encountered a Catholic diocese dominated by people who could be characterized as traditionalists. The traditionalist bishops possessed power of position which allowed them to declare the Catholic liberals and prophetic radicals to be not only not Catholic, but anti-Catholic. The bishops did not subscribe to Dulles' warning against hostility and recrimination of one strategy towards another.[18]

When I moved to Lincoln, I discovered a group of people who had been pushed to the doors of the Catholic Church yet they refused to walk out. These faithful and committed Roman Catholics had been speaking their truth to the power of the Roman Catholic hierarchy for many years. We became friends. They impressed me with their faithfulness and challenged me, through the example of their lives, to take even more responsibility for my faith. Their journey has been my journey now for seventeen years. The story of those struggling to be heard in the Lincoln diocese could be the story of many Catholics in the future. The conflicts described in this book are illustrative of the conflicts that exist in the U.S. Roman Catholic Church today.

Above all, *Crisis of Catholic Authority* is a story about voice: whose voice is heard and whose voice counts. In this book I tell the story of over thirty years of reform efforts in the diocese of Lincoln, Nebraska. The main feature of the story is the strong and courageous characters, but to understand the story, one must understand the elements: power, authority, and organizational structure.

In writing this book I do not intend to cast aspersions on the Catholic Church or any member of it. I believe that most, if not all, of the people mentioned in these pages, from the members of reform groups to the bishops of Lincoln have acted, and continue to act, in a manner that they believe to be correct and moral. These different perceptions are one phenomenon that makes the unfolding story of Catholicism in Lincoln, Nebraska so fascinating. My hope is that this book offers some areas for discussion so that we can move from baseless assumptions and name-calling to understanding.

A Communication Perspective

I approach the story of church reform in Lincoln, Nebraska as a scholar of communication. Communication is a relatively young field of study; it is interdisciplinary and draws quite heavily from sociology, psychology, and rhetoric. At the risk of oversimplifying, the study of communication is the study of messages: how messages are formulated, how they function and their effects. One reason I was so drawn to study communication is that there is virtually nothing that can't be studied from a communication perspective. Because it has played a significant role throughout my life, as a graduate student and as a professor, most of my research has focused on the Catholic Church. My main area of doctoral study was organizational communication. I am mainly interested in how humans use communication to organize.

I adopt a definition of communication articulated by Eisenberg and Goodall[19] called "balancing creativity and constraint." This approach asks the question: Does society create the individual or does the individual create society? The answer from this perspective is "both." According to this definition, social structure is created as humans act in patterned ways over time. This is the creativity referred to in the definition. Once social structure is created, we are then constrained by that creation. This approach is based on Anthony Giddens' idea of the duality of structure: structure is both an outcome of and a resource for interaction.[20]

People often operate with the assumption that certain social structures are inevitable when they are not. Every time we act in the same way, we uphold the structures as they stand. However, if we choose to communicate in new ways, we can change the structure. When we treat something that is a social construction as if it is "real," we are said to reify it. Gender roles offer a good example of this creativity and constraint. Traditionally, women were prohibited from holding positions of power in most organizations. This was a pattern of interaction over time and it created a certain societal structure that informed men and women of their role or place in society. While constrained by this structure, some women and men acted in new and creative ways that slowly changed our understanding of the role of women. `

For the purposes of this book, I assume that the structure of the Catholic Church is socially constructed through communication. This social constructionist perspective does not eliminate the role of the Holy Spirit in guiding the church. It does, however, emphasize the role of human beings as mediators of the Spirit. Humans find themselves situated in a particular place in history and culture. If we ignore history and culture, we close ourselves off to a more complete understanding of what is happening in the institution.

Organizational Structure

The structure of the Catholic Church as it exists today enables some to have their voices heard and silences others. Structure is, therefore, of primary importance to the story told in this book. Organizational structure includes "those aspects of an organization that are pre-specified for a given situation."[21] Some examples of organizational structure include flowcharts, policies, rules, and procedures. Organizational structure serves an important function; all organizations need some amount of structure.

Reification of the organizational structure of the Catholic Church has been extremely strong. Some believe that the structure of the church is as God intended. Because God intends that structure, the fruits of that structure must then also be as intended by God. Critics of this perspective note that the Gospels do not indicate that Jesus established any structure beyond naming Peter the Rock upon whom the church would be built.

I argue that the structure of the church must change to enable the voices of lay people to play a more dominant role. Without lay voices, the church will never be all it is called to be. In this book you will read the story of a group of people who received informal support from members of the hierarchy who either were powerless or felt powerless to actually take action to help these Catholics.

The structure of the Roman Catholic Church is complex with multiple levels that intersect in various ways. The Vatican provides the overarching structure of the church. Not even all bishops are pleased with the current structure of the church in that bishops from around the world have expressed their dissatisfaction with the treatment Episcopal Conferences, or groups of bishops, have received by Roman congregations.[22] That is, they have seen the power of the church more and more centralized at the Vatican.

However, on the diocesan level, though he operates within boundaries set by the Vatican, the bishop has control. There is a culture of support among the United States bishops; it is extremely rare for them to speak out against each other. Bishops are considered to be the sole teaching authority in their dioceses and they can listen to the laity or not; it is their choice. A pastor has control over his parish, though he works within the boundaries set by his bishop. The bishop can choose to be more or less involved in the behaviors and activities of the diocesan priests and in what happens on the parish level. Individual committees or groups within a parish work within the boundaries set by the pastor.

Lay people's voices are almost nonexistent at the highest levels of the church. The extent to which lay people have a voice at any level of church structure is dependent on their bishop and their priests. To some extent, those lay people who have no or few other options have begun to use the media to give voice to their thoughts and concerns about the Catholic Church. Communities of religious sisters and brothers often have their own structures within the larger organization that allow some freedom and voice in shaping, at least, their own communities.

Power and Authority

We can't look at the structure of any organization without also considering the role of power and authority in creating the structure. Power is part of the context in which organizational structure emerges.[23] If we consider that structure is created through communication, we have to realize that not everyone's voice has equal weight in that creation. There are few places where that is more evident than in the Roman Catholic Church. Not only are lay people's voices in general not heard, in particular, women's voices are almost never a part of the conversation on the macro level. Certainly women play a role in what happens in the life of some parishes, but only if the priests allow them that part. While some lay voices might be invited into certain discussions, dissenting views are kept at bay as often those invited have already passed the "litmus test" of orthodoxy.

Another relevant aspect of power to consider as it relates to organizational structure is discursive closure which refers to the suppression of conflict; alternatives are not entertained.[24] Discursive closure is evident in the Catholic Church when those who hold formal authority claim that what they say comes from God and they are, therefore, not to be questioned. For example, the Vatican has claimed that it does not possess the "authority" to ordain women. This claim attempts to silence any dissent on the matter. In effect, the authorities claim, "Our hands are tied."

There is hope. Lay people have a say in the structure of the church inasmuch as they choose to recreate that structure or not. That is, lay Catholics can maintain the status quo or they can choose to create a new Catholic Church structure by communicating in new ways.

Data Collection

Data for this book include documentary materials such as newspaper articles and editorials, letters, meeting minutes, and written recollections of meetings as well as thirty-seven interviews that took place during the summer of 2001. Most of those interviewed were members of Catholics for Active Liturgical Life or Call to Action Nebraska. Interviews were recorded and transcribed. I sent transcripts of the interviews to the interviewees for review and comment. When I quote from the interviews, I use the versions the interviewees sent back to me. In addition, when quoted, I adjusted the spoken and written words to make them more readable, eliminating words like "you know" and "kind of" and the like. I adjusted some letters, newsletters and written recollections to conform with publication style. Eight of the interviewees, two men and six women, requested that their names not be used in any report of my research.

In 2001, I attempted to interview the three bishops of Nebraska[25] but was granted no interviews. In response to my first letter to Lincoln bishop, Fabian Bruskewitz, I received a letter from Fr. Mark Huber, then-Chancellor of the Lincoln Diocese, who expressed that Bishop Bruskewitz's "full schedule would make it difficult for him to comply with your request before next year. If you write then, he might try to find time."[26] Fr. Huber also passed on to me some sources that the bishop thought I should review. Bishop Bruskewitz also "remarked that he was surprised that anyone would be interested in writing about the sect [Call To Action], since it is so insignificant." When I wrote a follow up letter to request an interview, I was told that an interview with Bishop Bruskewitz was "not possible."[27]

As I wrote this book, I also drew on my own experience as a member of the Diocese of Lincoln, Call To Action, and Call to Action Nebraska. I made every effort to express people's thoughts accurately. In addition, it is important to note that people's perceptions of the same events can be quite divergent. One person's account of an event may not reflect the reality of that event as experienced by others also involved.

I subscribe to the belief that all research and scholarship is influenced by ideology. I use the word ideology to refer to a set of assumptions and beliefs; we all have and operate under a set of ideological beliefs. By acknowledging my background and beliefs, the reader can frame this work for him and herself. To that end, I share parts of my own faith story.

My Faith Story

I don't remember learning much very specific about excommunication in my twelve years of Catholic education. As far as I knew, excommunication was saved for great sinners—Catholics who chose to do evil. While I knew people who only attended Mass on Christmas and Easter or who had grave doubts about just about everything the Church taught and practiced, I did not know anyone who had actually been excommunicated. If someone had suggested to me in my youth that some day I, myself, would be considered excommunicated by a large number of people, including my bishop, I would have laughed and considered the idea ludicrous.

I was born into a practicing Roman Catholic family. My parents, Dan and Marie Pokora were raised Catholics. My father grew up as a member of a Polish parish in Grand Rapids, Michigan and my mother grew up as a member of the Lithuanian parish in the same city. They married in 1966. My sister, Valerie, was born in 1967 and I was born in 1968. I received the sacraments of initiation (baptism, reconciliation, Eucharist and confirmation) at St. Jude Parish in Grand Rapids, Michigan. Catholicism was an integral part of the life of my extended family as well. For example, my parents, sister, and I would always attend Mass on the anniversary of my Grandpa Gedris' birthday and death. He had died before my parents were married and we observed these anniversaries with my grandma in religious ways.

As a child, I was a beneficiary of the reforms of the Vatican II and I knew no other way. I liked the folk music we sometimes sang in church; it seemed a simple and honest way for me to communicate with God. During my youth I saw lay women and men read the Holy Scripture and serve as Eucharistic Ministers. While I have childhood memories of boredom during homilies clearly geared toward the adults in the congregation, I also have memories of following along in the missalette during Mass even before I was old enough to read.

My sister and I attended St. Jude School. Unlike some of the stories Catholics tell about their years in Catholic school, my stories are overwhelmingly positive. I enjoyed school and learned a lot about Catholicism as I was growing up. As children we had opportunities to help plan liturgies by selecting songs and reading at Mass. I thought it was interesting to distract the teachers from the lesson at hand, especially the religious sisters, by asking them questions about religion and faith. I enjoyed watching them light up as they answered my questions.

My parents treated my sister and me and our faith seriously. They encouraged us to take responsibility for our spiritual lives, even as children. Two examples illustrate this point. When my sister was about to make her first communion, she was worried that she didn't really believe that the bread and wine became the body and blood of Christ. Her teacher taught her how important that belief was and she was told that she should not receive the sacrament if she did not believe. Transubstantiation is a difficult concept for a seven year old, especially one as serious as my sister. When she told my parents that she wasn't sure if she could make her first communion because of this, my parents did not respond as many, I suspect, would have. Though the first communion dress was purchased and the party planned, they encouraged Valerie to talk to a priest about her concerns. I went along. If my six-year-old memory of this event is accurate, the priest told us that faith was a journey and that because she was obviously taking the sacrament seriously, she could receive the sacrament. Looking back, I imagine he might have been pleased to talk to a child who cared so much.

The second example involves me. In fifth grade one of our parish priests came to our class to recruit boys to be altar servers. He spoke of what a great opportunity it was and how much the boys would learn about the Mass. He had a handbook that was given to all altar boys. I wanted that handbook. I wanted to learn more about the Mass. I wanted to be an altar server. I asked my teacher why girls couldn't be altar servers and she said, "Because Msgr. Brophy would never allow it." I was ten, but I wasn't stupid; this was no reason. When I went home that night I told my parents about what had happened. My dad said to me, "Why don't you start a petition? We could bring it to the bishop." I thought that sounded like a great idea. I don't know if I bowed to subtle peer pressure or if I thought it wasn't worth the effort, but I never followed through on the petition. Despite my lack of action, my desire to serve at the altar remained.

I was confirmed at fifteen years old. I remember the day I signed up for confirmation classes. My family lived close to church and I had walked to church that Sunday morning by myself; the rest of my family had attended a different Mass. The lector announced a sign-up opportunity for CCD and confirmation classes after all Masses. Even without them telling me, I knew my parents would never push me to be confirmed. They lived their lives in such a way that taught me that my confirmation was a personal decision. I signed up after Mass. Like most things involving my faith, I took confirmation seriously. I still remember standing in front of the congregation and the bishop and promising to be an adult member of the Roman Catholic Church. I eagerly anticipated receiving the fruits of the Spirit.

In high school I sang in the choir during school Masses. I also attended a camp for Catholic high school students after my sophomore, junior, and senior years. The camp was a week-long retreat experience which gave my contemporaries and me a genuine and deep faith experience. I left camp each year reveling in the beauty of Roman Catholicism as it touched my teenage life.

During my first two years of college I lived at home and attended Grand Rapids Junior College.[28] There weren't many faith opportunities at that age for me beyond attending Mass, but I was a team member on a

TEC (Teens Encounter Christ) retreat weekend for high school students. I transferred to Michigan State University for my junior and senior years of college. At MSU I became involved with the student parish, St. John's. I sang at one of the weekly Masses and became a lector and a Eucharistic Minister. I attended four retreats for students and young adults, the last one as a team member. One of these retreats had a huge impact on me. The parish brought in an outside team who led the retreat. One activity we did involved us getting in groups of about five and praying for the Holy Spirit to choose one of us to speak through. We had been focusing on the body of Christ ("the body is one and has many members"— I Corinthians 12:12) and the person who was chosen from our group shared how we were like a part of the body. I was told that I was a vocal cord. This revelation shaped how I see myself and my vocation. I try to open myself to the Holy Spirit so it might move through me. My job is to allow the Spirit to use me. The vocal cord does not create the message; it vocalizes the message so that others can hear and understand.

I made many friends at St. John's. Sometimes we would meet for Mass on Tuesday and Thursday evenings and then go out for frozen yogurt. In this way, I began to appreciate the benefits of daily Mass attendance. At this time I learned more about the rosary and prayed it regularly.

When I graduated from MSU, I moved to West Lafayette, Indiana to attend graduate school at Purdue University. During my six years at Purdue I was very involved at St. Thomas, the Catholic student parish. I was on the Tithing Committee and the Liturgy Committee. I sponsored five adults who joined the Catholic Church through the Rite of Christian Initiation of Adults (RCIA) program. I served on the RCIA team which meant that I frequently led "Breaking Open the Word" sessions during Mass and I planned, along with other team members, lessons designed to help the candidates and catechumens learn about the Roman Catholic Church. I joined a social concerns study group. I was a Eucharistic Minister. My second year in Indiana I lived in a house owned by the church, Antioch House, in community with other young women of the parish. For four summers during this time I returned to my home diocese in Michigan to be a team member for the camp I had attended when I was in high school. I attended Mass about four times a week. I became involved with a Focolare group that met monthly to discuss how we were living in love and unity with those in our lives. Many members of the Focolare group became close friends.

I was studying Communication and my faith played a role in my scholarship as well. In my Master's thesis I examined a Roman Catholic marriage preparation program. My doctoral dissertation examined organizational spirituality and how it intersected with communication and identity at a women's religious organization. I was frustrated by experiences I had in graduate school in which I felt I was judged negatively because I was involved in my church. The subtle message was that if thinking people actually believed in God, they wouldn't be so naïve as to belong to an organized religion.

I always took my faith and my religion seriously. I believed that an unexamined belief was not worth having. Therefore, I questioned why the Church had certain doctrines that did not make sense to me. Sometimes what I learned led me to accept the Church position. However, the more I learned about some practices, the less I agreed with them. For example, a male-only priesthood did not make sense to me as a child. As I grew and learned more about it, my conviction that the priesthood should be opened to women grew. Similarly, while I certainly understood the stated benefits of celibacy, I did not see why it was a necessity for the priesthood.

As my faith grew, so did my understanding that the Roman Catholic Church has changed over time. There are many stories of changes led by faithful and convicted people. While I did not expect to see change in my lifetime, I believed that change was inevitable and that I was to help lay the groundwork for that change. I never hid my convictions. While some of my friends and acquaintances did not agree with some or all of what I believed, I rarely, if ever, felt excluded.

During the spring of 1996 I wrote my dissertation and interviewed for academic positions. I was very pleased with my interview at Nebraska Wesleyan University in Lincoln. I liked the people I met and I felt the value I placed on teaching and community would fit well with this liberal arts university. Just before my campus interview, the bishop of Lincoln,

Fabian Bruskewitz, made national news when he issued extra-synodal legislation forbidding membership in a variety of organizations upon pain of excommunication. I was shocked by this action. I was not a member of any of the organizations Bishop Bruskewitz listed, but I was worried about moving to a diocese in which the bishop considered blanket excommunication a viable option for dealing with dissent. However, I felt called to Lincoln and the job at NWU. Just after I accepted the position, I saw a religious sister I knew and told her about my job. She was very excited for me until I told her where I would be moving. Her face fell. That worried me. A priest I knew told me that he had been to Lincoln and that I was in for a big shock. He seemed grave. That also worried me. Still, I held on to hope that I would find a parish in Lincoln.

Within my first month in Lincoln, I had attended three different churches. Even though I expected an experience different from that offered in my previous dioceses, I had no idea how different things were going to be. Some of the differences were easily identifiable. For example, in no church did the congregation receive the blood of Christ at Communion. When I asked a priest why, he told me they did not have enough people to help with communion. Eucharistic Ministers were not in use; instead, the Lincoln diocese utilizes acolytes who are, by definition, male only. Other differences were harder to describe, like the air of authority and exclusion exuded by the priests. I had a hard time imagining building the kind of relationship with one of the Lincoln priests that I had enjoyed in other dioceses. Mass felt lifeless to me. Rather than celebrating the Mass, the congregation seemed like observers. I was struck by the authoritarian attitudes conveyed in the homilies. I lost track of how many times I felt angry during Mass and how many times I held back tears.

I had heard that people in the Lincoln diocese were required to join the parish in whose boundaries they lived. This meant I would be required to join a parish with a priest who said (this word is used purposefully) the main Sunday Mass in thirty-five minutes. While I know that some people are grateful for a quick Mass so they can get on with their day, I look forward to spiritual fulfillment at Mass. I even enjoy a long Mass if I am swept away by prayer and song and meaning. I found none of this in that parish. I found a church not far away in which I was somewhat more comfortable and I talked to the pastor after Mass and told him I wanted to join. I told him where I lived. He said I would have to get permission from the pastor of the church where I lived because that church needed my money. While I certainly appreciate the financial concerns of parishes, my spiritual needs were treated as secondary to the money I would be expected to donate.

Before I moved to Lincoln, I thought about my need for a spiritual community. I had wondered if the Nebraska Call To Action group, one of the groups excommunicated by Bishop Bruskewitz, would be a place where I would feel spiritually fulfilled. I was familiar with Call to Action USA (CTA-USA) through my reading of the *National Catholic Reporter* (*NCR*). CTA-USA advertised their conferences in *NCR* and *NCR* sometimes reported on news that involved CTA. CTA supported reform of the Catholic Church including women priests, optional celibacy for priests, along with wide-ranging social justice issues. Because of these positions, I had felt ideologically drawn to CTA, but because of lack of money and time, I had never joined or attended any conferences. Additionally, though I am chagrined to admit it, before I moved to Nebraska, I was so comfortable in each parish I belonged to that I felt I did not "need" CTA. I considered finding the CTA community in Lincoln and I wondered how I might do that. As it turns out, I need not have worried. Within my first week at Nebraska Wesleyan, I learned that the kind Sociology professor, John Krejci, who helped me locate an apartment was the founding co-chair, along with Lori Darby of Omaha, of Call to Action Nebraska (CTAN). John invited me to a day-long retreat on November 2, 1996 and I attended. This retreat was my first Call to Action Nebraska gathering and very significant for me. I have many memories of that day and many of the people I met for the first time at that event are now dear friends.

I must share that even attending this retreat was a difficult decision for me. I had always been a faithful and dedicated Catholic. The threat of excommunication was very serious and the situation in which I found myself was painful. I knew that just attending the retreat would not lead to excommunication, but I found myself beginning to think about issues of authority and my own responsibility in ways that I had never done before. As I will demonstrate in this book, Bishop Bruskewitz held the ear of many Catholics in the diocese of Lincoln. He attempted to define members of Call to Action as outside the Church even though most members had been, like me, active participants in their parishes. In fact, many members of CTA-USA are priests, religious sisters, and paid parish and diocesan workers.

I was surprised to discover one day, early in my time in Nebraska, just how effective Bishop Bruskewitz had been in shaping my thoughts. I was attending a faculty meeting at Nebraska Wesleyan University. Before the meeting began, I found a seat in my usual spot, near the back. A friend called to me from the front of the room, "Come join me up here." I said, "come join me back here. All good Catholics sit in the back." Of course I was joking, but under my breath I said to myself, "not that I'm a good Catholic." I was taken aback, shocked by my own words.

While I became involved in Call To Action Nebraska soon after my move to the state, I did not officially join for quite some time. The threat of excommunication was profound for me and I did not want to do anything unnecessary or rash. The principle of the primacy of conscience teaches us that we are responsible to follow our consciences and I spent a great deal of time and energy considering what my conscience was telling me. I prayed. I talked to theologians and priests, I read opinions on the matter, and I discussed the situation with family and friends. I was determined to have a well-formed conscience. At the end of this long journey, I became a public member of both Call To Action Nebraska and Call To Action USA.

I made my involvement official by joining CTAN in July 1998. That moment is still vivid in my mind. I was in a taxi in Chicago with two CTAN friends, Patty and Mary Hawk. We were on our way to the first organizational meeting of the Next Generation of CTA-USA, a group of young people involved in Call To Action.[29] At the time, Patty Hawk served as President of the board of CTAN. I realized in that taxi that there was no looking back; the decision had been made. I handed Patty my membership dues. Not long after that moment I took leadership positions in both

CTA and CTAN. I served as a founding member of the Next Gen board of CTA-USA and I served as the President of the Board of CTA Nebraska. I have never regretted my decision.

This book tells a story of love and hope. Most members of Call to Action Nebraska love the Roman Catholic Church profoundly. If we did not, we would have left the Church long ago. Most members of Call to Action Nebraska hold a strong hope for a Church that more completely lives the teachings of Jesus Christ. We have hope for small changes and hope for large. We do not know when the changes will take place or if we will even live to see them, but we believe and hope in a future that will exist because of the work we do today.

Notes Chapter 1

1.   John Hooper, "Pope Benedict XVI: in his own words," *Guardian,*" September 15, 2010, http://www.guardian.co.uk/world/2010/sep/16/pope-benedict-xvi-own-words.

2.   For a discussion of Catholic responses to Vatican Council II, see Joseph A. Komonchak, "Interpreting the Council: Catholic attitudes toward Vatican II," in *Being Right: Conservative Catholics in America*, eds. Mary Jo Weaver and R.Scott Appleby (Indianapolis: Indiana University Press, 1995).

3.   "Bishop Bruskewitz Scores 'Para-Council' that Misunderstood Vatican II," *Southern Nebraska Register,* July 5, 1996.

4.   Mary Jo Weaver and R. Scott Appleby, *Being Right: Conservative Catholics in America,* (Indianapolis: Indiana University Press, 1995).

5.   Mary Jo Weaver, "Introduction: Who are the Conservative Catholics," in *Being Right: Conservative Catholics in America* edited by Mary Jo Weaver and R. Scott Appleby (Indianapolis: Indiana University Press, 1995), 4.

6.   James D. Davidson, Andrea S. Williams, Richard A. Lamanna, Jan Stenftenagel, Kathleen Maas Weigert, William J. Whalen, and Patricia Wittberg. *The Search for Common Ground: What Unites and Divides Catholic Americans* (Huntington, IN: Our Sunday Visitor Publishing Division, Our Sunday Visitor, Inc., 1997).

7.   Laurie Goodstein, "Dolan Chosen as President of U.S. Bishops' Group," *New York Times,* November 16, 2010, http://www.nytimes.com/2010/11/17/us/17bishops.html.

8.   Nancy Frazier O'Brien, "Cardinal reviews health reform debate as 'wound to church's unity,'" *National Catholic Reporter,* November 16, 2010, http://ncronline.org/news/cardinal-reviews-health-reform-debate-wound-churchs-unity.

9.   Joseph A. Komonchak, "A Smaller but Purer Church?" *Commonweal,* October 21, 2010, http://www.commonwealmagazine.org/blog/?p=10517.

10. Ibid.

11. Charles R. Morris, "A tale of two dioceses: From Lincoln to Saginaw," *Commonweal, 124,* no. 11 (June 6, 1997).

12. Avery Dulles, "Catholicism and American Culture: The Uneasy Dialogue," *America, 162,* no 3 (1990).

13. Ibid, 55-56.

14. Ibid, 56.

15. Ibid.

16. Ibid.

17. Ibid, 54.

18. Ibid.

19. Eric M. Eisenberg and H. L. Goodall, Jr. *Organizational Communication: Balancing Creativity and Constraint,* 4th ed. (Boston: Bedford/St. Martin's, 2004).

20. Anthony Giddens, *The Constitution of Society* (University of California Press), 1984.

21. George Cheney, Lars Thoger Christensen, Theodore E. Zorn and Shiv Ganesh, *Organizational Communication in an Age of Globalization: Issues, Reflections, Practices,* 2nd ed. (Long Grove, IL: Waveland Press, 2011), 18.

22. John R. Quinn, "Synod 2001 and the Role of the Bishop: The Working Document for the Synod has Some Striking Omissions," *America, 185,* no. 3 (July 30 – August 6, 2001).

23. Dennis K. Mumby, *Communication and Power in Organizations: Discourse, Ideology and Domination* (Norwood, NJ: Ablex Publishing Corporation, 1988).

24. Stanley A. Deetz, *Democracy in an Age of Corporate Colonization: Developments in Communication and the Politics of Everyday Life* (Albany, NY: State University of New York Press, 1992).

25. None of the three men who were bishops in 2001 remain in that post. Bishop Lawrence McNamara of the Grand Island Diocese died in 2004. The Archbishop of Omaha, Bishop Elden Curtiss, retired in 2009. Bishop Fabian Bruskewitz retired in 2012.

26. Letter from Fr. Mark Huber to author, July 31, 2001.

27. Letter from Fr. Mark Huber to author, January 23, 2003.

28. Now Grand Rapids Community College.

29. Today the group is called CTA 20/30.

CHAPTER 2

Early Organized Reform Efforts: Catholics for Active Liturgical Life

...I was really outraged by the idea that women were not going to be allowed to read. It just seemed like instead of going forward, it was backing up. And I think that was a big part of it. I had a wife and daughters.—Jerry Johnson, interview with the author.

Setting the Stage for Church Reform

By the time I moved to Lincoln, Nebraska, years of commitment to liturgical renewal, lay involvement, and Catholic social teaching (i.e., a key element of Catholicism that involves a commitment to justice for the poor[1]) had already been demonstrated by a group of Catholics in the Lincoln diocese. Catholics For Active Liturgical Life (CALL) was founded in October 1981 and disbanded during the summer of 1993. CALL was a lay organization made up of people heavily involved in the Catholic Church and committed to their faith. The members craved fulfillment through liturgical involvement—the same kind of involvement available in other United States dioceses—and worked to achieve this goal. While members of CALL attempted to achieve greater participation in their parishes, their efforts were thwarted by Bishop Glennon Flavin's preference for the pre-Vatican II church and, to some extent, his unwillingness to communicate with them.

Though CALL disbanded before I moved to Lincoln, I learned about the organization from some members of Call to Action Nebraska who participated in CALL. I did not fully understand what CALL experienced until I explored the archives of the group.[2] CALL's newsletter, *CallSpirit,* was particularly helpful in documenting the activities and positions of the group. Members of CALL must have known they were engaged in historically important work as they documented meetings with Bishops and kept extensive files of newspaper articles, letters, and papers.

Without this group of individuals who faithfully and doggedly sought to have a voice as lay people in the Roman Catholic Church and experienced the frustration and pain that goes along with such activity, Call to Action Nebraska might not have survived. Early in CTAN's existence, Lincoln members drew upon friendships forged through shared struggle in CALL. Many knew the pain of being ostracized in their parishes. These women and men had already spent years hoping and working for a more just Church.

The Context

In order to understand why Catholics for Active Liturgical Life was formed, one needs to know about Catholic life in the Diocese of Lincoln at the time of CALL's formation in 1981. At the time CALL was formed, Glennon P. Flavin was the Bishop of Lincoln. He had become a bishop in 1957; he was named to the Lincoln diocese ten years later serving as the Bishop of Lincoln, Nebraska from 1967 – 1992.

Bishop Flavin succeeded James V. Casey after Casey was named Archbishop of Denver. Bishop Casey served as Bishop of Lincoln from 1957 – 1967. While in Lincoln, Bishop Casey undertook a number of building projects, including the Cathedral of the Risen Christ. He is said to have "accomplished more for the Diocese of Lincoln in 10 years than any other comparable period in our history."[3] CALL member, Diana McCown, remembered Bishop Casey in an interview: "He was, I would say, liberal compared to what we have now, for sure. But even in that day and age, somewhat liberal and very out-reaching to the community. . . he was political. He was not closed in away from the society and he got to be very well known by the mayor, by the governor. . ."[4]

Bishop Casey was Bishop of Lincoln during the Second Vatican Council and he attended all four sessions of Vatican II. He appears to have been quite moved by his council experience. After Archbishop Casey's death, Permanent Deacon, Richard J. Bowles, is quoted as having said, "While attending the Vatican II Council in Rome, he [Bishop Casey] really caught the infectious enthusiasm of Pope John XXIII. In an archdiocese [Denver] used to a stern father, as Vehr and other previous bishops had been, Casey insisted that the laity take adult responsibilities, not just follow directions of priests and nuns."[5]

Charles Kelliher had been a priest in the Lincoln Diocese during Vatican II and he remembered that "Bishop Casey came back a changed man from the Council, and he was very progressive, or became very progressive, and implemented the Council. So that had a great influence on me."[6] Bishop Casey was quoted as having said, "I believe that all baptized people are to share equally in the work of the church. I do not see the clergy on an exalted level... The role of bishops and priests is to recognize the talents of lay people and call them out to take positions of leadership."[7]

Bishop Flavin's episcopacy exhibited a decidedly different character. While Bishop Casey might be characterized as moderate or even progressive, Bishop Flavin was known by those across the spectrum for his conservatism. Bishop Flavin was not eager to join in the liturgical reforms of Vatican II. Perhaps, like many who might be considered conservative Catholics, he considered the changes to be an outgrowth of a misunderstanding of Vatican II. Bishop Flavin is known for saying that if he "could put a wall around the Lincoln diocese," he would.[8] This demonstrates the bishop's, most likely well-intentioned, desire to protect Catholics in his diocese from what he considered to be outside negative influences.

Bishop Flavin was a devout man who lived a simple lifestyle;[9] he gave up his Bishop's house to a group of religious women, the Holy Spirit Adoration Sisters, for their use. Betty Peterson, widely considered the founder of CALL and long-time member of the Lincoln Diocese, reflected on Bishop Flavin in an interview. She commented:

> I think Bishop Flavin was so concerned about protecting his flock from what he perceived to be dangerous trends in the church. He was a very private man and I rather imagine that he found many of the Vatican II changes very difficult. . . . I think he was very comfortable with the church as it was and I think he was very sincere in protecting his flock from any tendency to stray from the orthodoxy of the church. I don't think there was anything mean spirited about him and he certainly wanted to control it [the diocese] but I think his intentions were good. But a little old fashioned.[10]

CALL member, Marilyn Seiker described Bishop Flavin as "intelligent, perhaps a little shy, but determined to 'keep the company store'—a man without vision, clinging to the past in which he was molded."[11]

Perhaps because he was a private man, Bishop Flavin was not open to interacting with media. In fact, he appeared to mistrust the local press.[12] I asked Anita Fussell, the Religion Editor of the *Lincoln Journal* at the time of CALL's founding, if she felt media coverage treated both CALL and the diocese fairly. She responded: "Yes, I did, because the diocese wouldn't talk to us. You know. We were really willing and able to give their point of view but, at that time, the diocese [diocesan] relationship with the newspaper was strained enough, for many reasons, that they just chose not to talk to us."[13]

Press reports often stated that Bishop Flavin would not comment on whatever issue was under discussion. The most frequent response from the bishop and the chancery was "no comment." This lack of response from Bishop Flavin appears to have made it difficult for the local media to represent the diocesan perspective. For example, the writer of a letter to the editor of a local newspaper in 1988 complained about the way the newspaper continually portrayed the Roman Catholic Church. The writer posited that articles involving the Catholic Church reinforced stereotypes and prejudices. The author ended his letter, "When the Lincoln press is prepared to really understand Catholicism and its traditions, the resources are available. Until then, its Catholic readership will be increasingly embittered by its condescending attitude."[14] The editors responded to this letter by explaining that they had tried numerous times to write stories that dealt with various aspects of the Catholic faith. However, Bishop Flavin "refuses to talk with the press nor will he allow most priests, nuns and others associated with the church to talk with the press under most circumstances."[15]

Some interviewees used the word "controlling" to describe Bishop Flavin; he did not appear to allow any priestly dissention or disobedience. Catholic apologist, Karl Keating, recounts an encounter with Bishop Flavin in the early 1990s.[16] Keating was seated next to Bishop Flavin at a luncheon during a study day for priests of the Lincoln diocese. Keating complimented Bishop Flavin "on the high quality of his men." According to Keating, Bishop Flavin "turned to me and said with a broad smile on his face, 'In this diocese we don't have even one dissentient priest.'" This may have been true at that time, however, as I will demonstrate, it wasn't always the case in the diocese.[17] It seems Bishop Flavin effectively stamped out the appearance of dissension and nurtured an environment of control and fear in at least some of his priests.

Charles Kelliher served as priest in the Diocese of Lincoln under both Bishop Casey and Bishop Flavin. He explained that during the Bishop Casey episcopacy, the young priests met regularly for educational, spiritual, and social purposes. According to Kelliher, Bishop Casey encouraged this activity. In contrast, Bishop Flavin forbade these gatherings. When asked why, Kelliher responded, "He wasn't in charge, he wasn't in control of it."[18] Kelliher explained that Bishop Flavin emphasized hierarchy, "it's like a ladder, rather than a circle."[19]

Because many members of CALL had been active members of their parishes for years, some had built relationships with their priests. At least one, perhaps more, of these priests shared information with CALL members, for example, by sending occasional copies of priests' newsletters and other pieces of information with them. Carol McShane, the first president of CALL, explained, "we would get information sometimes out of the blue; priests would send us messages from the priests' council or something."[20] Though CALL members shared with me the existence of these priests, years later they still protected the identity of their sources.

Bishop Flavin concerned himself with the image the priests in the Diocese of Lincoln projected. He required priests to be clean-shaven and to wear their clerical garb when they were in public. When discussing the issue of priests' outward appearance, Carol McShane commented:

> The parishioners would spy on them. So if a parishioner saw a priest at the movies in civilian clothes, they would call the bishop. . . And then they [the offending priest] would get sentenced to stay in the rectory and they would have to call into the Bishop every so many hours. . . And another priest got in terrible trouble for wearing sandals and he was diabetic and it was very important that his feet be able to get air. And so, I mean there were, it was very old fashioned. He was the boss, this bishop.[21]

Joan Johnson told a story about Bishop Flavin's concern with the physical appearance of priests in the Lincoln diocese:

> When we first moved to Lincoln. . . there was a priest who had come to Lincoln from Detroit to attend summer school at the University of Nebraska. He had gone through the channels to get permission to say Mass at one of the local churches, but when Bishop Flavin discovered that he had a beard, he rescinded the permission. So Father was saying Mass in one of the dorms where he was staying. Father Kalin [then-pastor of the University of Nebraska Newman Center] sent his secretary to one of the Masses, and when he verified that it was being done, reported it to Bishop Flavin who then, in turn, sent a letter requesting him to come to the Chancery.[22]

Bishop Flavin seems to have encouraged a separation between priests and the laity that reached beyond physical appearance. In a newsletter sent from Bishop Flavin to diocesan pastors, Bishop Flavin wrote, "In all public statements, especially in print, do not use nicknames for priests. They imply a buddy-buddy relationship with the laity. Such a relationship often negatively affects a priest's ministry to his people."[23] Perhaps Bishop Flavin felt a priest's authority is called into question if he was addressed informally.

Founding member and one-time president of CALL, Diana McCown, reflected on Bishop Flavin's relationship with some of the priests of the Lincoln Diocese, a handful of whom left the diocese in the early 1970s:

> The priests, of course, read our newsletter and were amazed at some of the things that were going on that they didn't know about. And I think it was one of those deals where they wanted us to succeed or at least to try to change things because they couldn't. They were powerless. There was a group of priests who left the diocese in 1973. . . the priests weren't happy. So this core group went to him and said "we want this and this" or "we're unhappy about this and this" and he would not deal with it. . . I'm not sure what he did to them, but they, many of them, left. There were like five or six, maybe more. . . So the priests weren't happy. They didn't like his style or his attitudes and the good thing was if you were a priest out in the diocese somewhere, you were okay because he didn't bother you too much. But the priests in the city, in this very definite region, were [bothered], he was on top of them all the time. And so they had to conform even if they didn't agree.[24]

CALL member Kay Haley reflected that this exodus of priests in the early 1970s led Bishop Flavin to discourage unofficial gatherings of diocesan priests. Haley said she learned from a fellow CALL member who was friends with many priests that Bishop Flavin "didn't like five or six of these guys to get together and, maybe, I think he was afraid they might plot or something."[25] Bishop Flavin's desire to control spread beyond his priests. His policies and behaviors also indicated his desire to control what lay Catholics in the diocese knew and experienced. Early issues of the CALL newsletter, *CallSpirit,* often included comments on the diocesan paper's lack of coverage of national and international Catholic news. This did seem to change over the years of CALL's existence and broader coverage of Catholic news in the diocesan paper were noted in *CallSpirit* as well.

Bishop Flavin's autocratic leadership style discouraged any kind of questioning from priests or laity. When discussing the atmosphere in the Lincoln diocese, John Sullivan, a self-proclaimed conservative, was quoted in the *National Catholic Reporter* as saying "We're talking about a whole style of leadership. It's the feeling that the laity have absolutely no rights and are unfaithful even if they ask 'your excellency, just explain to us your position. Just talk to us.' "[26] Bishop Flavin refused to talk with anyone who held a dissenting point of view. Phone calls and letters to the bishop went unanswered.[27] Another Bishop Flavin supporter, Joe Hanigan, is quoted as having said, "In this diocese, the bishop simply does not accommodate people. You have to live by the rules."[28] Members of the Lincoln diocese claimed that the bishop viewed dissent as disloyalty.[29]

Bishop Flavin dedicated himself and his work in the Lincoln diocese to two priorities: Catholic schools and vocations to the priesthood.[30] Much time and money were dedicated to both of these missions and these efforts led to a great deal of success. Both vocations to the priesthood and the Catholic school system grew and flourished under Bishop Flavin's leadership. Some measure a bishop's success by the number of seminarians he is able to recruit. By this measure, Bishop Flavin can be judged quite favorably.

Engagement with the Ideas of Vatican II

Bishop Flavin was appointed Bishop of Lincoln just two years after the close of the Second Vatican Council (1962–1965). Most members of CALL consider the years of Vatican II to be a time of personal spiritual growth; many of them began to take responsibility for their faith lives. While some changes in the Church were universal after the council (e.g. Mass in the vernacular), other changes were not adopted in the Lincoln diocese. I offer some CALL members' experiences with Vatican II to illustrate how important their faith life was to them and to demonstrate how they hungered for an adult faith experience. Some of these future CALL members lived in the Lincoln Diocese during Vatican II and others did not.

James V. Casey was Bishop of Lincoln at the time of the council. According to Betty Peterson, one of Bishop Casey's initiatives was to ask the Diocesan Council of Catholic Women to begin a study committee of Vatican II documents. Upon her pastor's recommendation, Peterson was appointed chair of that committee. When asked to recall her hopes for the future of the church at that time, Peterson said:

> I guess at that time I was just hoping that, first of all, that people would begin to think for themselves, especially women. And secondly, that there would be an awareness of social justice. . . One of the things that disturbed me when I came to Lincoln was, I noticed how the Catholic women never felt that they could study anything or do anything without Father being there. And I didn't understand that. Because, you see, I had belonged to a study club in Sioux City for years and we did all our own discussing and thinking and no priest was involved. And it really bothered me that these women had that feeling.[31]

During the years of Vatican II, Joan and Jerry Johnson were a young married couple with small children living in graduate student housing at the University of Minnesota. Joan Johnson explained how her husband, Jerry, attended classes at the Newman Center at the University of Minnesota where he was a graduate student. Joan shared:

> He would come home from these meetings and tell me about what was discussed and it fascinated me. The thoughts that people were putting forth about their faith [were] so different from my experiences—there was such a depth to these discussions. Of course, this was in the middle 60s and this was exactly the time that Vatican II was going on. The Newman Center adopted Vatican II almost from day one; there was no hesitation on their part to include the laity and to encourage them to be very active in their faith life as well as to put that faith into action.

It was a real faith community and it just was exciting to me. My faith just began to blossom and grow. I was excited to learn more about God. The more I learned, the more I read, the more awesome God became. It meant a lot to me. Then we moved to Lincoln and it was back to the old way of doing things. There was no identification or connection between my faith and my everyday experiences. It really caused a great deal of pain for a number of years. And we thought we were the only ones who felt this way.[32]

Kay Haley lived in Lincoln at the time of Vatican II and she followed the council closely by reading *Time Magazine*. Haley explained how the council led her to think about things she hadn't considered before like "Mass in the vernacular and all of a sudden we took the hats and said, 'off they go.'" Haley continued:

Shortly after the end of the Council. . . of course, we did have Mass in the vernacular and there was the movement to move the altars out and have the priests face the congregation. And all of a sudden it was okay to sing "A Mighty Fortress is our God," and some of those wonderful Martin Luther hymns. . . at that point Bishop Flavin came up here from St. Louis. And that's when everything closed down.[33]

CALL member, Mary Jo Bousek, moved to Lincoln in the early 1970s from Ames, Iowa. She describes the transition, "when we came here, it was a step backwards. It was a revelation. . . It just seemed very, very conservative."[34] Many Catholics who moved to the diocese of Lincoln felt shocked by what they found. One woman commented on her move in 1977. She said her husband asked, "'Is this the same church?' It was literally painful. I would come home from church in tears and say, 'Can I be Catholic in this diocese?'"[35]

One CALL and CTAN member describes how his time in the military opened his eyes. He served two years overseas in Germany and observed that Catholicism in Germany wasn't "as rigid." He learned that German Catholics observed more holy days than US Catholics and he concluded, "It's okay to be different. You can think for yourself."[36] He followed Vatican

II closely and felt that the council nurtured that same belief that it's okay to use your mind in religious matters.

Marilyn Seiker describes how in adulthood she "was challenged to examine this institution which was one of my major life stabilizers." She explains:

> When Francis and I married we were obedient in our acceptance of marriage as it was presented during our growing up years. . . And so, rhythm was the method for family regulation and the husband was the head of the household. Although there were strong women on both sides of my family, I depended on my husband. . . In eight years we had four little girls. My doctors suggested, "You've had four Cesarean sections. You're pushing your luck. Better start taking the pill. . . This was a time of real struggle, soul searching. . . Francis, understanding the Magisterium's position, and gifted with an ability to discern the logic of a matter, reasoned to his conclusion that contraception was morally acceptable. But he wasn't about to pressure me. I prayed through our dilemma and found peace with our mutual decision that I take the pill.[37]

Seiker remarked that this was the first time she made a conscious choice that was contrary to official church teaching.

Before the founding of CALL, future members were engaged in the Catholic Church on both a local and international level. These Catholics were waiting for the reforms promised by Vatican II to penetrate the figurative walls Bishop Flavin had erected around the Lincoln diocese.

New Lector Guidelines and The Founding of CALL

In the autumn of 1981, Roman Catholics in the diocese of Lincoln learned of new liturgical guidelines for the Lincoln diocese governing the use of readers and instituted lectors that were to go into effect by 1984. Bishop Flavin decided to expand the instituted lector program in the diocese and discontinue the use of other readers. Catholics in the diocese of Lincoln did not learn of the new policy from their parish priests or in the diocesan paper, the *Southern Nebraska Register*. Instead, the news reached

Catholics in Lincoln through an article published in the *National Catholic Reporter (NCR)* out of Kansas City.[38] After the *NCR* story, the local papers, the *Lincoln Journal* and the *Lincoln Star*, picked up the story leading to wide-spread knowledge of these changes in the Lincoln diocese.

Betty Peterson, founder of Catholics for Active Liturgical Life, was directly involved in informing the Lincoln papers about the new diocesan guidelines. Then a member of Sacred Heart Parish in Lincoln, Peterson read the *National Catholic Reporter* article after her parish priest, Oblate of Mary Immaculate, Dale Hardes, showed it to her. Here is Peterson's description of what happened:

> I can remember standing there in his office and putting [the article] down on the desk and saying… "[Bishop Flavin] hasn't heard the last of this." So I took that story and made copies of it and I dropped it off at three other friends'… So anyway, we got together and talked and then we decided to take the story to the *[Lincoln] Journal*… So Bonnie [Sittig] and I went down to the *Journal* and Anita Fussell was the religion editor at the time. And so she was interested enough, she said she would do a story… Well, this was I'll say on a Wednesday, and she said, "I'll get back to you." Saturday morning at 8:00 my phone rang and it was Anita and she said, "Betty, all hell is breaking loose. The *Omaha World Herald* ran a big story about this and we want to run this story tomorrow, full page." So, she said, "I need names."[39]

Peterson did not want her name printed in the story because she did not want her pastor to "get in trouble," but those who read the story and knew her reputation as a person who speaks out, called her.

One of the people who read the story in the *Lincoln Journal* was Carol McShane. McShane and Peterson were neighbors with children around the same age. McShane describes how she and her husband learned about the new lector policy:

> We had read in the paper that, in the Lincoln paper, that it was policy that women weren't going to read. And we never knew it was a policy, we just thought the Lincoln diocese was slow to allow women readers.

And it turned out that a priest in the diocese had leaked to the *National Catholic Reporter*... that there was this policy in the Lincoln diocese. This got picked up by the Lincoln [paper]. I'll never forget, it was a Sunday morning and I read that in the paper and I closed the paper, walked down the street—we lived just up the street from St. Theresa's—and I walked to the priest there and I said, "tell me this isn't true, I'm reading this in the paper, this is, this can't be true, it can't be a policy that women can't read." And he said it was. And I said, "What do you mean it's a policy? I mean this is happening all over the United States, how is it we can't read? Is it because we haven't been good? I is something wrong with the Lincoln people?" And he said, "This is the bishop's policy." Well, I was just dumbfounded.[40]

Somewhere amid the phone calls and conversations, Betty and others decided to hold a meeting of Catholics who were concerned about this new lector policy. Betty asked Carol McShane to lead the meeting. Betty and a friend called a number of banks to try to find one with a meeting room they could use, "And we finally found a bank that said they had had a cancellation for this, whatever, Thursday, Friday night... We said, we'll take it. So then we just called around and spread the word, and I think we had 55 people at that first meeting."[41]

The first meeting took place on October 30, 1981. The second meeting drew about one hundred people. These were the first of twelve years of regular meetings of the group that came to be known as Catholics For Active Liturgical Life (CALL).

Other Catholic Reactions to the Lincoln Lector Policy

Some Roman Catholics in Lincoln had a strong negative reaction to Bishop Flavin's new lector policy. The new rules Bishop Flavin intended to adopt had several components that some Lincoln Catholics found challenging or even heartbreaking. Below is a complete list of the requirements. These requirements applied to diocesan candidates for instituted lector and acolyte.

1. Must be male adults at least 21 years of age.

2. Must be possessed of outstanding qualities of virtue, loyalty to their pastor and Bishop, and love for the Church.

3. Their children must be in the Catholic schools when available.

4. Must enjoy a good reputation in the both the ecclesiastical and civic communities.

5. Must be physically, mentally, and emotionally capable of performing the functions of the ministry to which they aspire.

6. Must be possessed of organizational and leadership abilities.

7. Must be reasonably assured of maintaining residence in his parish for at least a year.[42]

An exception initially existed for women's religious communities.[43]

After the institution of these guidelines, the only people allowed to read scripture at Mass in the Lincoln diocese would be priests and instituted lectors who would partake in an extensive training program. In the Roman Catholic Church, instituted lectors, indeed, all instituted ministers, are, by definition, male. In practice, the "Rite of Institution of Readers" had been used as a step toward ordination for seminarians.[44] Women, and many men, who read the Scripture and Prayers of the Faithful during Roman Catholic Masses around the world serve as readers, not installed lectors. Bishop Flavin could argue that his intention was a fuller adoption of instituted lectors in his diocese, but the effect was a banning of women from proclaiming the word of God at Mass. During a time when the roles of women were expanding in society and, to a lesser degree, in the Church, the few women who had been readers found that their services were no longer wanted.

To complicate matters, the language of the announcement stated that this change was taking place to "emphasize the importance, dignity and seriousness of the role of reading the word of God."[45] While the diocese claimed that this was because instituted lectors go through an extensive training program as well as receive follow-up training, the wording seemed to imply that the bishop believed that it was the gender of the lector or reader that would enhance or diminish the dignity of the Mass. CALL member, Mary Jo Bousek, was a reader when the policy went into effect. She recalled, "It was very hurtful, frustrating, and a lot of us became very angry about it because they didn't mind taking our money and all of our cleaning. . . but, no, we couldn't be in front of the church at Mass. That ruined the dignity. . ."[46]

CALL argued that, even given the diocesan claim that the dignity came from the training and not the gender of the reader, "There seems to be no documentary mandate against offering suitable training for readers of either sex. To refuse to offer such training for readers locks out women. This creates confusion and causes anguish."[47] If the issue was simply a matter of training, then, and women were allowed to participate in training similar to that received by the instituted lectors, they could also be dignified contributors to the Mass.

The role of women in the Lincoln diocese was limited by even more than this lector policy. Carol McShane noted that women were forbidden to do fundraising in the diocese during Bishop Flavin's tenure because "if you have women asking for money, it's sort of a prostitute image. . . And when they would do DDP [Diocesan Development Program][48] Sunday, they would not let the women go door to door or do any of the fundraising." When asked how she knew this to be the policy, McShane explained that the information came from one of CALL's priest-informers.[49] Reflecting on a series of stewardship surveys taken while Bishop Flavin was in office, Rosalind Carr explained that, while the survey purported to inquire about time, talent, and treasure, "all they were interested in was [womens'] treasure." The only women's "talent" of note was cleaning the church. She concluded, "the talent that's wasted is just incredible."[50] Eighteen-year-old Jenny Allen was quoted in a *Lincoln Journal Star* article describing the difference between the Omaha and Lincoln dioceses regarding females. She explained that she had served as a candle bearer in Omaha and when her family moved to Lincoln, she asked a priest at the Lincoln Catholic high school, Pius X High School, why she could not be a candle bearer or altar server. "I was told women are not allowed on the altar unless they had a dust mop in their hands."[51]

While the fact that women would be barred from reading Scripture at Mass was the most divisive qualification for instituted lectors, there were other requirements that members of CALL questioned. For example, by requiring instituted lectors to send their children to Catholic schools, when available, some Lincoln Catholics felt that parents of public school children were being punished for making choices that they felt were best for their children.[52] In addition, by the very fact that some male parishioners questioned this new policy, their loyalty to the pastor and Bishop might be called into question, excluding them from the Instituted Lector program.

As Catholics upset by the new policy soon learned, individual bishops hold a great deal of authority and power in their dioceses. Short of Vatican intervention, Bishop Flavin was free to implement his new diocesan lector policy. Because it was unusual, the new lector policy made local and national news. Nebraska newspapers and national Catholic newspapers reported on the new policy and various Catholic responses. Papers published editorials and letters to the editor sections were filled with comments on what was happening in Lincoln.

Certainly some priests supported Bishop Flavin's new lector policy. A few priests from the Lincoln Diocese spoke to a journalist from the *National Catholic Reporter* for the article that broke the news to Lincoln Catholics as well as to a national audience. One unnamed priest who supported the policy reportedly said, "There is some reaction against [the policy] because it apparently discriminates against women, but I'm sure the bishop is just following the information that is coming from Rome."[53] Rev. James Cooper reportedly commented, "It is not a discrimination against women, but an advancement of the ministries program."[54]

While some people might have believed that the policy did not discriminate against women, comments from priests in the Lincoln diocese call that claim into question. An article on the new lector policy appeared in the November 5, 1981 edition of the *Wanderer*. In this article, Fr. Robert Vasa, then-Director of the Installed Lector Program, currently Bishop of Santa Rosa, California, is quoted extensively. He reportedly said,

Our Bishop has decided not to allow women, and that's that... until there is something more definite from the Vatican which orders women to participate, that's the way it stands... They're (women) allowed to be lectors but only by way of exception... The intention of the Church is that those persons who function as lectors and acolytes indeed be installed... It may sound chauvinistic, but men are to be preferred to women... I suspect you'd have to live in Nebraska in order to understand why.[55]

Not every priest in the Lincoln diocese felt the new lector policy was a good idea. Even though some people claimed that the policy had little to do with gender, others felt the policy was related directly to Bishop Flavin's feelings about the role of women in the Church. A few priests spoke under condition of anonymity to a journalist from the *National Catholic Reporter* about their feelings. One priest commented on how the new policy was unique to the Lincoln diocese and speculated on why Bishop Flavin initiated the policy. The priest felt that the new policy hurt the teaching authority of the Church. He is quoted as having said, Bishop Flavin "wants women in their place: in teaching and no other ministry."[56] Another anonymous priest reportedly said, "My impression is that the bishop is really uncomfortable with women doing anything other than the traditional duties they've been doing for so many years. This is more of a question of the role he sees for men and women, than a theological question."[57]

One of the most interesting reactions to Bishop Flavin's lector policy came from Archbishop Rembert Weakland of Milwaukee, then-Chairperson of the U.S. Bishops' Liturgy Committee, who spoke out strongly against Bishop Flavin's decision. Archbishop Weakland's comments are noteworthy in part because bishops rarely speak out publicly against another bishop's policies. Archbishop Weakland stated that he hoped no other bishop would follow in Bishop Flavin's footsteps and allow only men to read Scripture during Mass.[58] He referred to *Inestimabile Donum*, a document of the 1980 Vatican Congregation for the Sacraments and Divine Worship which lists roles women can perform in the liturgy including the role of reader of the Word of God and the Prayers of the Faithful. Archbishop Weakland continued, "No one will deny Bishop Flavin's right to do as he wishes in his own diocese, but I deeply regret that his action was taken without a broader consultation. It is indeed a step backwards and offensive."[59]

Two opinion pieces in national Catholic publications addressed Bishop Flavin's lector policy. In an editorial in the *U.S. Catholic*, the author likens Bishop Flavin to the Wizard of Oz who, when accused by Dorothy of being a bad man, replied, "Oh no, my dear, I'm not a bad man, I'm just a very bad wizard."[60] The editorial goes on to state:

> Consignment of women (and girls!) to second-class citizenship is, of course, outrageous… This arrogant discrimination against those who probably number more than half the membership of the church is surely a serious injustice. But it is also silly and sometimes comical. It is silly because there simply is no valid reason for it… The panic of the hard-liners, of course, is not induced by the specter of women lectors or altar girls but by their nightmare of women priests. And the high ground they think they have found is the fact that the present pope and several of his predecessors have said, "no" to the ordination of women. But a long line of popes said "No" to Mass in the vernacular while the last three popes have said "Yes" to non-Latin Masses so enthusiastically that those who have refused to accept this change have become apostates.[61]

The diocesan newspaper of Peoria, Illinois, the *Catholic Post*, published a similar opinion:

> Lincoln's Bishop Glennon Flavin is apparently basing his action prohibiting women lectors on a technicality in the law… The Bishop of Lincoln is being a legalist in insisting that the function of lector be reserved only to men… Once the taboo against women in liturgical roles was broken following the second Vatican Council, I believe no worthwhile purpose is to be achieved by re-introducing it… What the Lincoln diocese and its bishop are doing in this instance comes through to me as clearly discrimination against women. I think it should also

be a source of embarrassment to the Catholic faithful, both men and women, in that diocese. I've heard of pastors here and there withholding privileges and relaxations in law granted by higher authority, but it's something of a rarity for a bishop to do that. I believe that most bishops are only too anxious to pass on to their people whatever concessions they can where law is concerned... The action by the Bishop of Lincoln, Neb., in banning women lectors is arbitrary and regressive no matter how well-intentioned. It's a good example of the sort of thing that gives authority a bad name.[62]

Though supporters of the policy claimed that the policy was implemented to expand the installed lector program and not to discriminate against women, many commenters believed the new, out-of-step policy was an example of gender discrimination. This discrimination was built into the structure of the church as Bishop Flavin was able to rely on organizational rules to enact his new policy. Because women are not permitted ordination in the church and ordained ministers are the ones who make the rules and policies, the organization silences women in matters of rules and policies.

Readers of national publications chimed in on the diocese of Lincoln's lector policy as well. Some criticized the new policy and some supported it. A woman from Queens, New York wrote a letter regarding Bishop Flavin's new lector policy: "I do not understand why anyone should be in the least bit surprised at Bishop Flavin's decision to prohibit women from serving as lectors. His policy is in keeping with the ever-present attitude of the Church. The aura of male superiority was inculcated in all females as we first stepped across the threshold of the classroom in the parochial school."[63] A letter, published in the same publication as the above, written by a woman from the Diocese of Pittsburgh, expressed a different opinion: "Fortunately, in my hometown we have one terrific pastor who refuses to allow the ladies anywhere near the altar during Mass. In that church we have a beautiful, dignified Mass; while at a neighboring church the ladies are running around the altar, performing various and sundry duties, [and thus] one is hardpressed [sic] to feel one is attending Mass in the house of the Lord."[64] In another letter to *Our Sunday Visitor*, a priest wrote that the only women who will be offended by Bishop Flavin's new lector policy are women who themselves desire to be ordained deaconesses or priests.[65] While there are certainly many women who feel the call to ordained ministry in the Roman Catholic Church, such a statement is ludicrous in its overstatement. Many people were upset by Bishop Flavin's new lector policy because they desired to see each person, male or female, enabled to participate in the liturgy in a way that honored his or her God-given talents.

Many readers of the *National Catholic Reporter*, the paper to first break the story, wrote comments on Bishop Flavin's new lector policy. One priest mused that the "logical extension" of the policy could involve an even more male-focused church life "even to the annual Holy Week dusting of the church and the weekly laundry. This is absurd, of course."[66] Interestingly, the writer considers it absurd to imagine men doing the same cleaning in the Church that had been laid at women's feet for years.

A local newspaper, the *Lincoln Star*, published an editorial on the issue on November 3, 1981. The editorial position stated that while the editors had no expertise to comment on the ecclesiastics of the decision, they believe that women are the strength of every church congregation. Bishop Flavin's potential for angering women through this policy could lead to "the hottest potato to come his way since he has been in Lincoln."[67]

When the press in Nebraska picked up the issue of the new lector policy and covered the gatherings that soon became the organization Catholics for Active Liturgical Life, the differences of opinions of Catholics hit the mainstream media. Some Catholics expressed anger toward those expressing dissent for turning to the public press while others expressed agreement with the dissenters' position and supported them. The issues involved in the conflict played themselves out in the news and editorial pages of the local papers.

While letters in the national publication tended to discuss the issue of gender discrimination, opinions in the Lincoln papers tended to focus more on the issues of authority and obedience. Some letters backed the bishop; others disagreed with the new policy and supported the right of the members of CALL to question and protest. This focus on authority and obedience might be explained by the traditionalist's belief that Catholic identity is tied to obedience.

In one letter, Mrs. Cecil M. Cannon accused those who disagreed with the new lector policy of sabotaging the Church. She wrote,

> These protestors, with their rebellious spirit, are endorsing defiance of the pope... Dissidents... should not look upon [Bishop Flavin] as their enemy, but as their protector, their shepherd. Today's dissidents do not exhibit the intellectual honesty of yesterday's rebels. In the past, those who rejected church dogma felt compelled to leave the church. Today's rebels, enjoying the aid of the media, apparently relish the role of saboteur.[68]

Responding to this letter, Betty Peterson took issue with Cannon's use of the word "dogma" claiming that those who protest the new lector policy are not addressing an issue of dogma but rather a decree.[69] To this, Cannon responded, "Obedience to our bishop is a dogmatic matter."[70] This exchange highlights the narrow definition of Catholic held by traditionalists. The writer expresses the belief that those who question the bishop are not truly Catholic.

Other letters disagreed with the new policy and supported those who raised questions about it. For example, Diane Walkowiak wrote,

> In my years of attending Catholic school, I was taught never to question the authority of the Catholic Church. The years have since taught me that human powers tend to become autocratic, and need to be questioned at times... The courageous Catholics who are publicly disagreeing with the bishop are being lectured on how they should be submissive and not question the male hierarchy of the Catholic Church. If we never question their actions, how will they ever know how we feel?... Catholics have every right to put pressure on Bishop Flavin. It is my understanding that WE are part of the church, too![71]

Another woman who served as a reader in her parish wrote a letter to the editor in which she expressed her frustration, "But anyone knows that a woman is a woman is a woman forever and ever, amen… She shall cheerfully continue to do all the menial tasks until Kingdom Come? Then she will happily scrub the golden stairs with Holy Mary Mother of God."[72]

Eulalia Hansen, the President of the Lincoln Diocesan Council of Catholic Women (LDCCW), a group affiliated with the National Council of Catholic Women, wrote a letter to members of the organization in which she supported Bishop Flavin's new policy. The letter was dated November 1981. Hansen addressed the opportunities available for women in the diocese through the Diocesan Council of Catholic Women and explained that these particular works require "women's understanding, kindness, empathy and 'touch.'"[73] Carol McShane's response to Hansen's belief that there is work in the Church which requires a woman's touch was printed in a local newspaper article. McShane asked, "Doesn't that limit women to emotional support roles? What about social leadership, intellectual challenge, and cognitive reasoning?"[74]

In her letter, Hansen also wrote, "I guess I feel that my husband and sons can do this spiritual work [reading at Mass], why should I challenge them in that capacity? Let them do their part! Women do so many things that men can't and won't do (sometimes because they are content to just let us do it)."[75] Hansen offered her support for Bishop Flavin because of his office and expressed her opinion that those who disagree with the bishop's policy are like disobedient children. She wrote,

> Somehow when our Lord sent Bishop Flavin to be the Shepherd of the Lincoln Diocesan flock, I believe He gave him the graces and wisdom to faithfully guide us—just as He gave me my good Christian parents. Oh, at times way back, I thought, too, that my parents were all wrong and I was all right but I was taught to obey and respect and I'm thankful now that I've succeeded well—doing just that and keeping faith in God's plan. So, too, there are always sheep in the flock that want to stray for one reason or another but a wise shepherd watches and prays that they

will come back to the fold… Let's trust God—in His commandment: to love, respect, and obey![76]

Hansen's words indicate that she believes that if one trusts in God, one would believe that God's Shepherd on earth, the bishop, would act rightly. Therefore, those who do question the bishop are guilty of disobedience.[77] Hansen's analogy, however, does not acknowledge that just as some parents fail in their role, bishops might as well, and that is why we pass laws to protect children. In the Catholic Church, no one advocates for the laity neglected by their bishop.

Initial Meetings of CALL and Attempts to Communicate with Bishop Flavin

Catholics for Active Liturgical Life was formed specifically in response to the Lincoln diocese's new lector policy. However, members soon realized that a lack of communication in the Lincoln diocese was a major issue of concern, specifically, communication between the laity and the bishop. Members of CALL hoped to interact directly with Bishop Flavin but found him unwilling to meet with them to discuss their concerns or respond to them in any way.

Representatives of seven parishes from the diocese of Lincoln attended the original meeting of the group that became Catholics for Active Liturgical Life. Carol McShane chaired the first meeting of the group. The first gathering was largely informational and organizational. Those in attendance agreed to create a Steering Committee consisting of one representative from each parish. A trained liturgist, Sr. Rosalie VanAckeren, provided information on official Church positions and practices regarding instituted lectors and non-instituted readers. Those present voted to send minutes from this meeting to Bishop Flavin and request a response from him. Carol McShane, acting as temporary chairwoman for the group, wrote a letter that was included in the minutes she delivered to Bishop Flavin. In her letter she expressed the group's desire to meet with Bishop Flavin to discuss the situation: "The Steering Committee has met as charged [by those gathered at the October 30 meeting]. At this point we are united in our intent to convey to you that our expressions are of deep anguish and not those of simple rage… Please read these minutes; we wait, we pray, we hope for your positive response."[78]

Carol McShane attempted to hand deliver her letter and CALL meeting minutes to Bishop Flavin on November 4, 1981. When she called the chancery to arrange a time to deliver the minutes, she spoke to Fr. Robert Vasa, then-Director of the Acolyte and Instituted Lector Training Program and Assistant Chancellor (Bishop Flavin's Secretary).[79] McShane wrote down her recollections of her phone conversation with Fr. Vasa and her subsequent face-to-face meeting with him in the chancery in a transcript.[80] During the phone conversation, McShane explained to Fr. Vasa that she had been instructed to hand deliver the minutes of the meeting to either Bishop Flavin or his Vicar General, Msgr. Kealy. Fr. Vasa checked and informed McShane that Msgr. Kealy was currently present in the chancery. When McShane arrived at the chancery ten minutes after this phone conversation, she learned Msgr. Kealy had just stepped out and that Fr. Vasa would help her.

McShane also had opportunity to discuss with Fr. Vasa what she referred to as "the organization of concerned people in the Diocese." According to McShane's written report, the following conversation took place:

Vasa: The Bishop feels all the other Bishops do not rein in their laity because they do not have the courage.

McShane: Surely you speak in the extreme.

Vasa: No, once the laity get in there is no way to draw the (authority) line again.…

McShane: …We expect the chancery to treat us with charity as we will ever treat the chancery.

Vasa: Where do you expect to go with this? He won't change his mind.

CALL hoped to publish a position paper which addressed the issue of poor communication in the diocese of Lincoln as well as members' thoughts on the new lector policy in the diocesan newspaper. Carol McShane hand delivered the document on November 6, 1981 to Msgr. Thomas Kealy's secretary. At this time Msgr. Kealy was the editor of the diocesan paper, the *Southern Nebraska Register*. McShane contacted Msgr. Kealy by phone later that day to determine if he would publish the position paper. McShane wrote a recollection of her telephone conversation with Msgr. Kealy.[81] Msgr. Kealy began by stating that he did not know if the position paper would be printed but "probably not."

McShane: When will you know for sure?

Kealy: Wait till Friday (*Register* comes out on Friday).

McShane: I cannot; I need an outlet for this before then.

Kealy: I'm the editor in name only.

McShane: Who is the editor who would know then?

Kealy: I'm it if anyone.

McShane: You will not tell me if you will publish it?

Kealy: The Bishop is out of town.

McShane: May I call [the printers] to find out?

Kealy: They know nothing about this.

On November 10, after receiving no word from the chancery, McShane called the printer and learned that they had not received a copy of the position paper. McShane then delivered copies of the position paper to the editorial editors of the *Lincoln Journal* and the *Lincoln Star*.

On November 16, 1981, Carol McShane sent Bishop Flavin a copy of the CALL position paper. In the accompanying letter, she wrote:

This paper was adopted as the official document of CALL at its Nov. 13, 1981 meeting. The vote for said adoption was unanimous. I hope you will find its wording careful and its purpose clear. It is upon the points in this position paper that we wish communication with you. The steering committee of CALL requests a meeting with you at your earliest convenience.[82]

In a letter to Bishop Flavin dated December 7, 1981, McShane wrote about CALL's interest in matters related to liturgical wholeness. She expressed members' concern with education and administrative policy in the diocese. She concluded her letter, "Our efforts to communicate with you are sincere. I repeat our request to meet with you on these matters."[83] McShane called the chancery on December 8 before she attempted to hand deliver this letter. According to her written report,[84] "Father Vasa answered the phone. I told him that I wanted to hand deliver a letter and asked if I could come in 10 minutes. [Fr. Vasa said,] 'I wish you would never come; the Bishop is not going to change his mind.'" McShane hand delivered the letter.

In a letter dated January 24, 1982, McShane updated Bishop Flavin on the activities of CALL and CALL committees. McShane also provided a brief look at the agenda for the next CALL meeting. She wrote:

I am sending you this skeleton agenda early for two reasons: 1) so that you don't have to rely on newspaper reports after the fact; and 2) so that you have an opportunity to react to the agenda and consult with me.[85]

She concluded her letter:

Again, I repeat the desire of the Steering Committee and of the general body of CALL is to communicate with you. Will you not meet with us? Will you not speak to us? Will you not reconsider your position of silence?

McShane received no response from Bishop Flavin to any of her meeting requests.

The only response CALL received to their requests for communication with Bishop Flavin was in the form of an unsigned editorial in the

Southern Nebraska Register published on November 6, 1981, two days after Carol McShane left a letter and CALL meeting minutes at the chancery. The editorial addressed criticisms of the new policy. In addition, the author of the editorial addressed the second qualification for instituted lectors and acolytes, "Must be possessed of outstanding qualities of virtue, loyalty to their pastor and Bishop, and love for the Church." The editorial stated that this qualification "is quite significant in light of present developments. The men installed must be loyal to the pastor and the Bishop. It is difficult to see how anyone who would oppose the pastor, the Bishop, and their authority could be said to fulfill this requirement."[86] Additionally, the editorial ended, "It is hoped that the people of the Diocese will not be swayed by the false exaggerations of an inimical press, which obviously seeks to divide the Catholic community and to undermine the loyalty of Catholics."[87] Referring to this editorial, Carol McShane called it a statement but not a communication because, "Sadly, [Bishop Flavin] gives no indication that he has listened to the cry of his people."[88]

Fr. John Reedy responded to the *Southern Nebraska Register* editorial in a column published in the *Catholic Witness*, the Harrisburg, Pennsylvania diocesan paper, on November 25, 1981. He spent little time discussing whether women should be allowed to read during Mass stating, "Whatever the technicalities of ecclesiastical law, the action is so out of step with current practice and sensitivity that the issue hardly needs to be debated."[89] Instead, Fr. Reedy focused on the statement in the *Southern Nebraska Register*; specifically, Fr. Reedy addressed the second requirement of virtue and loyalty and the commentary on that qualification in the editorial. Reedy wrote:

> Opposition itself, even to a Pope, is not necessarily a sign of disloyalty to his authority, much less to the church. The authentic loyalty of the mature Christian is not that of unthinking conformity. God gave us intelligence and responsibility for decisions. We serve God and participate in the life of the church by using all the human qualities God has given us. I would regard it as disloyal to conform without comment to

an order I regarded as seriously wrong or unwise. To me, it would be disloyal to withhold from the superior my sincere, thoughtful disagreement... In the long run, I think a correct notion of religious loyalty is far more important than the question of whether women will be permitted to serve as lectors in the Diocese of Lincoln at this time.[90]

Tom Fox touched on this issue in the *National Catholic Reporter*. According to Fox, the debate in Lincoln cannot strictly be understood as a liberal/conservative issue.

The controversy rather stems from Flavin's unwillingness to acknowledge anyone—conservative, liberal or otherwise—who asks him to explain his autocratic directives, some clearly out of step with the National Council of Catholic Bishops and Rome itself.[91]

CALL member, Kay Haley, reflected on the first meetings of Catholics for Active Liturgical Life. She reported that the first few meetings attracted huge numbers but the numbers did not remain quite so large. Haley believes some people did not attend more meetings for two reasons: "I think a lot of people felt they were beating their heads against a brick wall and the other [reason] was I think a lot of people were afraid which is a terrible thing. To fear that someone might know that you went to this meeting and that maybe the parish priest might retaliate in some way. What an awful thing."[92]

While CALL lost some members and their desire to meet with Bishop Flavin did not come to fruition, the group thrived. Some members learned of CALL through social connections with the organizers; others read about the meetings in the Lincoln papers, attended a meeting and decided to join the group. Within their first several meetings, members of CALL chose a patron saint, St. Catherine of Sienna, who is known for strongly admonishing the pope for what she considered to be wrong action and encouraging him to reform. They adopted "Be Not Afraid"[93] as their theme song. Within the first year, CALL had a position paper, a constitution and by-laws, articles of incorporation and tax-exempt status. Because official diocesan channels were closed to them, the main way

CALL members communicated with others outside their organization was through their self-published newsletter, *CallSpirit*.[94]

Carol McShane served as the first president of CALL until the end of 1983. Other CALL officer positions included Vice President, Secretary, and Treasurer. Members of CALL formed ad hoc committees for Communications, Education, Liturgy and Finance. The Steering Committee met monthly in open meetings. General membership meetings took place monthly as well. These general meetings often included an expert speaker who helped educate members of the group on issues relevant to the Catholic Church. Some examples of topics covered by speakers at general meetings include: a historical perspective on women in the Catholic Church, a Catholic legislator's perspective on social issues; and identification of successful candidates for priesthood, diaconate, and religious orders. CALL also sponsored a variety of workshops including "A Day of Inner Healing" with Fr. Jim Schmitt, an evening of music and liturgy with Fr. Bob Dufford, S.J., and a family spirituality workshop featuring Mary Jo Peterson. A holiday gathering also evolved into an annual Epiphany Party.

Dedication to the Roman Catholic Church along with frustration with the liturgical circumstances in which they found themselves in the Lincoln diocese brought the members of CALL together. The support they offered and friendships that grew from their work together came to mean a great deal to many of the members. Along they way, many became dear friends and forged bonds that exist to this day. As Mary Jo Bousek expressed, "…we somehow did get together and we became good friends for a long, long time through our frustration and our hope that the Bishop would talk to us and see the error of his ways, which he, of course, never did. Never acknowledged us."[95]

Clearly, there was a big problem in the Lincoln Diocese.

Notes Chapter 2

1.   United States Conference of Catholic Bishops, "Catholic Social Teaching," 2012, http://www.usccb.org/beliefs-and-teachings/what-we-believe/catholic-social-teaching/.

2.   The archives of Catholics for Active Liturgical Life are located at the Nebraska Historical Society.

3.   Thomas J. Noel, "Casey: the Gentle Shepherd (1967 – 1986)," *Colorado Catholicism,* 1989, http://www.archden.org/noel/05000.htm.

4.   Diana McCown, interview with the author.

5.   Thomas J. Noel, "Casey: the Gentle Shepherd."

6.   Charles Kelliher, interview with the author.

7.   Thomas J. Noel, "Casey: the Gentle Shepherd."

8.   Thomas C. Fox, "Nebraska Bishop Cuts Off Dissenters: 'Autocratic' Leadership Frustrates Vocal Minority in the Lincoln Diocese," *National Catholic Reporter,* June 18, 1982.

9.   Ibid.

10.   Betty Peterson, interview with the author.

11.   Marilyn Seiker, interview with the author.

12.   Thomas C. Fox, "Nebraska Bishops Cuts Off Dissenters."

13.   Anita Fussell, interview with the author.

14.   Rev. Alfred N. Pettinger, letter to the editor, *Lincoln Journal,* January 17, 1988.

15.   Editorial response to letter to the editor of Rev. Alfred N. Pettinger, January 17, 1988.

16.   Karl Keating, "Up Front," *This Rock*, 7, no 2 (1996), http://www.catholic.com/thisrock/1996/9602up.asp.

17.   For example, Bishop Flavin expelled two Oblate of Mary Immaculate priests from the Lincoln diocese. Fr. Dale Hardes and Fr. Tom Kozeny served at Sacred Heart Parish in Lincoln beginning in 1980, a parish with a large Hispanic community. Frs. Hardes and Kozeny had a large impact on the Hispanic Catholic community. Anita Fussell reported in the *Lincoln Journal* ("Exuberant lay leaders describe flowering of…, June 6, 1982) that attendance at the Spanish Masses rose from 20 – 25 people a week before their arrival to between 125 – 250 people. After Fathers Hardes and Kozeny wrote to Bishop Flavin to express disagreement with the new lector policy, in the spring of 1982, Bishop Flavin wrote to Oblate Father Don Bargen in St. Paul, Minnesota, provincial superior of Hardes and Kozeny's order, to request that he transfer the two priests out of Lincoln (Anita Fussell, "Nebraska Bishop Ousts Justice and Peace-oriented Oblate

Priests," *National Catholic Reporter*, June 4, 1982). A good number of Lincoln Catholics were supportive of the social justice work done by Frs. Hardes and Kozeny and began a petition drive designed to express the wishes of the community to allow the two priests to continue their ministry. While there was not universal support for the priests, the one-day drive resulted in more than 1,400 signatures (Anita Fussell, "Teens deliver petitions to city's Catholic bishop," *Lincoln Journal*, May 31, 1982). Despite the groundswell of support, Bishop Flavin did not change his mind and the two priests left Sacred Heart Parish. Frs. Hardes and Kozeny told a reporter that Bishop Flavin treated them with respect, "except that we couldn't speak out. Now we are speaking out. It is the time to do it. We no longer need to hold our breath. If this were a healthy situation we could have spoken out long ago" (Anita Fussell, "Nebraska bishop ousts justice and peace-oriented Oblate priests," *National Catholic Reporter*, June 4, 1982).

18.   Charles Kelliher, interview with the author. Kelliher left the active ministry in the early 1970s and moved to Kearney, Nebraska in the Grand Island Diocese.

19.   Ibid.

20.   Carol McShane, interview with the author.

21.   Ibid.

22.   Joan Johnson, interview with the author.

23.   *Diocese of Lincoln Pastoral Bulletin*, XXIII, no. 6, (1989).

24.   Diana McCown, interview with the author.

25.   Kay Haley, interview with the author.

26.   Thomas C. Fox, "Nebraska bishop cuts off dissenters."

27.   Ibid.

28.   Ibid.

29.   Ibid.

30.   *CallSpirit* (April 1982) reported that five women from CALL attended a convention of Lincoln Diocesan Council of Catholic Women at which Bishop Flavin "said that the two priorities for this diocese were the same as they were 15 years ago: *Catholic schools and vocations.*" (emphasis in original)

31.   Betty Peterson, interview with the author.

32.   Joan Johnson, interview with the author.

33.   Kay Haley, interview with the author.

34.   Mary Jo Bousek, interview with the author.

35.   Leslie Wirpsa, "Lincoln in Eye of Church Storm: Threat to Oust is Outcome of Right-Wing Rule," *National Catholic Reporter*. April 12, 1996.

36. Interview with author, name withheld at request of interviewee.

37. Marilyn Seiker, interview with the author.

38. Roger Catlin, "Bishop 'dignified' Scripture Readings by Banning Women," *National Catholic Reporter*, October 16, 1981.

39. Betty Peterson, interview with the author.

40. Carol McShane, interview with the author.

41. Betty Peterson, interview with the author.

42. "Press Misrepresents Policy," *Southern Nebraska Register*, November 6, 1981.

43. Liz Schevtdhuk, "Lincoln prohibits women lectors," *Dubuque Witness*, Oct 22, 1981.

44. Don Zirkel, "No, Virginia, You May Not Lector in Lincoln, Neb.," *The Tablet*, October 31, 1981.

45. Don Zirkel, "No, Virginia, You May Not Lector."

46. Mary Jo Bousek, interview with the author.

47. CALL position paper, November 9, 1981, available in the CALL archives, Nebraska Historical Society.

48. DDP stands for Diocesan Development Program. Bishop Flavin started this fundraiser in 1971. Today the fundraiser is called the Charity and Stewardship Appeal. Information on this fund can be found on this website http://www.dioceseoflincoln.org/OfficesOrganizations/foundation_charity-stewardship.aspx.

49. Carol McShane, interview with the author.

50. Rosalind Carr, interview with the author.

51. Steve Buttry, "Catholics in conflict: Sex issues at crux of division," *Omaha World Herald*, May 13, 1996.

52. According to an unnamed and undated document in the CALL archives that addresses the individual requirements for becoming an instituted lector, Fr. Vasa, then-director of the instituted lector and acolyte program, reportedly said at some point that if a candidate for instituted lector or acolyte had a "valid excuse" for not sending his children to a Catholic school, that requirement would be waived. According to the CALL document, "Presumably, the pastor—and ultimately the bishop—would determine whether the candidate has a valid excuse."

53. Roger Catlin, "Bishop 'dignifies' Scripture readings by banning women," *National Catholic Reporter*, October 16, 1981.

54. "Catholics react to ruling: Women may not be lectors," *Hastings Tribune*, October 29, 1981.

55. "Lincoln Diocese Will Not Allow Women Lectors," *Wanderer,* November 5, 1981.

56. Roger Catlin, "Bishop 'dignified' Scripture readings by banning women," *National Catholic Reporter,* October 16, 1981.

57. Ibid.

58. Liz Schevtdhuk, "Lincoln prohibits women lectors," *Dubuque Witness*, October 22, 1981.

59. Ibid.

60. "The Examined Life: Roadblocks on the Yellow Brick Road," *U.S. Catholic*, January 1982.

61. Ibid.

62. Fr. Richard L. Mullen, "That ban on women readers," *Catholic Post*, November 1, 1981.

63. Margaret Quinlan, letter to the editor, *Our Sunday Visitor*, November 22, 1981.

64. Virginia Duffey, letter to the editor, *Our Sunday Visitor*, November 22, 1981.

65. Msgr. Tullio Andreatta, letter to the editor, *Our Sunday Visitor*, December 13, 1981.

66. Fr. Robert Zahrt, letter to the editor, *National Catholic Reporter*, Nov 20, 1981.

67. "Bishop in hot water," *Lincoln Star*, November 3, 1981.

68. Cecil M. Cannon, letter to the editor, *Lincoln Journal*, October 31, 1981.

69. Elizabeth A. Peterson, letter to the editor, *Lincoln Journal*, November 3, 1981.

70. Cecil M. Cannon, letter to the editor, *Lincoln Star*, November 17, 1981.

71. Diane Walkowiak, letter to the editor, *Lincoln Star*, November 4, 1981.

72. Genevieve Gergen, letter to the editor, *Lincoln Star*, November 24, 1981.

73. Eulalia Hansen, letter to LDCCW members, November 1981.

74. Anita Fussell, "Circulated letter supports bishop," *Lincoln Journal*, Dec. 9, 1981.

75. Eulalia Hansen, letter to LDCCW.

76. Ibid.

77. CALL addressed Eulalia Hansen's letter in its January 1982 newsletter. Someone from CALL contacted the past president of the LDCCW, Betty Lou Loudon, who said that the executive committee of the LDCCW was not consulted about this issue. Therefore, the position articulated by Hansen was her opinion only and not an official position of the LDCCW. Further, CALL pointed out that in 1979 the Executive Committee of the National Council of Catholic Women (NCCW) published a position paper on Women in the Church in which they support expanded ministries for women. Their position paper

stated, "We join in seeking the implementation of current liturgical ministries open to women and the approval of additional liturgical ministries, where they most appropriately serve the good of the whole Church. The national position seems to be at odds with Hansen's position. The January 1982 issue of *CallSpirit* noted that someone from CALL telephoned the headquarters of the National Council of Catholic Women and was told "that they at national level were 'greatly dismayed' by Mrs. Hansen's letter and urged that women of the Lincoln diocese study the entire NCCW position paper."

78.   Letter from Carol McShane to Bishop Flavin, November 3, 1981.

79.   Robert Vasa was consecrated Bishop of the Baker, Oregon diocese on January 26, 2000. He was appointed Coadjutor Bishop of Santa Rosa on January 24, 2010. He became the Bishop of Santa Rosa on June 30, 2011.

80.   Available in the CALL archives, Nebraska Historical Society.

81.   Ibid.

82.   Ibid.

83.   Ibid.

84.   Ibid.

85.   Ibid.

86.   "Press Misrepresents Policy," *Southern Nebraska Register*, November 6, 1981.

87.   Ibid.

88.   "Catholic group plans new action on policy," *Lincoln Star*, November 7, 1981.

89.   John Reedy, "Religious loyalty not blind obedience," *Catholic Witness*, November 25, 1981.

90.   Ibid.

91.   "Church authority misused," *National Catholic Reporter*, June 18, 1982.

92.   Kay Haley, interview with the author.

93.   Words and music by Bob Dufford, S.J.

94.   *CallSpirit* often included articles based on research done about the state of the diocese, quotations from other Catholic publications, letters to the editor, notices of meetings, reviews of public presentations, commentary on happenings in the Lincoln diocese and personal testimonials of Catholics' experiences in the Lincoln diocese. For example, one transplant to the Lincoln diocese wrote, "Our decision to move [to Lincoln] was difficult because we had heard how conservative things were in Lincoln... We came with hesitation, but it wasn't until we actually attended Mass that it hit us how difficult things were in the Lincoln Church. I spent most of that first Sunday in the cry room literally crying, weeping for the Church we had left behind, weeping for what the Church in Lincoln could be, weeping out of anger at what the people in the Lincoln Church are deprived of,

and weeping in frustration because of the way I was treated as a woman. Suddenly I found that I was not part of a Vatican II Church but back in the Church of my childhood. A Church that I thought had grown up, too… Never have I felt so powerless and frustrated, so angry and for the first time in my life, because I am lay and even more so because I am a woman, I experienced in a very minute way the oppression that minorities must feel. I had always glibly thought that when things are against you, you just have to work harder. You raise consciousness, you organize for change, you make things happen. I just had no idea how powerful oppression is, how oppression strips you of energy and fills you with anger and depression, and most of all often convinces you that there is nothing you can do to change things." Mary Clark-Kaiser, *CallSpirit,* 1987. At one point, over 1000 people received each newsletter.

95. Mary Jo Bousek, interview with the author.

CHAPTER 3

Working Within Church Structure: CALL

Nebraskan Catholics are not noted for their outspokenness. More often they "go along to get along." It is all the more noteworthy then that Catholics are speaking up in the local Nebraska press. They say they have no other place to bring their plight to public attention. The bishop won't listen. The diocesan newspaper will not print their letters. So a few hundred are raising their voices publicly. But for every one speaking out with name attached, many more express their private distress—but fear drawing attention to themselves and their children. Among those most upset are Catholics who have been active in the church for many years, clergy and laity alike, enduring silent pain.[1]—*National Catholic Reporter*

LIKE MANY NEWLY ESTABLISHED GROUPS, Catholics for Active Liturgical Life initially expended effort determining who they were and what they stood for. CALL members were not always of a like mind and early meetings involved negotiating the best way to approach the Bishop to achieve their main aim: women readers at Mass. The majority of the members of CALL placed a large value on ensuring that their actions and positions were faithful to the Catholic Church; they considered it important to work for change from within the institution. Indeed, they already were active, committed members of the Church.

Members of CALL did not view themselves as dissidents; they saw themselves as a group of people who wanted to practice their faith more actively in the ways permitted in every other diocese in the country.[2] They believed they were following the movement of the Holy Spirit and they claimed that what they asked for was nothing more than what every other Catholic in the United States already had. Many members of CALL were not accustomed to finding themselves in such a position. Carol McShane noted:

> Just coming to the meeting is a courageous act. . . We've known it wasn't a democracy since we were babes, but it's difficult. Our education tells us to do one thing and our upbringing tells us to do another. We're caught. Our reluctance to question authority makes it difficult to even say what we're doing. We're people speaking out, and for Catholics that's a big step.[3]

CALL member, Joseph Gabig, is reported to have said, "We've been unable through logic, through prayers, to get the bishop's attention. What I want him to know is that we're not rebels. We're not tearing anything down. We don't want to pull away. We want to be involved, to contribute."[4]

Members of CALL also considered their organization to be wholly Catholic; this identity was important to the members. A letter mailed to CALL members that addressed an upcoming discussion the group would have about a contentious issue stated, "This is what this group is all about—a laity who becomes informed and concerned *within the structure of the Church*" [emphasis in original].[5]

Bishop Flavin's Power to Define

While members of CALL did not consider themselves to be dissidents, Mother's Day, 1982 marked a turning point for the organization. Five of the then-seven Roman Catholic churches in the city of Lincoln published notices in their bulletins that stated that Catholics should not support or encourage Catholics for Active Liturgical Life. The text that appeared in the bulletin of St. John the Apostle parish, similar to what appeared in other parish bulletins, stated: "An organization known as CALL (Catholics for Active Liturgical Life) has been soliciting members of our parish to join their group. The Catholic people of our parish are advised that this is not an organization sponsored by the church. It is set up in opposition to the Bishop and must not be supported and encouraged by your member-ship and participation." In one parish, St. Joseph's, the priest announced "that an organization known as CALL... was harassing people to become members, and furthermore it was an illicit and illegal organization that parishioners *must* not belong to."[6] According to a written description of what happened at Mass that day, which some members of St. Joseph's Parish called the "Mother's Day Massacre":

> At the time Father [Holomon] made the announcement at this particu-lar Mass, one woman immediately arose with her children and walked out of Mass. Another who was sitting near the front of the church rose to challenge Father, "Father, CALL is not an illicit organization". *[sic]* Father ignored her at the time, so she sat down again, but she did man-age to speak with him after Mass. Nothing was resolved. Another tele-phoned Father that afternoon with a request to come and see him. He was too busy, he said. At that point she asked him to identify who it was that had been harassed, and he refused to do so. He then said he would like to meet with Parish leaders of CALL, but wanted to wait a month until he returned from a trip. When pushed he finally arranged a meet-ing for three days later. At the meeting, Father apologized for not letting at least some of the Parish CALL members know about the impending announcement and said perhaps the words he used from the altar were too strong...[7]

Carol McShane was informed of one of the discussions a St. Joseph's parishioner had with Fr. Holomon after the "Mother's Day Massacre." According to the notes McShane took of what she was told, Fr. Holomon told the parishioner that Bishop Flavin had a meeting scheduled with Carol McShane. According to Fr. Holomon, when McShane "went to the press," Bishop Flavin cancelled the meeting. McShane wrote, "As a meet-ing between me and the Bishop had neither been arranged nor cancelled,

I called Fr. Holomon asking him to retract his statement. Fr. Holomon said: 'I can't; I got it from the Bishop.'"

On May 9, 1982, Carol McShane wrote a letter to Bishop Flavin requesting information about the announcements that appeared in the parish bulletins. She wrote:

> The similar wording leaves me to believe the basic message originated from the Chancery. The true intent of this message is not clear. In short, was the message which was generally published in the Lincoln parishes hortatory or was it mandatory? Are the Catholics of Lincoln being advised or commanded? I await your reply. Should there be no reply, I will assume the message of May 9 is hortatory in intent.[8]

Bishop Flavin did not reply. At their May 18, 1982 meeting, the CALL Steering Committee decided to seek advice from a canon lawyer and church authorities.[9]

Even though Bishop Flavin did not tell Carol McShane that Catholics were required to cease their association with CALL, the bulletin and verbal announcements had the ability to shape the perception of CALL in the minds of Catholics in the pews. Presumably, many Catholics who did not know much about CALL and did not know any members of CALL concluded after the announcement that members of CALL were dissidents and the organization dangerous. This perception had the potential to create a filter through which all further information about CALL would be screened. Bishop Flavin possessed the power to define CALL as an "illicit and illegal" organization in the minds of many Catholics. Diana McCown recalled, "Whenever we would go somewhere, for instance, I'd go to meetings, workshops, whatever. . . you get to talking to people and people would make comments about 'that awful group of women.' So, we were looked on pretty negatively. CALL was."[10]

An Unreachable Bishop

While the main reason Catholics for Active Liturgical Life formed was the new instituted lector policy, once they began meeting, CALL focused on other issues that impacted the lives of Catholics in the Lincoln diocese including a lack of availability of the Eucharist for the homebound and institutionalized, low-quality Confraternity of Catholic Doctrine (CCD) for Catholic children who did not attend Catholic schools, the state of the Newman Center at the University of Nebraska at Lincoln and a lack of financial accountability. Their main concern, as stated in several public statements, however, was the lack of communication between the Bishop and the laity; communication was essential to address the other problems.

Members of CALL felt the laity needed a way to express their concerns to the bishop. The CALL Position Paper stated: "Catholics for Active Liturgical Life (CALL) seek to improve communication within the Diocese of Lincoln, and between the people of the Diocese and Bishop Glennon P. Flavin... There is in the Diocese not only a lack of communication that alienates, there is also a lack of liturgical wholeness that isolates."[11] As demonstrated, Bishop Flavin refused to meet with those who questioned his decisions. A large number of lay people with concerns about their diocese felt they had no recourse.

The Lincoln Diocese's new lector policy highlighted Bishop Flavin's view of a bishop's authority. The bishop is to be obeyed, not questioned. Bishop Flavin fulfilled his duties as bishop, but by refusing to meet with people who raised questions about his policies or actions, he did not meet the needs of the community of believers. CALL hoped to dialogue with the Bishop; they appeared to believe dialogue would result in understanding and they hoped it would result in a more fulfilling liturgical life for them in the diocese of Lincoln.

Members of CALL continued to reach out to Bishop Flavin for years and they addressed new concerns that came to their attention. As described below, CALL appears to have exhausted every official means at its disposal. The bishops, priests, theologians, and canon lawyers to whom CALL turned continually answered that while they sympathized with the plight of CALL, only Bishop Flavin had authority to change the situation.

Reaching Out to Diocesan Priests

After unsuccessfully trying to meet with Bishop Flavin and consulting with priest and bishop contacts outside the diocese about their situation, CALL decided to reach out directly to the priests in the Lincoln diocese. In August 1982, CALL sent a letter to diocesan priests to request their support. The letter from CALL explained, "Originally our policy was to avoid directly involving our diocesan priests in our quest for active participation in the liturgical life of our parishes for fear of putting you in a difficult situation… We hope to address our deep concerns for spiritual vitality to the bishop. He has up to this point in time refused to hear, let alone answer, our questions."[12] The letter addressed several problems in the church including sexism which, it explained, resulted in some diocesan women's anguish, the anguish of men who do not send their children to Catholic schools but use, instead, the CCD programs, and the deprivation caused by the lack of Extraordinary Ministers of the Eucharist. The letter further stated and asked:

> Members of CALL intend to continue to seek the grace-filled nourishment offered by our Church. To that end we are attempting to reach out to adult Catholics who want a full understanding of the roles of clergy and laity in the post-Vatican II Church. We are researching Vatican II documents and statements by the bishops in matters relating to the American laity. We are also planning guest lectures and a lending library. But priests provide the crucial link between the people of God in each parish and Bishop. Therefore we ask for your help. Would you like to address our group? Are there other ways in which you might help us? Are there any ways that we might help you?[13]

Along with this letter, CALL sent an addressed, stamped envelope the priests could use to respond, a copy of the CALL position paper, copies of correspondence with the Apostolic Delegate and the current CALL newsletter. Priests were encouraged to contact members of CALL and informed that members of CALL would contact them. The October

1982 CALL newsletter reported that clergy response to this letter was minimal.

Reaching Out to Archbishop Sheehan

While traveling during the summer of 1982, several people from Lincoln had the occasion to discuss the situation in the Lincoln diocese with a number of prominent priests and bishops, including Bishop Gumbleton of Detroit. According to Betty Peterson, Bishop Gumbleton suggested a small group from the Lincoln diocese meet with Archbishop Daniel Sheehan of Omaha.[14]

Peterson wrote to Archbishop Sheehan on July 25, 1982. Archbishop Sheehan readily agreed to the meeting although he failed "to see what could come out of such a meeting."[15] He suggested that the group meet instead with Msgr. Kealy, then-Vicar General of the Lincoln Diocese. Peterson responded to Archbishop Sheehan: "people in this diocese who wish to express concerns feel that the chancery office is not open to us. Time and time again, we have been told to 'write a letter.'... We realize that you may not be able to *do* anything to help us, but we need to talk to you—and we hope you will listen" [emphasis in original].[16] Archbishop Sheehan agreed to meet with the group from Lincoln.[17]

Four members of the Diocese of Lincoln—Betty Peterson, Dolores Cardona, Gene Morton, and Jerry Johnson—drove to Omaha, Nebraska to meet with Archbishop Sheehan on September 29, 1982. The persons who attended the meeting were not representing CALL or any formal group or organization.[18] The Lincoln Catholics had a variety of topics on their agenda.[19]

When the group discussed the lector and Eucharistic minister issue with Archbishop Sheehan, Archbishop Sheehan said he had discussed these issues with Bishop Flavin and he found Bishop Flavin "adamant." According to Johnson, Archbishop Sheehan could not understand Bishop Flavin's position. However, Archbishop Sheehan recognized that, as a local bishop, Bishop Flavin had the authority to make those decisions.

The four Lincoln Catholics reportedly felt the meeting was a positive experience. Johnson wrote: "[Archbishop Sheehan] was sympathetic throughout and we really found no major points of disagreement. The four of us left with a very positive attitude toward him… At one point in the meeting he said something to the effect that we should just keep doing what we are doing."

Reaching out to the United States Bishops

As continuing attempts at communication and dialogue with Bishop Flavin proved fruitless, members of CALL began a project "detailing and documenting what we perceive as diocesan concerns and policies peculiar to the Lincoln diocese."[20] The documentation was sent along with a letter to a group of eighty-six United States bishops and the Apostolic Delegate to the United States. These bishops were chosen because they were bishops in the Midwest United States, members of the Administrative Board of the National Council of Catholic Bishops, and/or they were bishops who made public statements concerning the areas addressed in the document. Members of CALL hoped that these bishops would intercede for them with Bishop Flavin and encourage him to implement the spirit of Vatican II. CALL addressed five areas of concern: religious education, the laity, the press, priests, and religious and ecumenism. Authors of the packets rooted their comments in the Vatican II document *Christus Dominus* (Decree on the Bishops' Pastoral Office in the Church). The information packets were mailed in October 1983.

The letter[21] sent to the bishops and signed by the four officers of CALL began:

> The People of God in the Diocese of Lincoln seek your assistance. We plead for your consideration of the continuing dilemma we encounter with Bishop Glennon P. Flavin. Our concern is the divergence between the national Conference of Catholic Bishops' positions on renewal through Vatican II and the Lincoln diocesean [sic] policies which

appear to be a direct result of Bishop Flavin's intransigence in the implementation of these decrees.

The letter stated that "the sacred power of the bishop within this diocese" was not in question; rather, the "spirit with which he uses that power" was in question. The letter also stated CALL members addressed issues "in the spirit of love for our Church and with deep concern for the spiritual well-being and growth for the entire diocese."

Issues raised in this letter to the bishops were supported with documentation in the form of letters, reports, newspaper articles, etc. However, the issues addressed by CALL as early as 1983 in this documentation remained important areas of concern for CALL throughout the organization's tenure. Therefore, I include some extensive descriptions and quotations.

Religious Education

In documenting concerns about religious education, CALL focused on Confraternity of Christian Doctrine (CCD), adult education, and the Newman Center at the University of Nebraska in Lincoln. The authors of the information packet explained the great support Bishop Flavin lavished on the Catholic school system while youth who attended public schools received very little. CALL members claimed that the CCD programs in the diocese were largely ignored. The information provided in the packet explained that the diocese had no office through which CCD programs were coordinated or from which CCD catechists could seek support.

Also documented was the fact that a few programs that showed a great deal of promise in the 1970s were terminated, seemingly because they were considered a threat to the Catholic school system. Sr. Patricia Hennessey, former Director of Religious Education at St. Teresa Parish, wrote a letter explaining her experience with CCD in the diocese of Lincoln.[22] Sr. Hennessey had signed a three-year contract with St. Teresa Parish during which time the CCD program expanded and grew.

According to the letter,

> In January, 1974 I approached Msgr. Kaczmarek about renewing my
> contract in the parish for at least another year. I felt good about my
> work, had received no complaints from Msgr. and so had no suspicion
> that I was not to be rehired. Msgr. suggested to me that I look elsewhere
> for work. I was very surprised and told him that I would really like to
> stay in the parish. He replied that he could not rehire me, and could not
> give me any reason for not doing so. He said it was not his decision, it
> was the decision of higher authority. I stated that, in justice, I had a right
> to know why I was not being re-hired. Msgr. replied that I owed obedi-
> ence to the Bishop... The [St. Teresa] CCD Advisory Board wrote to
> Bishop Flavin to ask if there was a change of policy in the diocese con-
> cerning CCD programs. They requested information from him so that
> they could plan for the following school year. The answer they received
> stated that they should trust their pastor and his decision. Members of
> the Board then asked to meet with Msgr. Kaczmarek but I don't think
> they were ever able to see him... It is my understanding that any of
> the teachers who taught in the CCD program while Dolores [Peppard,
> BVM] and I were directors were not permitted to teach the following
> year... Sr. Loretta, whose last name I can't remember, was also not re-
> hired at St. John's parish at the same time. . . Bishop Flavin believed that
> all those children at that end of town could be bussed to St. Teresa's for
> school. He definitely wanted all children in a Catholic school, thus his
> non-support for CCD programs.

Addressing the same situation, St. Teresa parishioner, Edward F.
Vitzthum, explained in a letter[23] that funding for the CCD program was
ended at the time when Srs. Hennessey and Peppard's positions were
terminated. In addition, the priest who directed the CCD program was
transferred to another parish. In his letter, Vitzthum wrote:

> It does not take a great deal of intelligence to bring this sordid situa-
> tion into proper perspective. The numerical success of the St. Teresa's

CCD program was apparently perceived by the hierarchy as a threat to the parochial school in the parish. A viable CCD program might not be compatible with long-term development. Ergo, there was only one choice: destroy the CCD program... It is now more than 10 years since this unconscionable chain of events occurred. Predictably, the subsequent track record of our "Holy Mother, the Church" in serving the spiritual and religious growth needs of public school students is equally sordid... It is quite true that parents can opt to send their children to Catholic schools. However, parents have an awesome responsibility to make choices and decisions in the best interests of their children. When our children were at the age to begin the primary level of their education, we decided that our parish school had neither the human or physical resources available necessary for adequate educational preparation... The point is that other parents continue to have to make that critical decision, and if they opt for public school education for their children, "Holy Mother" in the diocese of Lincoln makes every effort to penalize both parents and children.

As illustrated by the above excerpt, diocesan programs and support seemed to indicate that Bishop Flavin wanted each and every Catholic child to attend Catholic schools. Marilyn Seiker, a member of CALL and a mother of four children who belonged to a rural parish in the Lincoln diocese, wrote of a time she approached Bishop Flavin and mentioned to him a local Methodist program that was meeting the needs of the youth.[24] Wrote Seiker:

I suggested the additional need for a Diocesan-sponsored enrichment program for our young people. Bishop Flavin commented, "I don't want to hear about what those Methodists are doing, why don't you put your children on a bus and bring them into our Catholic Schools in Lincoln?" Elmwood is located 25 miles from Lincoln. Many of our people live at greater distances. They are integrally involved in four good public schools... Teachers [in our CCD program] are mothers, who feel wholly inadequate. The Pastor does not actively participate in the program. Neither he, nor the mother-teachers receive any inspiration or practical help from the Diocese.

Carol McShane summed up the difficulty in finding good CCD education in the Lincoln diocese:

> There were a couple of nuns that came into St. Theresa's once and they were excellent and people all over the city would send their kids to CCD at St. Theresa's. The bishop shut that down. . . So the options for Catholic education for your kids gets slimmer and slimmer. So a lot of people just opted out. They just went to the Methodist church or the Episcopal church. So we lost bunches of people at that point.[25]

Clearly the decision of where to send one's children to school is complex, as demonstrated by Joan Johnson:

> When we first moved to Lincoln in 1968, we tried to enroll the children at the Cathedral. They had room for one of them, but not the other two. We didn't want to split the children up, so we enrolled them at the public school and they went to CCD classes. A year later we moved to our present house which was a block from a public school and three miles from the nearest Catholic school at the time, so we decided to keep them in public schools. At that time we had become aware of what was going on this diocese, and we were not sure we wanted them educated in a pre-Vatican II diocese. But we soon found out that if your children were not enrolled in the Catholic school in your parish, you were definitely a second-class Catholic.[26]

Members of CALL became aware of a young man, Tom Ferguson, who moved to the Lincoln diocese from another state and tried to get a Teens Encounter Christ (TEC) program started in the diocese. Ferguson had experienced the life-giving TEC retreats and, learning of the dissatisfaction of many people in the diocese with the lack of programs for young people, Ferguson attempted to start TEC in the diocese. Of the planning process, Ferguson wrote, "I had never been confronted with so much opposition and negativism in my life."[27] Ferguson decided to make an appointment with Bishop Flavin. According to Ferguson:

> When I arrived at the Chancellery *[sic]* I was greeted and sent right in. I wondered how I got in so quickly until I found out that Fr. Danko had told him about my previous experience in a monastery in South Dakota for a year. I had mentioned to Fr. Danko that I was still considering the Priesthood. The Bishop wasted no time getting into a talk about the priesthood in his diocese. He told me how he doesn't put up with long hair or facial hair and that his men go to the strictest seminary, a seminary where they don't teach "that crazy liturgy stuff." After about 25 minutes we finally got around to TEC. I mentioned that I thought TEC was a good program for the youth of the Diocese. He said they are all good programs, however a strict hand must be over them or they will get out of hand. He said these programs are built on sand because they contain emotional spiritualism which he claims is no good. He said, "I go to these Bishops meetings and hear them talking about their problems. I don't have any of those problems. I run a tight diocese."

CALL members were also concerned about the state of adult education in the Lincoln diocese. Of course, adults who were selected to be part of the acolyte or installed lector program were to receive on-going training. However, these educational programs were limited to people who fit the ministry requirements (i.e., males who send their children to Catholic schools, etc.). In addition, because acolytes and installed lectors were invited by their pastors to participate in the program, the average layperson could not attend a training session for educational purposes alone. According to reports by CALL, very little was offered to adults to enrich their faith.

A former seminary professor, Fr. Anton Morgenroth C.S.Sp., did offer programs in parishes for adults, but, "His presentations challenge even the most intellectually gifted and best educated and so do not attract the average lay person."[28] Additionally, the bishop frowned on adult Bible studies that met without a Catholic priest. One parish even published in its bulletin a notice that adults were not to meet to study the Bible without a priest present. This was noted in the April 1982 CALL newsletter: "Can you believe this appeared in a church bulletin: 'Bible Study Classes without the supervision of the priest are by order of the bishop not to be allowed.'" Bishop Flavin's desire to control the activities of the laity appear to indicate a lack of trust in the intelligence and good will of the laity.

Included in the section on religious education, CALL discussed problems they saw with diocesan campus ministry at the University of Nebraska. Prior to 1970, faculty and staff of the University of Nebraska worshipped with the students at the University's Newman Center. In 1970, Bishop Flavin declared that only students were to worship at the Newman Center and the faculty and staff were informed that they were no longer welcome. Faculty and staff were to worship at the parishes to which they belonged by virtue of residence.

A number of faculty members from the University of Nebraska were members of CALL. They learned from talking with students that

> large numbers of these young people [UNL students] refuse to attend Mass there [the Newman Center] and instead go to a downtown parish near the campus. Many others, particularly those from outside the diocese, refuse to attend Mass in Lincoln. The atmosphere at the Newman Center is best described by its dress code: no jeans at Mass, coats and ties for men, dresses and nice slacks for women. The primary goal of the Newman Center is the bishop's top priority—vocations to the religious life… the climate at St. Thomas is such that many students come away with frustration and bitterness… Bishop Flavin's overriding concerns with vocations to the religious life and his apparent fear of the intellectual approach to our faith has resulted in the Newman Center becoming a very narrow, cliquey place.[29]

Faculty expressed concern that students were receiving the message that academic inquiry and religious faith were incompatible, that "a university is a corrupting secular institution."[30] Students could attend the University of Nebraska for years and never know that there were Catholic faculty and staff of the institution who cared about them. The students "do not have before them models of persons who, committed to inquiry and criticism, are nevertheless faithful Catholics; nor do they have models of persons who, out of faith, undertake lives devoted to intellectual pursuits."[31]

The Laity

In the section of the materials sent to bishops covering the laity, CALL addressed the issue that brought them together: the installed lector policy that placed unusual restrictions on who could read Scripture at Mass. Among other issues addressed in this section, CALL was also deeply concerned about the availability of the Eucharist in the diocese. The report focused on the lack of opportunity of the homebound and institutionalized Catholics to receive the Eucharist. This had been a large concern of CALL's which seemed to come to their attention when a CALL member, Rosalind Carr, was visited by her father who was unable to attend Mass. Carr attempted to arrange communion for her father but was unsuccessful.

In the diocese of Lincoln, only priests were allowed to take the Eucharist from churches to Catholics who were unable to attend Mass. The diocese does not utilize Extraordinary Ministers of the Eucharist (EMEs). Even acolytes, trained and installed ministers who assist the priest at the table and distribute communion, were forbidden this duty. According to Bishop Flavin, the Church "specifically forbids the use of Extraordinary Ministers of Holy Communion when a priest is available. The fact that this instruction is disregarded in some places outside the Diocese does not permit me to disregard it here in the Diocese of Lincoln."[32] A difference of opinion seems to have existed between what is meant by the availability of priests. Overworked and overextended priests often found themselves able to visit the homebound and institutionalized only once a month. For Catholics who had been weekly or even daily communicants, monthly communion was quite a reduction in a very important sacramental participation.

Religious Sisters in Lincoln utilized a Sisters' Council (later disbanded) to request the ability to distribute communion in nursing homes once a week. Bishop Flavin refused. According to the CALL document sent to bishops, "The elderly, homebound, and institutionalized are neglected not so much by their priests as by their bishop's refusal to permit, encourage, and build a lay apostolate to assist an overworked, overextended, and in some cases, burned-out and/or elderly clergy."

At the time Rosalind Carr wrote to the Bishop expressing her concern regarding her father's inability to receive the Eucharist during his visit, Bishop Flavin responded that if Catholics in nursing homes were denied communion, then he would like to know about it.[33] In response, Carr and fellow CALL member, Joan Johnson, engaged in a survey of nursing homes and other institutions in the Diocese of Lincoln. Specifically, they were concerned with learning how often priests visited the institutions and presided at Masses or offered the Eucharist. In the report of their survey they wrote,

> With every telephone call, with every contact, it became apparent to us that the Catholic Church we love and respect is not loved and is certainly not respected in many of the communities we contacted. We heard again and again that Catholics are ignored by their Church... If the needs of residents of institutions are not being met, what of the spiritual needs of those who are bedridden or homebound?... It is probable that a pattern of neglect and indifference similar to the institutional one blankets the diocese. This lack of concern is symptomatic of the attitude of the official church in Lincoln.[34]

The report of the survey was sent to Bishop Flavin in August 1982. When CALL sent its packet of information to the bishops a year later, they noted that nothing had been done to improve this situation.

The final concern of this section addressed the lack of communication with Bishop Flavin. CALL members noted, "When the laity seek clarification on diocesan policy or question arbitrarily made decisions, Bishop Flavin refuses to reply or to acknowledge receipt of letters and will not communicate by phone or permit interviews with his people."[35] Some Catholics expressed their frustration that CALL turns to the local papers, an act that seemed disloyal to them. But, CALL pointed out, the secular press is the only means Catholics have of communication with the bishop.[36]

Jerry Johnson, a member of CALL and a University of Nebraska at Lincoln (UNL) faculty member, recalled the policy that prohibited faculty from worshipping at the Newman Center. He said, "what it boiled down to, he wanted, he wanted to have control over things and he wanted to have control over the kids and to be able to run the thing the way he wanted without a lot of outside influence from the faculty."[37] Another CALL member and UNL faculty member, Jim McShane, also commented:

> I've never understood it. In my worst moments I have believed that there is sincere opposition to the notion that you can keep your mind and keep your faith at the same time. And the only way to be sure that there's no confusion about that is to keep the faculty, who have kept their mind and their faith, out of the Newman Center. . . This is not a diocese which is theologically astute it seems to me. And the insistence that we bring all our young people here who are going to be trained as priests. . . very scary to know they have to accept this blind authority. And authority is based on will and clarity. I assume they clear any issue of any ambiguity. . . CALL was based on very different principles, it said: Look, we live in a wide church and if we look at what happens in other parts of the church, we understand that this is not what the church has to be, there are other options.[38]

The Press

CALL noted that Bishop Flavin refused to speak with the media and that the laity were embarrassed by how the Roman Catholic Church was represented in the secular press. The diocesan paper, the *Southern Nebraska Register*, was poorly edited with limited amounts of national and international news of religious significance. CALL members sent examples of articles to the bishops that supported their claims about the diocesan paper, including misplaced and misleading headlines, as well as copies of articles in the secular press.

Priests and Religious

In their communication with the bishops, CALL claimed that priests in the diocese do not have the kind of relationships with Bishop Flavin as described in the documents of Vatican II. As active Catholics in the Lincoln diocese, many CALL members had close relationships with priests and knew of their concerns. Many members of CALL were concerned with protecting their priest friends from the bishop's response should the bishop discover that they had talked of their dissatisfaction with members of CALL. CALL wrote: "Because of the delicacy of this particular topic, we have enclosed very little documentation; everything we report has come from several priests. Some of the reports have been given anonymously, others by priests who spoke or wrote openly but asked not to be quoted. There is a definite atmosphere of fear of speaking openly on this subject."[39] CALL identified a lack of a council of priests through which priests can gather and express their concerns. A Priests' Senate did exist, but Bishop Flavin set the agenda for the meetings and chaired the meetings.

Bishop Flavin appeared to control a great deal of priests' lives. For example, he was "overly concerned with clerical dress and clean shaven faces."[40] In addition, in 1983, Bishop Flavin, "demanded that all priests make their retreats at the diocesan retreat house in Waverly [Nebraska]... He charged them $100 each... It was nothing but a review of the Baltimore catechism." Bishop Flavin attended and frequently walked the halls. Several priests exhibited frustration and anger at such a session, saying it was *not* a spiritually uplifting experience at all."[41] In addition, priests appeared to be overworked, in part, because of a lack of lay involvement in the parishes. This lack of involvement was a result of limits placed by Bishop Flavin on lay participation. In addition, Bishop Flavin "punished" priests who "dare to differ" with diocesan policies by sending them to small parishes where they have infrequent contact with other priests.[42]

CALL reported that religious sisters in the Lincoln diocese formed a Sisters' Council in the early 1970s. The council ceased to exist in 1975. Apparently, the council was formed with the intention of participating in social justice issues. Reportedly, these activities did not receive approval from Bishop Flavin and "the council became lifeless and pointless."[43] Bishop Flavin encouraged religious sisters to "obey, wear their veils, and 'be a *real* sister.'"[44] Religious sisters who were Eucharistic Ministers in other dioceses were forbidden to continue in that ministry when they moved to Lincoln.[45]

The life of seminarians from the Lincoln diocese also appeared to have been closely controlled. A priest tells a story "when some prominent theologian was visiting the seminary, an order by phone came from the chancery office in Lincoln that no Lincoln seminarian was to attend the lecture."[46]

As noted above, the Newman Center at the University of Nebraska in Lincoln, under the direction of Fr. Leonard Kalin, was a large recruiting ground for the priesthood. "Since [Fr. Kalin's] conservative, non-ecumenical, and guilt-provoking views come across in his sermons and dealings with the students, the young men who enter seminary training from this diocese often have problems."[47] In addition, conservative men from other dioceses are attracted to the Lincoln diocese. CALL provided an example of such a priest, eventually assigned to teach religious education at the Catholic high school in Lincoln. When this priest was still a deacon, he said during a homily in which he addressed the infallibility of the Pope, "When Christ promised the Holy Spirit, he did not promise it to all of us. He did not promise it to theologians. . . He only promised it to Peter and the Apostles."[48] A CALL member who heard this homily discussed this point with the deacon after Mass "reminding him that all of us receive the Holy Spirit at Baptism and again at Confirmation. He was also questioned about his remarks that the Holy Spirit was not promised to theologians— his angry answer, 'I've had it with theologians up to here!'"[49]

Ecumenism

According to the document produced by CALL, Bishop Flavin tried to isolate Catholics in the Lincoln diocese from outside influences and therefore kept ecumenism a low priority. The CALL document provides many examples of times when the Catholic Church chose not to participate in activities that would involve non-Catholics. For example, in response to a request for clergy to serve on a chaplaincy corps for the Lincoln Police and Fire Department, Bishop Flavin responded that "his priests were too busy."[50] Another example involves the formation of a Lincoln Urban Ministries program by the Lincoln Fellowship of Churches. The program was designed to serve the poor and elderly. "Refusal by the pastor of an inner-city parish to become involved at all plus the lack of response from the chancery office is another example of lack of concern for social problems and inter-faith endeavors."[51]

CALL acknowledged several ecumenical dialogues and services that were successful. CALL asserted, however, that their success was not due to official diocesan support. Rather, interested and committed Catholic laity contributed to the success of these projects.

Meeting with Bishop Flavin

In November, 1983, CALL elected Diana McCown to be their new chairperson. McCown remembers being asked to consider standing for the position. She explained that the members of CALL felt they might have a better chance at receiving a response from Bishop Flavin if they changed leadership. In the early days of CALL, Carol McShane would carry letters to the chancery and sit in the lobby and wait to hand deliver them to the bishop. According to McCown, "he wasn't about to come out into the room with that wild woman. And not necessarily Carol, but anybody who was, you know, disagreeing. . ."[52] McCown continued, "[The CALL membership] thought somebody new would at least have a better chance with trying to work something out with the bishop because he would never see Carol; he just would not. And it was because she was aggressive early on, you know. He knew she was sitting out in the office."[53] It is interesting to note that McCown perceives that the bishop interpreted waiting quietly for hours to see him as an aggressive rather than a faithful act.

On January 14, 1984, McCown wrote to Bishop Flavin in her new capacity as President of CALL. Her letter stated:

> The organization of CALL—Catholics for Active Liturgical Life—has now been in existence for over two years. It was begun because of increasing disappointment and frustration concerning some Diocesan policies. Other incidents since then have led to a further widening of the gulf between many of us and our bishop. As the new president of CALL, I feel the necessity of attempting to narrow this gulf, and open the lines of communication. I have the hope that you would find time for a visit with me in the near future. I know that your calendar is quite full, but possibly a face-to-face discussion could be the beginning of a reconciliation between some very distressed Catholics and you, their Shepherd... I eagerly await your answer.[54]

Bishop Flavin responded to McCown in a letter dated January 20, 1984. He wrote, "I will be happy to visit with you on the condition that you come as a member of the Diocese of Lincoln and not as a representative of a group of dissidents."[55]

McCown recounted a piece of information that helped prepare her for her meeting with Bishop Flavin:

> I had also been educated about seeing the bishop because, and I'm thinking a priest friend told me this. In fact, I know a priest friend did. That when you go to visit the bishop, if he feels it might be an uncomfortable situation, about fifteen minutes into the visit, the phone will ring and he will answer the phone and if he doesn't want you there anymore, he will say, "I'm sorry but I have to go, such and such is going on" and you'll be dismissed. If he wants to continue, then he will say, "Well, have them call back" or he'll make some comment like that. And that this was a standard procedure. . . And so, and certainly that happened. Fifteen minutes after I got there it was one of those situations where the

phone rang and I kind of smiled and he said, "excuse me" and answered the phone and made some comment, "No, I'm not free right now. I'll talk to them later." So then I knew that evidently what I was saying may not have been agreeable to him, but he didn't find that I was going to cause him any problems.[56]

McCown wrote that the meeting with Bishop Flavin was a "simple and frank exchange of ideas" and she believed "we achieved a degree of understanding."[57] McCown told Bishop Flavin by letter that the membership of CALL had been considering a formal conciliation attempt available through the National Council of Catholic Bishops (NCCB). However, based on the promise of the meeting between McCown and Bishop Flavin, the membership "voted to suspend the conciliation filing until late April, in favor of a possible dialogue. . ."[58] McCown continued by asking Bishop Flavin to meet again with her along with the CALL Vice President, Gordon Peterson. She wrote,

> Please consider this request as coming from the CALL membership, to try to solve our problems at the local level. Bishop Mahony [chair of the conciliation committee of the NCCB] has suggested this solution, before we consider filing for conciliation. We hope and pray for guidance from the Holy Spirit for you and all our bishops who must lead the Church in these changing times.[59]

The bishop did not respond to this letter from McCown. McCown sent a certified letter to Bishop Flavin dated April 28, 1984 in which she asked again for a meeting.[60] She again received no response. McCown commented on the lack of response, "So [Bishop Flavin] decided that [one meeting] was all we needed because he knew that I wasn't going to change and he certainly wasn't going to change."[61]

Conciliation Attempt

When CALL received no response from Bishop Flavin to the letters they sent him, CALL formally requested conciliation through the National

Conference of Catholic Bishops (NCCB).[62] The NCCB had instituted a process by which Catholics could attempt to resolve their differences involving alleged violations of rights;[63] a committee of bishops, the Committee on Conciliation and Arbitration, was named to oversee this process. Bishop Roger Mahony, Bishop of Los Angeles at the time the process was initiated, chaired the NCCB committee. CALL filed their petition in July 1984.[64] Ten members signed the petition with the President of CALL, Diana McCown, listed as the main petitioner.

The petition listed six instances of violation of the rights of Catholics in the Diocese of Lincoln. First, Bishop Flavin refused to communicate with the petitioners. Second, the institution of the installed-lector only policy was more restrictive than necessary. Third, Bishop Flavin neglected the needs of public school children through his non-support of CCD programs. Fourth, through refusing to utilize Extraordinary Ministers of the Eucharist, Bishop Flavin did not meet the sacramental needs of the people of the diocese. Fifth, Bishop Flavin did not participate in ecumenical activities. Sixth, Bishop Flavin limited the participation of laity in their churches.

Prior to filing the petition for the conciliation process, members of CALL first carefully considered whether the process would be appropriate for their situation. Gordon Peterson, then-Vice President of CALL, discussed the conciliation procedures with Bishop Mahony. In a letter thanking him for this discussion, Peterson assured Bishop Mahony "we will do our level best, during March and April, to establish a dialogue with Bishop Flavin so as to solve our problems at the local level, however, if that does not bear fruit, it is quite likely that we will have to file a petition with your committee…"[65]

Bishop Mahony was in Africa when the petition arrived at his office. He acknowledged receipt of the petition when he returned in a letter of August 9, 1984. In this letter Bishop Mahony informed Diana McCown that he had talked to Bishop Flavin by phone and sent him a letter along with a copy of the petition. Bishop Mahony informed McCown that the next step was for Bishop Flavin to respond.

On October 26, 1984, McCown wrote to Bishop Mahony. She expressed a question on the minds of the petitioners regarding the appropriate amount of time to wait for a response to the petition. McCown explained that Bishop Flavin knew the conciliation would be attempted because she had informed him by letter that, if he did not respond to them, the petition would be filed. McCown wrote, "Since Bishop Flavin has shown a past history of refusing to respond to us, we strongly suspect that he will take the same stance with your Committee."[66] McCown explained, "for at least three years, and even longer, we have been faced with a Bishop who is not responsive to his faithful… We are genuinely hurting here."[67]

Bishop Mahony responded to the letter from Diana McCown on November 7, 1984. In his letter, Bishop Mahony wrote:

> I did receive a response from Bishop Flavin in which he respectfully declined to participate in our conciliation process… When one party declines, there is very little that our Committee can do additionally. However, in your case I have elicited the help of another Bishop who is a good friend to Bishop Flavin and together we are attempting to move towards some type of resolution of the matter.[68]

Diana McCown wrote back to Bishop Mahony on January 7, 1985 asking for an update on the progress made, or not made, by the bishop's friend. McCown assured Bishop Mahony that the petitioners "will continue to work from within the structure of our Church where the Holy Spirit leads us."[69]

Bishop Mahony wrote to both Bishop Flavin and Diana McCown on January 25, 1985. In this letter Bishop Mahony acknowledged "It has now become apparent that it will not be possible to utilize the conciliation services of this Committee in this matter."[70] McCown responded on March 12, 1985 thanking Bishop Mahony for his efforts. She stated, "Our disappointment is even greater when we realize the pain that continues to exist in this diocese among the laity, and even more deeply among the priests."[71] Bishop Mahony responded in a letter dated March 27, 1985 in which he wrote: "I appreciate the very Christian tone expressed in your letter… I am confident that your own faith and prayer will be acknowledged by the Lord according to His plan and His time. The greatest test of our discipleship with the Lord is our ability to work together even in the midst of many difficult and trying circumstances."[72]

After Bishop Flavin refused to participate in the conciliation process, CALL decided to make its attempt and the bishop's refusal known in the community. Gordon Peterson told a reporter that the petition was filed in an attempt to force Bishop Flavin to communicate with members of CALL.[73]

Before CALL decided to make their conciliation attempt and Bishop Flavin's refusal to participate public, they explored other channels available to them. For example, they contacted Archbishop Sheehan of Omaha and requested a meeting during which they could obtain his advice on how they could improve their situation.[74] At the meeting, Archbishop Sheehan agreed to pursue a few avenues. Archbishop Sheehan wrote to Bishop Mahony and he discussed the situation with Papal Nuncio Archbishop Pio Laghi, who, in turn, asked Archbishop Sheehan to discuss this situation with Bishop Flavin.[75]

McCown expressed CALL's gratitude for Archbishop Sheehan's willingness to help. She wrote, "Because of such Shepherds as you, the whole Church benefits and grows; and because of you, we have been silent in reference to the conciliation attempt and other solid evidences of impropriety by this administration."[76]

When the time during which Archbishop Sheehan said he would consult with Bishop Flavin expired (summer 1985), Diana McCown again wrote to Archbishop Sheehan to request the outcome of the consultation. She wrote that the CALL Steering Committee voted to publicize the conciliation attempt.[77] Archbishop Sheehan responded that he could not say whether any changes would occur in the Diocese of Lincoln but that "Bishop Flavin agreed to take these matters under consideration."[78] Archbishop Sheehan seemed to indicate in the letter, however, that Bishop Flavin would not change his policies until the Pope changed the *Moto Proprio* upon which Bishop Flavin relied almost totally regarding his view of canonical ministries, including that of lector.

CALL's attempt to communicate with Bishop Flavin and its attempt to utilize existing avenues for reconciliation had failed due to the bishop's unwillingness to participate. Once again, while the group received sympathy from others, no one CALL contacted had the authority to require Bishop Flavin to meet with members of his diocese or change any of his policies. Reflecting on this failed conciliation attempt, Kay Haley commented:

> I think it's wonderful for a bishop to be in charge of his diocese, but it's also like it's his very own little kingdom and he's like a little king and that's the way he wants to treat it. He alone has authority and the Archbishop in Omaha can't do anything. He's answering only to the Pope. So it can be a real problem if you have a man like Bishop Flavin who wanted to build a fence around the diocese. . . and the abuse of power and I think that's the thing that makes me angry is this flagrant abuse of power. . .[79]

Another Meeting with Bishop Flavin

Even though CALL's attempt at a formal conciliation process had failed, CALL did not stop trying to resolve their disagreements with Bishop Flavin's policies through direct communication. Gordon Peterson, then-Vice-President of CALL, wrote to Bishop Flavin on January 10, 1986 and requested a meeting between him, Diana McCown, President of CALL and Bishop Flavin. In his letter, Peterson wrote:

> Surely Christ dwells in us all, including his laity. He does not dwell solely in the religious, clergy or hierarchy. When we lay people express our concern for the good of the Church, we do so out of love for both Christ and the Church, and out of some degree of divine inspiration. By failing to even listen to us, you are overlooking part of God's message. In refusing to trust in your laity, you are also displaying a lack of trust in God, i.e., you demonstrate that you feel God has not sent you good and helpful lay people. For the last four years, members of CALL have tried to get you to listen. During those four years you have steadfastly refused, except for one meeting with Diana McCown on January 26,

1984 (almost two years ago)… I am asking you to be open and to let God's presence be felt by you through your laity.[80]

The Bishop's secretary contacted Gordon Peterson and told him that Bishop Flavin "would be willing to meet with me alone (McCown excluded) so long as I would assure the Bishop that I would attend as a 'private individual' and not as a member of some 'dissident group.'"[81]

According to Gordon Peterson, Bishop Flavin spent most of the thirty-five minute meeting complaining "about the negative attitude of CALL and the 'dissention' it has caused."[82] According to a written report of the meeting, "At several points in the interview he referred to us as a bunch of protestants with a small 'p.'"[83] Peterson reported that the bishop did not address any solutions to the concerns Peterson raised.

During this meeting Peterson addressed the issue of dialogue with Bishop Flavin. Peterson shared that, as an attorney, he found the best way to solve problems is through dialogue. "I told him that what I would like to do is see these problems between himself and CALL be put to rest and that the only way to do that was to really talk it out. At several points in the conversation, I told him that we are not saying that we are necessarily right, that we certainly think we're right, but that we would like to have a chance to express ourselves and talk things out with him."[84]

The bishop agreed to meet with Peterson again, alone. When Peterson asked if he could bring Diana McCown along, the bishop reportedly said that he already knew what she wanted so there was no need for her to attend the meeting.[85] Four days before that meeting was to have taken place, the bishop's secretary called Peterson and cancelled the meeting informing Peterson that Bishop Flavin had received and read the latest *CallSpirit* and did not see a need to talk to Peterson. This issue of *CallSpirit* included a report on the deterioration of the Catholic Social Services Bureau. Peterson came to the conclusion that

I *believe* (although I certainly do not know) that [Bishop Flavin] is under some pressure from "higher authority" to talk to us, and that is really the only reason he saw me, or agreed to the second meeting he later cancelled. The visits are really only "token" visits for him. He seems to have no understanding (either intellectual or emotional) of the fact that criticism is a normal and healthy human way of bringing about change or adjustment. He simply takes all criticism as a personal attack, gets angry, and can't seem to get beyond that anger.[86]

Letters of Acknowledgment and Support

When members of Catholics for Active Liturgical Life were unable to reach Bishop Flavin, they contacted other bishops, theologians, priests, church officials, and Canon lawyers to seek advice on how to improve their situation. Many of those contacted responded to CALL. While CALL was ignored in its own diocese, CALL received encouragement and support for their activities from other parts of the Roman Catholic Church. These responses demonstrate that the members of Catholics for Active Liturgical Life were not out of step with much of the Church in the United States. For example, Ladislas Orsy, SJ, from the Department of Canon Law at The Catholic University of America wrote, "I would do anything to help you because I think that one of the greatest needs in the Church is to restore to the laity their right position in the Christian community."[87] Reverend Ronald F. Krisman, Executive Director, Secretariat for the Liturgy commented, "I am gratified always to read of the deep faith of so many people in the diocese, and I am hopeful that the leadership of the diocese might soon come to tap into the rich resource of the peoples' goodness and willingness to be involved in the full life of the Church."[88] However, the letter writers acknowledged that there was little they could do to help. Reverend John A. Gurrieri, the Executive Director of the Bishop's Committee on Liturgy noted, "As you know, the Bishops' Committee on the Liturgy has no authority or competence in a local diocese… Therefore, I know no other way to advise you than to counsel you along the same paths you have been following."[89] Bishop Thomas J. Gumbleton wrote, "As I'm sure you know, I have no easy answers for you. There is nothing I can do to change the mind and heart of the leadership within Lincoln."[90]

Still, some offered hope, even if undefined. For example, Ladislas Orsy commented, "The fact that no legal remedy is available to you does not mean that the voice of CALL should not be heard. Good ideas are bound to break through; they cannot be stopped for long."[91] Augustinian John E. Rotelle encouraged, "Keep trying and persevering. The good that you are doing now along with the suffering, will always be rewarded."[92] Bishop Gumbleton urged members of CALL not to lose heart:

> In fact, the whole future of the Church in Lincoln depends on how long you can bear the hurt and the suffering that you and others are experiencing. You are fighting "the good fight" and as in most cases like that, it is difficult, if not sometimes impossible, to see the light at the end of the tunnel.[93]

Bishop Joseph L. Imesch of Joliet wrote, "I am certain that things will change. I only wish that I could say when."[94]

And Yet Members of CALL Hope

Catholics for Active Liturgical Life was founded because Bishop Flavin instituted a new policy that effectively barred women from reading scripture during Mass. Though Bishop Flavin's policy differed from every other diocese in the United States, the bishop appeared to believe that he was being faithful to Church teaching. CALL spent a great deal of time researching and documenting its position and rooting its argument in Church documents. The interpretation of Church teaching CALL offered was clearly, at the time, the more prevalent one. When women were barred from reading Scripture in the Lincoln Diocese, women were reading throughout the United States and in other countries as well, including at Papal Masses.

Even those who disagreed with Bishop Flavin's policy believed he had the authority, as Bishop of Lincoln, to institute the policy. This authority raises important questions about the structure of the Roman Catholic Church: What does it mean that a bishop can ignore attempts at communication from the people he is supposed to lead? How can it be that CALL members had no recourse to address their problems?

Members of CALL were relieved of teaching duties in CCD programs and trustee positions in parishes.[95] CALL members nominated to run for positions in their parishes were not allowed to run for those positions "on orders from the Bishop."[96] Diocesan officials derisively referred to members of CALL as "Call Girls". Diana McCown reflected on her own inability to serve her Church in her "Letter From Our President" column in *CallSpirit*:

> Those of us who represent CALL in an official capacity are most restricted as we are most well known. After many years in the CCD program, I have not been allowed to teach in recent years, even on a substitute basis, though I am a teacher by profession. I am allowed to continue in the choir, serve coffee and clean the church. I was allowed to prepare the lamb and set tables for our Holy Thursday Passover Supper, yet could not read in this most personal of our community celebrations, even in the church basement! My gift of my talents to my church has been discarded.[97]

McCown explains, though, that she is using her talents in other ways, "to enlighten and inform, to bring God's message to the modern world through Vatican II." Indeed, one writer to *CallSpirit* commented, "I am sure that you have done much more good with your newsletter than you would have done reading at Mass in your parish churches."[98]

Ten years into CALL's existence, members still expressed hope that they would be blessed with an inclusive church. In a reflection on Advent, Marilyn Seiker wrote: "And will this be OUR YEAR, too? The year when we People of God in the Diocese of Lincoln regain our freedom from imposed laws—the year we are empowered to grow again toward Christian maturity, graced by the Holy Spirit, in the LIGHT which is our legacy through the Second Vatican Council."[99] The first time I read this passage by Seiker, I was deeply moved because of the beauty of hope expressed in the statement but also because, in hindsight, I knew it was not CALL's year. Indeed, it never was. I knew what was to come.

Notes Chapter 3

1.   "Church authority misused," *National Catholic Reporter*, June 18, 1982.

2.   Betty Peterson described the members of CALL as "for the most part, people deeply involved with the parishes and very supportive of the church." Roger Catlin, "'Prayer': Group's weapon against lector restriction," *National Catholic Reporter*, November 27, 1981.

3.   Patty Beutler, "Catholics organize committee," *Lincoln Star*, November 11, 1981.

4.   Thomas C. Fox, "Nebraska Bishop Cuts Off Dissenters: 'Autocratic' Leadership Frustrates Vocal Minority in the Lincoln Diocese," *National Catholic Reporter*, June 18, 1982.

5.   Letter from CALL Steering Committee to CALL membership, February 19, 1982.

6.   Written description of what happened that day available in the CALL archives, Nebraska State Historical Society.

7.   Ibid.

8.   Carol McShane, letter to Bishop Flavin, May 9, 1982.

9.   Associated Press, "Catholics told not to support CALL," *Lincoln Star*, May 24, 1982.

10. Diana McCown, interview with the author.

11. CALL Position Paper, November 9, 1981.

12. Letter from CALL to Lincoln diocesan priests, August 1982.

13. Ibid.

14. Betty Peterson, letter to Archbishop Daniel Sheehan, July 25, 1982.

15. Archbishop Daniel Sheehan, letter to Betty Peterson, August 2, 1982.

16. Betty Peterson, letter to Archbishop Daniel Sheehan, September 15, 1982.

17. Archbishop Daniel Sheehan, letter to Betty Peterson, September 17, 1982.

18. Betty Peterson, letter to Archbishop Sheehan, Sept 23, 1982.

19. My information about this meeting comes from handwritten notes about the meeting made by Jerry Johnson which he provided to me. Topics of discussion at this meeting included: the Hispanic community in Lincoln, the Newman Center at the University of Nebraska, seminary training of priests in the Lincoln diocese, the pain felt by some priests in the Lincoln diocese, the instituted lector program, and Lincoln's lack of Eucharistic ministers. According to Johnson's notes, Archbishop Sheehan had

"misgivings about the Newman Center." Archbishop Sheehan had heard that students apparently reported that Fr. Kalin, the pastor at the Newman Center, had said negative things about the Omaha diocese. In addition, Fr. Kalin had reportedly convinced some young men from the Omaha diocese who were considering the priesthood and studying at the University of Nebraska at Lincoln "to study for the priesthood through the Lincoln diocese" instead of Omaha. According to Johnson's report of what Archbishop Sheehan told them, when Archbishop Sheehan approached Bishop Flavin about the negative comments about the Omaha diocese, Bishop Flavin responded that Fr. Kalin "must have been misquoted."

20. "86 Bishops Hear CALL From Lincoln," *CallSpirit*, Nov-Dec 1983.

21. Letter available in the CALL archives located at the Nebraska Historical Society.

22. This letter was included in the packet of materials mailed to the bishops and is available in the CALL archives in the Nebraska Historical Society.

23. Ibid.

24. Ibid.

25. Carol McShane, interview with the author.

26. Joan Johnson, interview with the author.

27. Packet of information provided to the bishops.

28. Ibid.

29. Ibid.

30. Ibid, I. F-1.

31. Ibid.

32. Quoted in packet of information provided to the bishops, Section II.

33. Bishop Glennon Flavin, letter to Rosalind Carr, July 19, 1982, included in packet of information sent to bishops.

34. Rosalind K. Carr with assistance from Joan Johnson, "A Survey of Catholic Contact With Institutionalized Persons In the Lincoln Diocese," August 1982, submitted to His Excellency Bishop Glennon P. Flavin.

35. Packet of information provided to the bishops.

36. Ibid.

37. Jerry Johnson, interview with the author.

38. Jim McShane, interview with the author.

39. Packet of information provided to the bishops, Priests and Religious section, p. 1.

40. Ibid, p. 2.

41. Ibid, p. 2.

42. Ibid, p. 3.

43. Ibid, p. 3.

44. Ibid, p. 3.

45. Ibid, p. 3.

46. Ibid, p. 4.

47. Ibid, p. 4.

48. Ibid, p. 4.

49. Ibid, p. 4-5.

50. Packet of information provided to the bishops, Ecumenism section, p. 2.

51. Ibid, p. 2.

52. Diana McCown, interview with the author.

53. Ibid.

54. Diana McCown, letter to Bishop Glennon Flavin, January 14, 1984.

55. Bishop Glennon Flavin, letter to Diana McCown, January 20, 1984.

56. Diana McCown, interview with the author.

57. Diana McCown, letter to Bishop Glennon Flavin, March 16, 1984.

58. Ibid.

59. Ibid.

60. Diana McCown, letter to Bishop Glennon Flavin, April 28, 1984.

61. Diana McCown, interview with the author.

62. Today it is called the United States Conference of Catholic Bishops.

63. Betty Stevens, "10 Catholics: Bishop nixed our petition," *Lincoln Journal*, October 10, 1985.

64. Ibid.

65. Gordon Peterson, letter to Bishop Roger Mahony, March 9, 1984.

66. Diana McCown, letter to Bishop Roger Mahony, October 26, 1984.

67. Ibid.

68. Bishop Roger Mahoney, letter to Diana McCown, November 7, 1984.

69. Diana McCown, letter to Bishop Roger Mahoney, January 7, 1985.

70. Bishop Roger Mahoney, letter to Diana McCown, January 25, 1985.

71. Diana McCown, letter to Bishop Roger Mahoney, March 12, 1985.

72. Roger Mahoney, letter to Diana McCown, March 27, 1985.

73. Betty Stevens, "10 Catholics…."

74. Diana McCown, letter to Archbishop Daniel Sheehan, March 12, 1985.

75. Archbishop Daniel Sheehan, letter to Diana McCown, July 2, 1985.

76. Diana McCown, letter to Archbishop Sheehan, July 5, 1985.

77. Diana McCown, letter to Archbishop Sheehan, September 12, 1985.

78. Archbishop Sheehan, letter to Diana McCown, September 16, 1985.

79. Kay Haley, interview with the author.

80. Gordon Peterson, letter to Bishop Flavin, January 10, 1986.

81. Gordon Peterson, letter to Archbishop Sheehan, March 3, 1986.

82. Ibid.

83. Gordon Peterson, written report of meeting with Bishop Flavin on January 28, 1986.

84. Ibid.

85. Ibid.

86. Gordon Peterson, letter to Archbishop Sheehan, March 3, 1986.

87. Letter from Ladislas Orsy, SJ, to Carol McShane, February 21, 1983.

88. Letter from Reverend Ronald F. Krisman to Gordon Peterson, May 24, 1990.

89. Letter from Reverend John A. Gurrieri to Carol McShane, March 12, 1982.

90. Letter from Bishop Thomas J. Gumbleton to "Friends in Lincoln," June 24, 1982.

91. Letter from Ladislas Orsy, SJ, to Carol McShane, February 21, 1983.

92. Letter from John E. Rotelle, O.S.A., to Carol McShane, May 28, 1982.

93. Letter from Bishop Thomas J. Gumbleton to "Friends in Lincoln," June 24, 1982.

94. Letter from Bishop Joseph L. Imesh to Betty Peterson, March 5, 1985.

95. Packet of information sent to bishops, 1983.

96. Diana McCown, *CallSpirit*, Letter From Our President, May-June 1986.

97. Ibid.

98. "Open Line, *CallSpirit* Winter Issue 1986-87.

99. Marilyn Seiker, "We Look To the Light," *CallSpirit* Vol. X, No. 4, 1991.

CHAPTER 4

CALL Disbands

For the first time since we had come to Lincoln, we felt that we were part of a group of deeply committed Catholics who wanted to be part of the Vatican II church. They were deep thinkers about their faith and how it could be applied to their everyday lives. I am not as bright as some of them, or maybe as talkative, but that did not matter to any of them. I have never felt as accepted in a group for who I was as I felt with this group. They just wanted to have an active part in their church, each according to the gifts that God had given them. And all of us were being put in the same small box, by a man who was threatened by who knows what. . . [The bishop put] absolutely no trust in the direction that the Holy Spirit would lead all of us. But it was still wonderful to belong to a really Catholic community that felt the same way we did.[1]—Joan Johnson

CATHOLICS FOR ACTIVE LITURGICAL LIFE provided an opportunity for committed Catholics who believed they had a right to be heard in their own church to build relationships with each other. Many of these relationships were personal and caring; the members formed a new community.[2] Members of CALL and readers of *CallSpirit* became better educated about the Church. They read the Documents of Vatican II and Catholic periodicals. They used every avenue open to them to raise questions about issues that directly impacted their lives and the lives of other

Lincoln diocesan Catholics. CALL members also learned how powerful a bishop is in his own diocese. As Joan Johnson noted, "We were naïve enough to think that the hierarchy outside Lincoln would intervene by acting as intermediaries."[3] After intensive work documenting life in the Lincoln diocese and sharing their concerns with authority figures outside the diocese, they received sympathy but not much else.

According to Canon Law, when a bishop reaches the age of seventy-five, he must tender his resignation. Members of Catholics for Active Liturgical Life eagerly awaited the retirement of Bishop Flavin and hoped for a new bishop who embraced the Vatican II reforms enjoyed in other U.S. dioceses and allowed the laity more responsibility in their parishes. Joan Johnson recalled:

> At some point we figured out when his [Bishop Flavin's] 75th birthday was, when it would be mandatory to resign. We figured we would weather the storm because a replacement would surely be better. We were wrong on both counts. In fact, it took a year longer than that to have a replacement named and boy were we ever wrong about a better environment to follow.[4]

While members of CALL had no official influence in the choice of their next bishop, they studied the process by which bishops were chosen and wrote letters to church officials outlining what they considered to be the needs of the Diocese of Lincoln. When Fabian Bruskewitz from Milwaukee, Wisconsin was named the new Bishop of Lincoln, members of CALL learned as much as they could about him. They heard he was considered conservative. CALL received a letter from a Catholic man in Milwaukee who warned them to "be careful. This man is not what you need, what you're hoping for. Be careful."[5] Yet CALL members remained cautiously optimistic. Reflecting on that time in an interview, Carol McShane stated, ". . .we were sure that it couldn't get any worse. We were just absolutely sure. . . So we were very happy when Bishop Bruskewitz was coming. We sent him letters. . . I went to his installation, and we wanted to meet with him. . . "[6]

Bishop Bruskewitz was consecrated Bishop of Lincoln on May 13, 1992 and he served in that capacity until his retirement on September 14, 2012. Bishop Flavin continued to live in the Lincoln diocese until his death on August 26, 1995. Bishop Flavin left a legacy in his strong emphasis on vocations and in his insistence on priestly conformity. Bishop Flavin ordained a large number of men to the priesthood and these men were educated at the most conservative seminaries. Some claim the priests' conservative education ensures Catholic orthodoxy will live on in the diocese.[7]

After his arrival in Lincoln, Bishop Bruskewitz told the members of the Lincoln diocese that he would take at least a year to meet with many people and assess the diocese.[8] Shortly after his consecration as bishop, Bishop Bruskewitz asked the priests of the Lincoln diocese to read a letter from him at all Masses on June 6 and 7, 1992. In this letter, Bishop Bruskewitz honored the efforts of Bishop Flavin and greeted the members of the diocese and asked for their fidelity and prayerful support. Looking ahead to actions he would take in his capacity as bishop, Bishop Bruskewitz stated:

> It has been said that to lead is to decide, which means of course, that as my ministry is carried out, decisions will have to be made. Some of these decisions, doubtlessly, will be painful and difficult to accept on the part of some people. It is especially in moments such as that that I will have to call upon the well-known loyalty, humility, and docility of the people of this Diocese in doing my mission as God gives me to see that it should be done.[9]

The descriptors the bishop chose to highlight in this context are fascinating: loyal, humble and docile. While I am sure it is not an inclusive list of Bishop Bruskewitz's highly valued Catholic characteristics, the list is instructive of how Bishop Bruskewitz believes the people of the Lincoln diocese should respond to his decision-making authority.

Within several months of becoming Bishop of Lincoln, Bishop Bruskewitz made a slight change to the lector policy by allowing religious sisters to read Scripture at Masses in their community convents, if no installed lector was present. This new policy was communicated to the pastors of the diocese in a Pastoral Bulletin, the priests' newsletter. In this bulletin, Bishop Bruskewitz outlined the requirements including that "The Sister doing the reading has rehearsed the pronunciation, phrasing, diction, etc. and is suitable for this task."[10]

Bishop Bruskewitz expressed concern with what could happen if news of this modification was made public. As stated in a Pastoral Bulletin: "This disposition is given on an experimental basis only and will be withdrawn if it is the subject of 'publicity', abuse, etc. Priests who offer holy Mass in convent chapels should quietly inform the Sisters about this and advise them to give this no 'publicity'. On special, great, or solemn occasions, Sisters should be encouraged to invite in an instituted lector."[11] Bishop Bruskewitz demonstrated his belief in the preference for installed lectors by suggesting that the sisters look outside their own community for readers on "special, great, or solemn occasions."

CALL's Interactions with their New Bishop, Fabian Bruskewitz

While both Bishops Flavin and Bruskewitz were known for their conservatism, Bishop Bruskewitz demonstrated that he possessed a few traits that were significantly different from Bishop Flavin. First, Bishop Bruskewitz did not ignore the media. Second, Bishop Bruskewitz exhibited a biting or caustic tone regarding ideas about which or people with whom he disagreed. Diana McCown, who met and talked with both bishops, reflected on this difference, "He was a much different person than Flavin—much more aggressive, much more negative, much more cutting, even in face-to-face dialogue."[12] The matter was addressed in an editorial in the *National Catholic Reporter*. Bishop Bruskewitz is described by some as "kind in personal relationships but also fear-driven and authoritarian, an autocrat needing to enforce a conformity of practice and belief that is neither healthy nor wise."[13]

Diana McCown met with Bishop Bruskewitz shortly after his arrival in Lincoln. McCown contacted Bishop Bruskewitz in her capacity as President of CALL to request the meeting and Bishop Bruskewitz agreed. McCown reflected on this meeting:

> He just wanted to know all about CALL. What it did. . . And we talked about the church and we talked about the fact that CALL Catholics were active Catholics, that we had not left the church. We weren't working from the outside, that we were active and continued to stay active within our parishes and that it was a group of people who really wanted change in the church. Not because they wanted the change but because it would be good for the church to have that change. And there again, the whole thing, the focus was on women readers, that was the focus. . . people would say, "Well, did he tell you anything about what he's going to do?" He didn't commit in any way. He would just ask questions… He wanted names, he wanted the names of the people in the group. He said, "Well, how many people are in the group?" And I said, "Well, we don't have an active membership list. We don't take a membership in CALL." But, I said, "Our newsletter goes to over a thousand people in the diocese." And he said, "Well, do you have the names of the people who are in the Lincoln area that you know?" And I said, "I'm sorry bishop, but I can't give you any names." I said, "That would be going against their confidence. I can't give you any names." And so, he was a little, little put off with me by that, that I didn't give him names. I wasn't about to, of course. And I said, "You have my name, you know who I am." So that was one thing he was pushing for. He questioned the fact that we would go against the authority of the bishop, of any bishop. That the bishop was designated by the Pope and that the Pope was the representative of St. Peter and the bishop was the representative of St. Peter and Christ to us. . . At any rate, he really wanted, he wanted the inside dope about CALL. That's what he wanted. He didn't want to know if we were right or wrong or what our reasoning was behind doing this.[14]

After this meeting, McCown sent materials to help Bishop Bruskewitz understand the attempts CALL made to resolve their conflicts with Bishop

Flavin. She included the packet of information sent to selected bishops and archbishops in 1983 and a copy of the petition for conciliation along with *CallSpirit* newsletters that reported the conciliation attempt. Finally, she included a copy of the letter CALL sent to selected bishops and archbishops regarding their assessment of the needs of the diocese as a new bishop was in the process of being chosen.

McCown requested another meeting with Bishop Bruskewitz and the CALL Steering Committee in early 1993. Bishop Bruskewitz responded to this request with a long letter that, though it began and ended with pleasantries, exhibited an acrimonious tone. McCown reflected, "You would almost think it was satire if you didn't know it was the bishop writing to people in the diocese. It was very cutting. It was very terse. It was very, on the border of insulting. And he didn't know us. He knew me, but he didn't know us."[15] He requested further information on whom, specifically, would attend the meeting and how the Steering Committee members were selected to serve. He inquired as to the nature of the "further dialogue" requested, specifically the goal of the dialogue. "I do not like simply to dialogue for the sake of dialogue which, my experience tells me, is a waste of time."[16] He requested an agreed upon agenda for the proposed meeting.

In the letter, Bishop Bruskewitz wrote that he would be happy to discuss Vatican II with the CALL Steering Committee. He wrote: "However, from reading at least your last several issues of the publication entitled *CallSpirit,* I find not the slightest indication of any knowledge about the documents of the Second Vatican Council. It appears to me that those who publish this brochure are unfamiliar with the Second Vatican Council, but simply use 'Vatican II' as a pretext and a convenient expression for their primary activity of Bishop-bashing."[17] In this segment of his letter, Bishop Bruskewitz highlighted the ongoing battle over interpretation of the Second Vatican Council.[18]

Bishop Bruskewitz ended his letter with a long explanation of what he had learned about perceptions of CALL in the diocese:

I have had occasion to encounter many people who are out-spoken in opposition to your organization claiming that it is entirely unrepresentative, but consists basically of disgruntled feminists, left-wing liberals, anti-clericals, and general discontents, bound together only by the negative factor of opposition to the Diocesan regulation in regard to Instituted Lectors doing readings at Eucharistic Liturgies... Many priests have told me that they are convinced that your organization stands in violation of Canon 300 in the Code of Canon Law of the Catholic Church, and, although one or the other of their priest-brothers, perhaps embittered for some reason or another, might be allies of your organization, the overwhelming majority of the priests of the Diocese of Lincoln, are opposed to your group. I am especially amazed by the large number of women who continue to approach me at various times, and say in quite emphatic terms that they are opposed both to your organization and to its goals, insofar as these can be discerned. Many women, for instance, have told me that they would ordinarily be in favor of women participating in the Mass by being lectors, but they are constrained from supporting this development in the Diocese of Lincoln because it may give some people an illusion of making concessions to your group, which they see as fundamentally repulsive. Given that attitude, as you can see your group may actually be an obstacle to further development toward having women lectors. I would not say that the above statements represent my thinking, but at the same time, I would not want to dissociate myself from them.[19]

Canon 300 in the Code of Canon Law states, "No association is to assume the name Catholic without the consent of competent ecclesiastical authority according to the norm of Canon 312."[20] Canon 312 grants authority to "erect public associations" to "the diocesan bishop in his own territory" and explains that "written consent of the diocesan bishop is required for the valid erection of an association..."[21]

Responding to this letter, Diana McCown expressed her sadness at receiving "such a harsh letter from my Bishop."[22] McCown reiterated the CALL Steering Committee's desire to meet with Bishop Bruskewitz even though it seemed to her that they had been "pre-judged by hear-say." McCown wrote of the various ways in which members of the CALL Steering Committee were involved in their churches:

> These Catholics are particularly faithful and ardent in their devotion to the Holy Mass and the reception of the Sacraments, especially the reception of the Body of our Lord in the Holy Eucharist. I am happy to say that more active and faith-filled Catholics could be rarely found anywhere. We definitely are *not* "disgruntled feminists, left wing liberals, anti-clericals, and general discontents" as imputed by some. We have never in the past created a stir in anything more reactive than marching on freezing January Saturdays in the Walk for Life, or actively respecting the "whole cloth" of life by standing up against the death penalty. You have mis-taken *(sic)* us as malcontents because we asked for, both privately and publicly, that which other Catholics take for granted... Be assured, I would never have lent my support to an anti-Catholic group, or a group determined to undermine all that I have believed in my 54 years. My rights and beliefs as a Catholic by far supersede my rights as a woman. This has only been a women's issue insofar as some of my rights as a Catholic, who happens to be a woman, have been denied. My greatest desire is to be of service to my Church and my God, to whom I owe everything. If the talents that I have to offer as teacher and trained reader are not utilized, my life and the life of my Church are the poorer for it.[23]

Bishop Bruskewitz agreed to meet with selected members of the CALL Steering Committee, though he wrote, "I find it difficult to suppose that you will be saying anything more than has already been expressed in the communications and publications of your organization over the past years."[24] Bishop Bruskewitz wrote that he would like the conversation "to take place in the context of three recent publications."[25] These books, published by Ignatius Press, were *The Politics of Prayer: Feminist Language and the Worship of God* by Helen Hull Hitchcock, *Women in the Priesthood?: A Systematic Analysis in the Light of the Order of Creation and Redemption* by Manfred Hauke, and *Ungodly Rage: The Hidden Face of Catholic Feminism* by Donna Steichen. All three of these books address the issue of women in church from a conservative viewpoint. In a response to Steichen's book, *Ungodly Rage*, Rosemary Radford Ruether wrote

> Steichen draws an inflammatory picture of Catholic feminists as a "demonic conspiracy" against the Catholic church. She not only employs stock diatribes against feminists as "lesbians," "antifamily" and "antilife" but also as "witches" in league with the devil. Using a technique of guilt by association, Steichen draws a fallacious picture of post-Christian *wicca* feminists as pagan devil-worshipers and then claims that all Catholic feminists are in league with these "witches" as secret promoters of an anti-Catholic worldview. For Steichen the promoters of this demonic conspiracy include not only prominent feminist theologians and activists... but virtually every nun and laywoman of even moderate feminist leanings operating in Catholic parishes, schools and diocesan offices. . . As Steichen said in a talk at St. Lawrence Church in northern Virginia in early October, the entire middle management of the church, priests, nuns and laymen and laywomen, are made up of these "secret apostolates."[26]

If Bishop Bruskewitz actually believed what was written in these books, one could understand his likely fear for the future of the Catholic Church.

Those who were to meet with the bishop dutifully obtained the books and read them. They were confused, though, as the books had little or nothing to do with the issues to which they had committed themselves in CALL. While CALL addressed women readers, it had not taken a position on the ordination of women. McCown said,

> Well we got the books and they were all so, they were awful. The one, of course, was about the fact that feminism was taking over the church, it was trying to. And that the feminists, the raging, wild feminists, are trying to disrupt the church totally because they want to have control because then they will put goddesses in place of. . . I mean, it was insulting to ask us to read those books. And the other books were all of a type.

Definitely conservative, ultra-conservative, definitely anti-women. . . And it was like, it was the tirade of somebody who felt that the church was being lost to all these liberals.[27]

Jim McShane, who also read the books recalled them as "poisonous." McShane reflected further:

And people who had been engaged in CALL for a long time and who had been looking forward to the coming of the new bishop as a time of renewed vitality for the diocese were terribly disheartened by the response of the new bishop. "Read these awful books and see yourselves in them" was the first thing, in effect, [he] said to us. And the second thing he, in effect, he said was something, was about the "ugly bishop bashers" the third thing he said was "I'm not going to talk to you." And his way of saying "I'm not going to talk to you was simply by not answering his mail. Now if you say to somebody, or give them to believe, I don't remember the precise language, "You and I disagree. I want you to see where I'm coming from. Read this material and then we'll talk." And you read the material and you say "We read the material, now we'll talk." And you discover that the talk consisted of reading the material. This isn't quite straight. And many people lost hope.[28]

CALL sent a letter to Bishop Bruskewitz dated March 17, 1993 informing him that they had read the books and they requested a meeting. As indicated above, despite the compliance of the CALL Steering Committee to the bishop's wishes, Bishop Bruskewitz declined to meet with the group.

In an interview, Diana McCown reflected on that time in her life and told the following story:

I was at home baking bread, I was kneading bread, and it was after I'd sent the second letter to him [Bishop Bruskewitz] in reference to those books. And I had the feeling of being a martyr. It's strange how these things come. But I had the feeling of being a martyr. It just came over me all at once. I was kneading bread like this and I was thinking about

that letter and thinking about some of the horrible things he had said,...
And thinking that he was capable of doing things, and maybe it was a
forewarning of an excommunication down the line. But it was, I think
thinking of what he could possibly do to me, to my family, to us, in
retaliation. That was the feeling you got from having read his letters,
what else he could do. And this altruism just flooded over me, this thing
of saying, I will put myself on the line. If he wants to martyr me, fine.
Because I really believe in this cause. It's so strong for me. I really believe
in it and I will be glad no matter what happens, no matter what he does
to me, I will be glad that I did this. And it was the first time that I can
really say in reference to CALL that I had this altruistic feeling of, I'm
not the important thing, it's what we accomplish is the important thing.
And even if I suffer for it, I had the feeling it was like maybe the martyrs
felt when they were actually up against the emperor who said, give up
your faith or be killed. And it was that feeling, it was just, and it was
strange. It was, you know, I suppose it was the Holy Spirit. It was just
like it flooded over me at that moment while I was kneading bread at
home.[29]

The Lector Policy Changes

After the reported period of discussion and prayer, Bishop Bruskewitz
decided to allow non-instituted readers in the Diocese of Lincoln. The
priests were informed of this change in policy through a letter addressed
to all Diocesan priests and marked "confidential." Members of CALL
received a copy of this letter from one of the priests who was on the bishop's mailing list. The letter from Bishop Bruskewitz was lengthy and it
spelled out quite carefully his thought process. Bishop Bruskewitz began
the letter reviewing the current policy and commenting on the positive
aspects of the instituted lector policy. In addition to his perception of
the positive effect the instituted lector program had on the personal and
spiritual lives of the lectors, Bishop Bruskewitz wrote: "Another positive
aspect has been the absence of the feminization of religious practice. In

some parts of the world, men choose to remain aloof from religious practice or on its margins because the culture proclaims the practice of religion
is not 'virile' but rather something that is basically effeminate."[30] Bishop
Bruskewitz implies in this paragraph that when women are involved
in public ministry, men chose to remove themselves from involvement
because the ministry is not considered masculine. Bishop Bruskewitz also
discussed the lack of correlation between including women as readers
and improved church life.

Along with the benefits of the existing lector policy, Bishop
Bruskewitz addressed what he saw as a danger that could come from a
change in the policy. Bishop Bruskewitz weakly supported some gender-
based concerns, but he feared that a change in policy would send the
message of appeasement: "Certain aspects of 'women's rights' have a kind
of legitimacy, e.g. equal pay for equal work, but there are aspects of the
feminist 'movement' in our culture which are inimical to our Catholic
Faith. Changes in our diocesan regulation may be seen by some as an
appeasement of radical feminists and a concession to undesirable cultural
pressures."[31] Clearly, Bishop Bruskewitz did not want to give the impression that CALL could claim any responsibility for a change in diocesan
policy. He appeared to have feared that a change in policy would offer
legitimacy to CALL he did not think they deserved. Bishop Bruskewitz
also demonstrated his lack of knowledge of the complexity and richness
of feminisms as the activities and concerns of those involved in CALL
cannot be accurately described as part of the radical feminist movement.

Next, Bishop Bruskewitz addressed the negative side of the existing
instituted lector policy. First, Bishop Bruskewitz noted that when the policy was initiated, women who had been reading at Mass were prohibited
from continuing in that ministry. Second, Bishop Bruskewitz acknowledged that the Lincoln diocesan policy was unique.

> Almost all (perhaps all) of the other dioceses in the world have under-
> stood the instituted ministries as maintaining a direct relationship with
> Holy Orders. I know of only a very few dioceses where permanent insti-
> tuted lectors are used for the liturgy, and I know of no other diocese

where this is done exclusively. This causes difficulty, misunderstanding, and hurt when people move into our Diocese from another place.[32]

Third, Bishop Bruskewitz explained that he conducted informal inquiries of diocesan priests into the matter and found the majority of priests to be in favor of allowing women to serve as non-installed lectors.

Bishop Bruskewitz addressed some questions with which he grappled as he considered a change in policy. First, he wondered if allowing non-instituted lectors might harm the instituted lector program. Second, would a change in policy give the impression of a negative judgment on the current policy "and would this be an act of injustice and ingratitude?"[33] Presumably, Bishop Bruskewitz did not want Bishop Flavin to feel bad about this change. Third, the bishop considered what the Holy See and older and more experienced bishops thought about a potential change in policy. Fourth, he questioned if a change in policy might be considered a type of reward to those who had been working for this change. The bishop's words for those who had been working on this change were quite harsh, however: "Would any change in this regulation appear to be a 'reward for disobedience' or imply a giving in to 'political pressure' especially from ugly bishop bashers (e.g. 'CALL')?"[34] Bishop Bruskewitz clearly demonstrates his negative assessment of CALL and, presumably, of others who chose to work toward reform of the lector policy.

After laying out these questions, Bishop Bruskewitz explained that he decided to change the existing policy. "This new regulation (or more accurately, set of regulations) could be a permanent arrangement, or a step to another arrangement, or simply an experiment that can (and if necessary, will) be called back."[35]

Bishop Bruskewitz listed twelve regulations regarding the new policy. One point the bishop made in these regulations is that "If the instituted lector program in our Diocese falters, the use of extraordinary lectors will be curtailed or eliminated."[36] Non-instituted lectors were to be used "on an occasional basis." Instituted lectors were required to read during at least one Sunday Mass at each parish. If the parish had no instituted lectors, the priest was required to read all the Scripture at the Mass. If the parish had only one Sunday Mass, an instituted lector was to read at that Mass. "On greater and more solemn occasions, especially when the bishop is present, instituted lectors should be used."[37]

Those allowed to serve as non-installed lectors were subject to certain requirements as well. Besides being known personally by the pastor or thoroughly investigated:

> People who belong to forbidden societies (e.g. Freemasons) or who are in associations which are inimical to the Church or to the Bishop, or who are living in a way that is not in conformity to the Catholic Faith (e.g. divorced and remarrieds, homosexuals, etc.) or who oppose the doctrine of the Catholic Faith (e.g. those who hold to the possibility of women priests) are totally unsuited to be lectors and must be excluded from this function. Readers must be dedicated, pious Catholics known for their loyalty to the Holy Father and the Bishop.[38]

The only doctrine specifically mentioned by Bishop Bruskewitz addressed the issue of women's ordination. Also, dedicated and pious Catholics are defined by their loyalty to the institution's leaders and not by, for example, their joy, kindness, loving nature, or dedication to serving the poor.

The bishop included a dress code for instituted and non-instituted lectors in the twelve regulations. Men were required to wear a jacket and tie and refrain from wearing shorts instead of pants. "Women are to wear dresses (no slacks, shorts, etc.) which are modest (proper length, not too tight, not suggestive in front, not sleeveless, etc.)."[39]

Bishop Bruskewitz explained that he did not want excessive attention given to this change in policy, "It is my desire not to have this matter given undue publicity. It is not a secret, but I want it to come into practice with as much quiet and lack of publicity as possible."[40] The bishop may have thought that publicity could diminish the sacredness of the Mass. He may not have wanted Bishop Flavin to feel bad about the change. He may also have feared that it could draw attention to CALL and their efforts to change the policy. As previously noted, he did not want anyone to think the change was implemented as a result of CALL's efforts.

The letter from Bishop Bruskewitz concluded with words of support and gratitude to the priests in the diocese who supported the instituted-lector only policy. "In no way is this modification to be understood as any kind of reproach to them."[41]

Catholics for Active Liturgical Life learned of the change in policy when it was announced in the *Southern Nebraska Register*. The *Lincoln Journal Star* covered the change as well. Diana McCown again wrote Bishop Bruskewitz and addressed the tone that he took in his letter to diocesan priests.

> We are astounded that you would put into writing, and therefore on indelible record, your term for us (CALL), "ugly bishop bashers." This term is inimical to your role as defined in THE DOCUMENTS OF VATICAN II (*Christus Dominus,* Chapter II, No. 16): "Let him be a good shepherd who knows his sheep and whose sheep know him. Let him be a true father who excels in the spirit of love and solicitude for all…" The very fact that we have spoken out against a bishop's local policy which was in contrast to the rest of the Church seems to have made us anathema to Bishop Flavin and to you. In no way does our dissent discredit our apostolate in our beloved Church, nor should it damage our relationship with our bishop. All of our correspondence with Bishop Flavin and you and all of our *CallSpirit* issues were appropriately within the structure of the Catholic Church. At no time could we have been justifiably accused of being "ugly bishop bashers" by any but the most biased of people… As stated in the past, we are *not* "radical feminists seeking to overthrow the Church in favor of witchcraft and other substitute deities. Like you, we reject these tendencies. We are a group of *faithful,* caring, active Catholic men and women who want to see our Church grow in nurturing within its members a living faith in Jesus Christ.[42]

McCown expressed her regret that members of the CALL Steering Committee had not had the opportunity to meet with Bishop Bruskewitz and address the "rumors and falsehoods"[43] the bishop had heard from others about the members of CALL.

Catholics for Active Liturgical Life Disbands

With the news that Bishop Bruskewitz would allow women, in some circumstances, to read Scripture at Mass, the issue that brought CALL together was brought to a type of resolution. While members of CALL were frustrated by the tone Bishop Bruskewitz set with them and their concerns, they were happy that women would once again be allowed to read Scripture at Mass. The CALL Steering Committee decided on July 1, 1993 to publish the last *CallSpirit*. *CallSpirit* staff wrote, "Now is the time for us to direct our energies and time to other works for the Church and to our own spiritual enrichment."[44]

In the last issue of *CallSpirit*, the Call Steering Committee listed changes made in the diocese over the thirteen years of CALL's existence. While the committee did not claim to have been responsible for the changes, they noted that their persistence was justified by the fact that many of the causes they championed were addressed. For example, "Women will now be allowed to read Scripture at Mass [began August 1, 1993]… Eucharistic ministers may now take Holy Eucharist to the homebound and those in nursing homes [began in November 1992]… Response to the Catholic Hispanic community has improved… Our new bishop has urged pastors to establish parish councils… Diocesan CCD outreach has been renewed…"[45] The CALL Steering Committee also listed changes they hoped to see in the future. Included in their list were liturgical renewal, full disclosure of diocesan finances, prioritizing peace and justice issues, etc.[46]

Members of CALL shared their thoughts about CALL's role in the Diocese of Lincoln in the last *CallSpirit*. Rosalind Carr wrote:

> Our record is in *CallSpirit* for all to see. All we espoused is right there in print. Our cries were for the Lincoln Diocese practices to become the same as those of the one, holy, catholic (universal) church. Our

perfectly just and moral requests are now being vilified. We are being called all sorts of names by those who happen to think we shouldn't have cried out. We have nothing to be ashamed of and a great deal to be proud of.[47]

Mary Jo Bousek shared that the discrimination and autocracy of the Lincoln Catholic Church might have caused her to "revert back to her Protestant heritage to find the loving Jesus that I used to know."[48]

Reflecting on ten years of CALL, Diana McCown in her "Letter From Our President" expressed the good that came from involvement in CALL. While she acknowledged the problems that made the last ten years miserable, she also stated:

Has this been a journey of travail and tears? Has nothing good come from our commitment to address these problems?... NO!... Our happiness of the past ten years was in the service, the love, the seeking. Our lives as lay persons became more meaningful, more focused, more poignant and more spiritual. In our striving for equality and respect, we became stronger and more knowledgeable in our faith. We formed new and lasting friendships and we became members of a base community... best of all, we the laity have formed a support group for ourselves. We as church are asked to be Christ to each other; and within CALL we have fulfilled that quest... Our trust is in the guidance of the Holy Spirit, and we will continue wherever the Spirit leads...[49]

During an interview, McCown reflected on change in the diocese. She shared this:

When we first started CALL and we'd tried all the avenues, everything we could think of to make this change happen and nothing seemed to work, I remember Betty [Peterson] saying to me, she said, "Well, I will probably never be able to read again." She said, "I'm old, and when this bishop is gone, I probably will be too old and I probably will never be able to read again. I've resigned myself to that." And so she did. She read again after the change, then she read. And so her prediction that she would be too old or doddering or maybe not even here when the change happened was wrong. And she did get to read again.[50]

Notes Chapter 4

1.   Joan Johnson, interview with the author.

2.   Anita Fussell, "McCown of Cortland New President of Lay Group CALL: Diocese Said to Lack Vatican II Spirit," *Lincoln Journal and Star*, Nov 20, 1983.

3.   Joan Johnson, interview with the author.

4.   Ibid.

5.   Diana McCown, interview with the author.

6.   Carol McShane, interview with the author.

7.   Thomas C. Fox, "Nebraska bishop cuts off dissenters: 'Autocratic' leadership frustrates vocal minority in the Lincoln diocese," *National Catholic Reporter*, June 18, 1982.

8.   Diana McCown, interview with the author.

9.   Bishop Fabian Bruskewitz, Diocese of Lincoln Pastoral Bulletin, Vol I, No. 1, May 27, 1992.

10. Bishop Fabian Bruskewitz, Diocese of Lincoln Pastoral Bulletin, Vol. I, No. 7, August 19, 1992.

11. Ibid.

12. Diana McCown, interview with the author.

13. "Catholics of Lincoln flounder in atmosphere of fear," *National Catholic Reporter*, April 5, 1996.

14. Diana McCown, interview with the author.

15. Ibid.

16. Bishop Fabian Bruskewitz, letter to Diana McCown, January 15, 1993.

17. Ibid.

18. See Joseph A. Komonchak, "Interpreting the Council: Catholic Attitudes toward Vatican II," In Mary Jo Weaver and R. Scott Appleby (Eds.) *Being Right: Conservative Catholics in America*, Indianapolis, IN: Indiana University Press, 1995.

19. Bishop Fabian Bruskewitz, letter to Diana McCown, January 15, 1993.

20. Code of Canon Law, http://www.vatican.va/archive/ENG1104/__P11.HTM, accessed December 13, 2010.

21. Ibid.

22. Diana McCown, letter to Bishop Fabian Bruskewitz, January 24, 1993.

23. Ibid.

24. Bishop Bruskewitz, letter to Rosalind Carr, March 17, 1993.

25. Ibid.

26. Rosemary Radford Ruether, "Book Says Catholic Feminists Like Pagan Devil-Worshipers," *National Catholic Reporter,* December 11, 1992.

27. Diana McCown, interview with the author.

28. Jim McShane, interview with the author.

29. Diana McCown, interview with the author.

30. Bishop Bruskewitz. letter to priests of the Diocese of Lincoln, June 1, 1993.

31. Ibid.

32. Ibid.

33. Ibid.

34. Ibid.

35. Ibid.

36. Ibid.

37. Ibid.

38. Ibid.

39. Ibid.

40. Ibid.

41. Ibid.

42. Diana McCown, letter to Bishop Fabian Bruskewitz, July 19, 1993.

43. Ibid.

44. "To Everything There Is A Season," *CallSpirit*, Vol. XII, No. 2, 1993.

45. "Changes that CALL Hoped For," *CallSpirit*, Vol. XII, No. 2, 1993.

46. "Changes We Still Hope For," *CallSpirit*, Vol. XII, No. 2, 1993.

47. Rosalind Carr, "Our Readers Share Some Thoughts," *CallSpirit*, Vol. XII, No. 2, 1993.

48. Mary Jo Bousek, "Our Readers Share Some Thoughts," *CallSpirit,* Vol. XII, No. 2, 1993.

49. Diana McCown, *CallSpirit*, Vol. XII, No. 2, 1993.

50. Diana McCown, interview with the author.

CHAPTER 5

The Founding of Call To Action Nebraska

We acknowledge that the church is not a democracy, but that does not require us to concede that it is a tyranny.[1]—Jim McShane

THOUGH CALL DISBANDED as an official organization, many former members continued to nurture the friendships they had built.[2] Former CALL members formed a network of people in the Lincoln diocese interested in reform in the Catholic Church. When some members of CALL became interested in the organization Call To Action, they easily shared their enthusiasm with like-minded individuals.

While members of Catholics for Active Liturgical Life (CALL) came together when the Lincoln diocese's new lector policy that barred women from reading scripture at Mass was initiated, no such event precipitated the creation of Call to Action Nebraska. The main goal of CALL members had been to achieve the same level of lay participation found in other dioceses. They never took any position contrary to official teaching of the Catholic Church. In contrast, Call To Action urges reexamination and reformation of what members consider unjust Church policies and positions rooted in the structure of the Catholic Church. Many founders of Call to Action Nebraska believed in the importance of dialogue in the Catholic Church. They believed that the hierarchy of the Church should consult the laity about their experiences. Because the laity had not been heard by their two bishops, many former CALL members recognized this to be a vital need.

Call To Action USA

The mission of today's national Call To Action organization is to work for social justice inside and outside of the Catholic Church. The history of the organization dates back to 1973 when the United States Conference of Catholic Bishops (USCCB) organized a two-year dialogue initiative on the subject of justice.[3] The name for the national phase of the dialogue process, "Call To Action," was drawn from Pope Paul VI's May 14, 1971 Encyclical letter, *Octogesima Adveniens,* in which he wrote, "It is to all Christians that we address a fresh and insistent call to action."[4] In this encyclical, Paul VI quotes from his 1967 Encyclical On the Development of Peoples:

> Laymen should take up as their own proper task the renewal of the temporal order. If the role of the hierarchy is to teach and to inter-pret authentically the norms of morality to be followed in this matter, it belongs to the laity, without waiting passively for orders and direc-tives, to take the initiatives freely and to infuse a Christian spirit into the mentality, customs, laws and structures of the community in which they live.[5]

About two-thirds of the United States dioceses participated in local dialogues or in hearings. The USCCB received over 800,000 feedback sheets.[6] Head of the Call To Action conference, Cardinal John Dearden, spoke of the people who shared their stories in the regional hearings in words memorable to Jane Wolford Hughes, Director of the Institute for Continuing Education of the Archdiocese of Detroit. Hughes quoted her recollection of the words spoken by Cardinal Dearden about those meet-ings, "You would never be able to recapture the intensity of feeling, the joy and the pride, the pain and anguish, the hope and trust—that was sensed in those people."[7]

The consultative process culminated in a Call To Action convention held in Detroit in October 1976. The event coincided with the United States' bicentennial celebration. Among the conference delegates were representatives of diocesan leadership, lay parishioners, and Catholic organizations.[8] The three-day conference resulted in twenty-nine general recommendations. In addition, delegates advocated ongoing, structured communal dialogue.[9]

The United States bishops responded to the 1976 Call To Action conference by emphasizing their role as "authentic teachers." They pronounced a number of the topics raised through the process to be "illegitimate subjects for further conversation" including opening ordination to the priesthood to women and those who are married, an examination of the restriction on birth control, homosexuality, and separated and divorced Catholics.[10] The U.S. bishops concluded their involvement in Call To Action after the Detroit convention.

Roman Catholics in the Chicago area had been left out of the Call To Action process because the Archbishop of Chicago, John Cody, did not allow his archdiocese to participate. In response, a group of Chicago laity established an organization called Chicago Call To Action. This grassroots organization held its first convention in 1978. Around four hundred people attended and a major topic addressed was "the autocratic decision-making style and policies in the Chicago archdiocese."[11] Chicago Call To Action met yearly and though it appealed to some people beyond the Archdiocese of Chicago, for many years the base of Call To Action remained Chicago.

Among its other work, Call To Action developed a series of musical dramas in the 1980s that highlighted the teachings of the United States bishops on economic justice and world peace. Though Call To Action was no longer a bishop-sponsored organization, CTA performed these dramas hundreds of times around the country in Catholic parishes and at diocesan conventions and even for the U.S. Catholic Conference itself. Because of this ministry, in 1987, Cardinal Joseph Bernardin awarded Call To Action a Vatican World Communications award.[12]

In 1987, members of the Chicago Call To Action group traveled to

Rome to observe a synod on the "role of the laity." According to theologian Bernard Cooke, this event can be viewed as CTA's inspiration to become a national entity.[13]

The Call To Action board wrote a pastoral letter entitled a "Call for Reform in the Catholic Church" in 1990 in which they laid out the organization's platform.[14] Theologian Hans Kung read the letter from the podium at a national conference on "The Future of the U.S. Church" and reportedly said he had "never seen a better declaration of the motives and goals of the progressive church."[15] Call To Action purchased a full-page advertisement that ran in the *New York Times* on Ash Wednesday. The advertisement featured a Call for Reform and included the names of over 4,500 signers.[16]

The Call for Reform remains Call To Action's basic platform. Many of the issues in the platform were addressed in the recommendations from the 1976 Detroit Call To Action conference.[17] According to the CTA-USA website:

- We appeal to the institutional church to reform and renew its structures. We also appeal to the people of God to witness to the Spirit who lives within us and to seek ways to serve the vision of God in human society.

- We call upon church officials to incorporate women at all levels of ministry and decision-making.

- We call upon the church to discard the medieval discipline of mandatory priestly celibacy and to open the priesthood to women and married men…so that the Eucharist may continue to be the center of the spiritual life of all Catholics.

- We call for extensive consultation with the Catholic people in developing church teaching on human sexuality.

- We claim our responsibility as committed laity, religious and clergy to participate in the selection of our local bishops, a time-honored tradition in the church.

- We call for open dialogue, academic freedom, and due process.

- We call upon the church to become a model of financial openness on all levels, including the Vatican.

- We call for a fundamental change so that young people will see and hear God living in and through the church as a participatory community of believers who practice what they preach.[18]

After the 1990 publication of the Call To Reform in the *New York Times*, interest in Call To Action around the United States grew. A few months later, over 25,000 people had signed on to the Call for Reform.[19] The television news program, *60 Minutes*, covered Call To Action in January 1995.[20] In a year's time, membership doubled from 2,500 to 5,000.[21] Roman Catholics in Baltimore organized the first local chapter of Call To Action and CTA expanded rapidly. Within two years, the organization added twenty-five regional affiliates.[22]

Call To Action in Nebraska

Some members of Catholics for Active Liturgical Life were aware of, or even involved in, the original Call To Action gathering in 1976. For example, CALL member John Krejci served as a delegate at the first Call To Action convention in Detroit. In addition, a number of Nebraskans were among the signers of the CTA *New York Times* Ash Wednesday advertisement.

Joan Johnson recalls seeing an advertisement for the 1994 Call To Action annual conference in Chicago in the *National Catholic Reporter*. She and her husband, Jerry, decided to attend. They did not know anybody else planning to attend the conference, but they quickly became acquainted with other Nebraskans because attendees are encouraged to sit by state at the opening session of each national CTA conference. Fr. Tom McCormick, a priest who had transferred out of the Lincoln diocese, visited the Nebraska area. Fr. McCormick had baptized one of Joan and Jerry's daughters and he had a connection to almost everyone in attendance from Nebraska. Fr. McCormick's ties to the many Nebraskans helped them meet and get to know one another. That evening, the Johnsons met

Nebraskans from the other two dioceses in the state: Omaha and Grand Island. Reflecting on that first conference, Joan Johnson said: "It was a fantastic feeling that we were with other people who felt as we did. I really felt that the speakers were speaking directly to me as they challenged all of us to live and grow in our faith. I came back so energized and excited and, of course, shared that excitement with the other members of our CALL faith community."[23] The Johnsons stayed in touch with people they met at that conference. For example, in early 1995 Charles and Jeanine Kelliher, a couple from the Grand Island diocese who attended the Chicago conference, visited the Johnsons in Lincoln and together they reflected on their conference experience.

Meanwhile, a group of Omaha Catholics had started a pro-Vatican II group they called Weavings. Call To Action founding member, Mel Beckman, explained that Weavings was a group that was interested in staying "behind the scenes." However, Beckman commented, "I felt that a more actively challenging group was needed, not because it's better but because it was needed in addition to the work behind the scenes."[24] Some members of the Omaha diocese considered developing a coalition with the name Future Church Coalition that Beckman explained would "propose changes in the church in positive ways and offer loyal opposition to church policies which prevent women from ministering fully in the church, prohibit marriage for priests or make the church less collegial than it should be."[25] A group of people interested in an active coalition like this met in March 1995 and continued to meet throughout that year. In an interview, Beckman described this group as "low key." In the fall of 1995, Lincoln Catholics began to attend these meetings and those involved formed a statewide group rather than a group exclusive to the Omaha Archdiocese. That statewide group decided to affiliate with the national Call To Action organization and become Call To Action Nebraska.

Not all members of CALL joined Call To Action Nebraska. For example, Mary Jo Bousek explained that she was busy with other things and "reasonably content" at her parish, "You know, it's not like it should be, not like other places in this country. But, probably about as good as I was going to get here in Lincoln and I think also I was just tired of fighting the bishop."[26] Diana McCown shared that she did not necessarily agree with everything on the CTA national agenda. She explained, however, that she did agree with the general "thrust of the group." Having gotten to know so many of the people while working with CALL, she "had a lot of faith and trust in their opinions and how they felt."[27]

Soon-to-be members of Call To Action Nebraska from the Grand Island Diocese had been involved with Call To Action on the national level. For example, Charles Kelliher had signed his name to the 1990 *New York Times* advertisement. He and his wife, Jeanine, regularly attended CTA conferences. Current CTAN president, Teresa Hawk, from Chadron, first learned about Call To Action when her parish priest told her about the group and the national conference. Her first exposure to the group occurred when she attended the conference her priest advocated.[28]

Call To Action Nebraska Meets

On February 3, 1996 the group convened the first state meeting of Call To Action Nebraska at Mahoney State Park which is located between the cities of Lincoln and Omaha, just inside the boundaries of the Lincoln diocese. The heading on the brochure for the event stated, "WE ARE THE CHURCH: What if We Meant What We Said?" Seventy-five people attended this meeting on a memorably frigid day; the temperature dipped to twenty below zero, Fahrenheit. The gathering included much discussion, a keynote speech given by theologian Sr. Maryanne Stevens, a presentation on Call To Action by then-CTA-USA Co-Director, Dan Daley, steering committee elections and Mass at which Fr. Jack McCaslin, a priest from the Omaha archdiocese, presided. A few days after this meeting, Call To Action Nebraska had seventy-two paying members or member couples and twenty-four non-member contributors.[29]

Reflecting on that first meeting, Omahan Lori Darby said,

> It felt very comfortable. It was exciting to see that there were seventy-five or eighty people who were interested enough to spend a Saturday with us, hear [Sr. Stevens] speak in the morning and then do some business

in the afternoon, celebrate Mass and go home. I remember being really energized and excited. Wow, there's hope here. . . I was excited to be a part of the leadership of it. We had no idea how we [the Steering Committee] were going to design it, what the leadership was going to look like. After that day we were even, no one was president, no one was chair, we were just eight or ten or twelve folk from all the dioceses who planned to meet again to talk about what we should do next.[30]

Lori Darby noted that two people attended the meeting at the request of Bishop Bruskewitz; their job was to observe what happened and report back to the chancery. Darby stated, "That never occurred to me, ever in a million years, that people would be that interested. Because it [our meeting] didn't seem that radical."[31] The Lincoln diocesan observers were two undergraduate students from the University of Nebraska at Lincoln, one male and one female. Because of their youth, these two stood out in the crowd. As they left the meeting before the closing liturgy, another attendee engaged them in conversation. The two students said at that time that they would report "what they had seen and heard" to Msgr. Timothy Thorburn.[32]

Lori Darby remembered that a number of attendees from the Lincoln diocese expressed concern that the bishop had sent observers. She recalled that some Lincoln Catholics believed this might indicate that Bishop Bruskewitz "wasn't wanting to listen to us, he wasn't wanting to develop a relationship with us, he was there to get whatever he could and then to use it against the people there."[33]

Just a few days after the day-long organizational meeting at Mahoney State Park, Fr. Jack McCaslin received a letter from Msgr. Timothy Thorburn, the Chancellor of the Lincoln Diocese. Fr. McCaslin, a priest of the Omaha Archdiocese and long-time social justice advocate, had presided at the Call To Action Mass at the February 3rd gathering. Church regulations stipulate that a priest must seek permission from the local bishop before he celebrates Mass in a diocese other than his own. As Mahoney State Park falls just inside the Lincoln diocese, Fr. McCaslin had presided at a Mass outside his home diocese. The text of the February

8, 1996 letter to Fr. McCaslin states that the Bishop of Lincoln wanted the following information communicated to Fr. McCaslin:

> You have no faculties to celebrate or perform any liturgical or ecclesiastical acts or functions in the Diocese of Lincoln, including the celebration of Holy Mass, the hearing of confessions, and preaching. You are forbidden to celebrate or perform any liturgical or ecclesiastical acts or functions in the Diocese of Lincoln, and this prohibition is in perpetuity. This communication is also a canonical warning. Any violation of this prohibition will be punished with a decree of excommunication.[34]

The letter was copied to then-Archbishop of Omaha, Elden Curtiss.

When Fr. McCaslin did not seek permission to preside at the Mass at Mahoney State Park, he circumvented Bishop Bruskewitz's authority. Fr. McCaslin violated the rule that a priest is to receive permission from the local bishop before he presides at Mass and Bishop Bruskewitz's response was rapid and severe: lifetime prohibition from ministry in his neighbor-diocese and threatened excommunication. Fr. McCaslin reported that he responded to Bishop Bruskewitz by suggesting that Bishop Bruskewitz consult the Gospels to see how Jesus led.[35]

Announcing the Formation of Call To Action Nebraska

In a February 9, 1996 letter to fellow newly-elected members of the Call To Action Nebraska Steering Committee, Mel Beckman noted that both Fr. Jack McCaslin and Mel's wife, Mary Ann Beckman, had been contacted by the Chancellor of the Omaha Archdiocese, Fr. Michael Gutgsell. Fr. Gutgsell asked them about Call To Action. According to Mel Beckman, both McCaslin and Mary Ann Beckman assured Fr. Gutgsell that the members of Call To Action Nebraska were "a good group of people."[36] Mel Beckman continued, "We should probably make some contact with the three [Nebraska] bishops soon. We didn't think they needed to be the first to know about CTA Nebraska but they probably should not be the last to know either."[37] Clearly, at least two of the three Nebraska bishops,

Bishop Bruskewitz and Archbishop Curtiss, were already aware of that first Call To Action meeting.

The first meeting of the Call To Action Nebraska Steering Committee took place on February 24, 1996 three weeks after the first general meeting. Msgr. Thorburn sent the same two people who had attended the February 3rd meeting to the first meeting of the newly-elected Steering Committee to continue to act as observers and report back to the chancery. According to the meeting minutes:

> The first forty-five minutes of the meeting were spent in a discussion of whether a young couple known to be reporting to the Lincoln Diocese should be allowed to be present as observers at the meeting. Steering committee members wished to have open meetings but they were seriously divided as to whether that openness should extend to persons who do not share the goals of the organization or who would, by their presence, clearly inhibit candid discussion.[38]

The decision whether or not to allow the young couple to remain at the meeting was a difficult one. Lori Darby reflected on the visitors and the subsequent discussion in an interview: "Even to me who was young, they were young. . . I mean college age, certainly, but not any more than that. That's my recollection. So we deliberated. . . forty-five minutes at least trying to decide. Because we were very sensitive to being accused of being closed. See right off the bat, 'You're not open.' And struggled mightily with that."[39] The Steering Committee opted to have Jim McShane and Barb Adkins talk directly to the guests and share the dilemma with them. Joan Johnson remembered that the committee members were relieved when the couple decided to leave.[40]

Confronted with this difficult decision scenario at their very first meeting, the Steering Committee developed a policy on open meetings. According to the policy, any person is permitted to attend any general membership meetings. Non-members who intend to report their observations to some other person or entity are requested, as a matter of courtesy, to identify themselves to one of the co-chairs. Members are allowed to observe Steering Committee meetings but non-members are asked to request permission to attend before the day of the meeting.

In a March 4, 1996 letter addressed to Msgr. Thorburn, Jim McShane wrote of his struggle with the decision about whether to allow these observers to attend the Steering Committee meeting. He believed Msgr. Thorburn placed the young people in a difficult position that they may not have fully understood.

> . . . I had misgivings about admitting persons to our deliberations who were there not for their own benefit, nor to support the purposes of [Call to Action Nebraska], but primarily to serve as your informers. I was concerned about open discussion. But I was also worried about the burdens those young people would bear if their unsubstantiated reports became the basis of canonical sanctions imposed with little or no due process on accused persons. As you no doubt know, I explained to them some of the moral dilemmas your request for their admittance posed; and I asked them to bear with us some of the burdens your request presented. To their credit, they seemed to understand the bind we were in and they accepted a share of that burden. From my conversation with then [sic] I was impressed by their sincerity, courage, intelligence and good will. I cannot accord your role such admiration. The college students report that you were worried about the tone our meeting might take and felt the need to have direct information about it... I pass over in silence the judgments appropriate to your unwillingness to do your own dirty work. But sending those two young people unannounced into that situation suggests to me an appalling lack of care and respect for them.[41]

Msgr. Thorburn responded to McShane's letter on March 7, 1996. Rather than address the misgivings expressed in McShane's letter, Msgr. Thorburn appears to taunt McShane with what he perceives to be hypocrisy exhibited by the Call To Action Steering Committee. He wrote:

> You were nice to them, as I had no doubt you would, but the bottom line was that your group simply would not let them attend. You were

not very open and liberal. . . Because your group has presented itself as a Catholic organization which addresses Catholic issues, the Catholic Church has every right to make an assessment, through highly educated lay representatives, of your organization… be assured that observers from the Catholic Church will attend any open meetings (if any more open meetings are held) of Call-to-Action that take place in the Diocese of Lincoln. While I may attend myself some time, I am surprised that you would object to having lay representatives attend. We are in, after all, the post-Vatican II Church.[42]

Among other business at the February 24th meeting, the CTAN Steering Committee designated John Krejci of Lincoln and Lori Darby of Omaha co-chairs of Call To Action Nebraska. The Steering Committee adopted an initial policy that called for one male and one female co-chair who come from two different dioceses in Nebraska. They also discussed announcing the formation of Call To Action Nebraska to the three state bishops as well as the media.

That day, the Steering Committee agreed to send letters to Archbishop Curtiss of Omaha, Bishop Bruskewitz of Lincoln, and Bishop McNamara of Grand Island officially announcing the formation of Call To Action Nebraska. Reflecting on those letters, Lori Darby of Omaha said:

God we were so naïve. And I truly, truly believe that all of us were this naïve. No one set this up to get the bishop ticked off. No one did. We, all these letters did was say, "Hi. We're here. We're meeting. We thought it'd be polite to let you know. We really love the church but we disagree with some things and we want to meet together as a group of people." Very innocent, we thought. Oh God, we thought that was innocent.[43]

The complete text of the March 6, 1996 letter to Bishop Bruskewitz read: "We are in the process of forming Call To Action, Nebraska, an affiliate of the national Call To Action organization. As we go through the organizing process, we are trying to bear in mind the words of Pope John XXIII, 'In essentials, unity; in other things, diversity; in all things, charity.'"[44] Call To Action Nebraska recieved responses from Archbishop

Curtiss and Bishop Bruskewitz. Here is the complete text of Archbishop Curtiss' March 12, 1996 letter:

> I have your March 6 letter announcing plans to form an affiliate group in Nebraska Call To Action. I do not accept the agenda of "Call To Action" and I will not recognize any organization which proposes its agenda in the Archdiocese of Omaha. I will make it clear, if you attempt to tie your organization to the Church, that you do not represent the Church or its teaching.[45]

Bishop Bruskewitz dated his response March 18, 1996:

> A priest-friend of mine, who had formerly been a Protestant minister, said that the difference between a dissenting Catholic and a Protestant is that the Protestant has integrity. This comes to mind as I reply to your communication addressed to me under date of March 6, 1996. Your organization is intrinsically incoherent and fundamentally divisive. It is inimical to the Catholic Faith, subversive of Church order, destructive of the Catholic Church discipline, contradictory to the teaching of the Second Vatican Council, and an impediment to evangelization. Of course, your slogan, which you claim to have from the mouth of Pope John XXIII, is not relevant to the issues at hand, since neither you nor your group possess the competence, ability, or authority to determine authentically what is essential or non-essential in Catholic doctrine, Catholic moral teaching, or Catholic Church law. Please advise any Catholics from or of the Diocese of Lincoln, who are members of your group, that such membership constitutes a grave act of disrespect and disobedience to their lawful Bishop. This letter is to be considered a formal canonical warning to them about this matter. After April 15, 1996, appropriate ecclesiastical censures will be imposed on those Catholics from or of the Diocese of Lincoln who attain or retain membership in your organization.[46]

While both bishops are clear that they do not support the agenda of Call To Action Nebraska, Bishop Bruskewitz attacked the character of the group's members. Although Bishop Bruskewitz did not know who were the members of CTAN, in claiming that CTAN members possess no "competence, ability, or authority to determine authentically what is essential or non-essential in Catholic doctrine," the bishop appears to believe only those given authority by the Church through ordination and achieved position in the Catholic hierarchy have the competence, ability and authority to speak on Catholic doctrine. A group of lay Catholics is, therefore, necessarily devoid of this competence, ability and authority. No amount of education, experience, discussion, thought, prayer or inspiration by the Spirit appears to have any impact on the matter.

On March 16, 1996, the *Lincoln Journal Star* and the *Omaha World Herald* ran stories on the new Nebraska organization. The *Lincoln Journal Star* quoted from the CTAN press release that stated: "Call To Action, Nebraska, believes the church is always in need of reform and renewal as she strives to answer more fully her calling to be the People of God on earth... Toward that end, the organization provides Catholics in Nebraska a participative structure through which they can share their convictions and changes and activities needed in the church."[47] In the *Omaha World Herald* article, Lori Darby explained: "We are not disgruntled, grumpy Catholics who want things to go our way. We understand and respect the authority of the College of Bishops. We want a dialogue. We can't just assent to teaching that we, in good conscience, have serious doubts about."[48]

Bishop Bruskewitz Issues Extra–Synodal Legislation

Looking back at Bishop Bruskewitz's letter, designed to be a "formal canonical warning," as well as the media attention provided by the article in the *Lincoln Journal Star*, perhaps Bishop Bruskewitz's next move should not have come as a surprise. Without the benefit of hindsight, however, members of Call to Action Nebraska and, indeed, many people all over the country were astounded by what Bishop Bruskewitz did next.

In March 1996, the national Call To Action organization had around 15,000 members. Of those, about 5,000 members were priests or vowed religious. Six of them were bishops,[49] including Bishop Raymond Lucker of New Ulm, Minnesota, Thomas Gumbleton, Auxiliary Bishop of Detroit, and retired Bishop Charles A. Busswell from Pueblo, Colorado.[50] Though thousands of Roman Catholics in good standing retained membership in Call To Action, the diocesan newspaper, the *Southern Nebraska Register,* published extra-synodal legislation that threatened members of Call To Action in and of the Lincoln Diocese with excommunication. An editorial entitled "Dissipating Ambiguities" was published alongside the extra-synodal legislation in which the rationale for the legislation was explained. The text of the extra-synodal legislation follows:

> All Catholics in and of the Diocese of Lincoln are forbidden to be members of the organizations and groups listed below. Membership in these organizations or groups is always perilous to the Catholic Faith and most often is totally incompatible with the Catholic Faith.
>
>> Planned Parenthood
>> Society of Saint Pius X (Lefebvre Group)
>> Hemlock Society
>> Call to Action
>> Call to Action Nebraska
>> Saint Michael the Archangel Chapel
>> Freemasons
>> Job's Daughters
>> DeMolay
>> Eastern Star
>> Rainbow Girls
>> Catholics for a Free Choice
>
> Any Catholics in and of the Diocese of Lincoln who attain or retain membership in any of the above listed organizations or groups after April 15, 1996, are by that very fact *(ipso-facto-latae sententiae)* under interdict and are absolutely forbidden to receive Holy Communion. Contumacious persistence in such membership for one month following the interdict on part of any such Catholics will by that very fact *(ipso*

facto-latae sententiae) cause them to be excommunicated. Absolution from these ecclesial censures is "reserved to the Bishop." This notice, when published in the *Southern Nebraska Register,* is a formal canonical warning. By mandate of the Most Reverend Bishop of Lincoln[51]

The legislation was signed "Reverend Monsignor Timothy Thorburn Chancellor, March 19, 1996."

The accompanying editorial asserted the "authority and sacred power" of a bishop and the responsibility of the faithful to closely follow their bishop. The editorial explained that the extra-synodal legislation was enacted to dissipate the ambiguities regarding the acceptability of the groups in question:

> Despite the fact that the anti-Catholicism of most of these organizations
> and groups is frequently open and apparent, some of their members and
> leaders have been trying to sell their evils to the unwary or uninformed,
> and sometimes to give the impression that the Catholic Church is divided
> or undecided about some of these groups and organizations. . . Let us pray
> that all Catholics in the Lincoln Diocese will be obedient to our Bishop
> and let us pray as well for the conversion of any who may dissent and thus
> incur the serious sins and ecclesial penalties listed in the legislation.[52]

According to the editorial, Bishop Bruskewitz "engaged in extensive consultation over many months with innumerable inquiries and discussions" regarding the extra-synodal legislation and he felt it was his duty to protect the Catholic faith in this way. Msgr. Thorburn confirmed that the impetus behind the legislation was media coverage of the founding of Call To Action Nebraska.[53] Bishop Bruskewitz reportedly told a reporter that he wanted to "warn parishioners" that Call To Action is "too progressive."[54] In an interview with Catholic News Service, Bishop Bruskewitz stated that he discussed the legislation with his priests' council but not with the other two bishops in Nebraska.[55] He did report that he discussed the matter informally with several bishops.[56]

In the editorial, Bishop Bruskewitz appears to equate Church hierarchy with the entire Catholic Church. This illustrates a fundamental difference between Bishop Bruskewitz and members of Call To Action Nebraska who view all the baptized to constitute the Catholic Church. When Bishop Bruskewitz wrote that the Catholic Church is not divided or undecided, he is clearly not including the laity because a large percentage of the United States laity hold positions that differ from official church teaching. According to a book published shortly after Bishop Bruskewitz's legislation went into effect, forty-seven percent of highly-committed Catholics demonstrated some support of women's ordination.[57] More recently, polls show a divide between official Catholic Church teaching and the beliefs of Catholics. Though the Catholic Church is opposed to artificial contraception, a Gallup poll found that 82 percent of U.S. Catholics find birth control to be morally acceptable.[58] Also, while the Catholic Church is against allowing gays and lesbians the right to legal marriage, a 2011 Pew Research Center poll found that 52 percent of United States Catholics favor that right.[59] According to another 2010 Pew poll, seventy-seven percent of Catholics believe "There is more than one true way to interpret the teachings of my religion."[60] Much of Call To Action's platform has wide support among the United States Catholic laity. Jesuit theologian Rev. Thomas Reese noted, "The church has tried to marginalize these kinds of people—isolate them as being opposed to Catholic teaching. But when you look at the polls, you see that Call To Action is concerned about what many Catholic faithful are concerned about—so the church fears them."[61]

Because many practicing Catholics disagree with official church teaching on a number of issues, Msgr. Thorburn said the time had come to confront the issue. He stated, "The church has been tolerant too long about a lot of things that touch the hearts of those who believe. It's a time where people have to decide what they believe in and why they believe in that and be honest and make the consequential step."[62]

Some lay the blame for these dissenting opinions on bad catechesis. Bishop Robert Vasa reportedly shared this belief in a conversation with Leigh Casler that was written in the National Catholic Reporter. According to Casler, when she asked Bishop Vasa about the role of an individual's conscience when making decisions, Vasa told her, "If a person was properly catechized, his or her conscience would be formed by the Catechism and would naturally follow all the church teaching and that an individual's conscience was only valid if it was in line with church teachings."[63] In other words, Catholics who reach conclusions different from official church teaching necessarily have an improperly formed conscience.

While it may be true that Bishop Bruskewitz's actions were taken out of concern for the souls of members of these twelve organizations, his manner did not appear to indicate concern for the suffering endured by the individuals impacted by the legislation. According to Msgr. Thorburn, the extra-synodal legislation was intended to be "medicinal."[64] Members of CTAN note that Canon Law is not very clear on the concept of a medicinal penalty. They note, "standard dictionary etymologies suggest that something is medicinal if it offers a reflective healing response to an illness, if it is so measured as to be commensurate to the problem it is to rectify, if it does no harm, and if it is administered in a caring manner."[65] Many of those impacted by the legislation did not experience the action in this caring way. As John Krejci noted in an interview, "We wish [Bishop Bruskewitz] would have been more pastoral and less legal. . . ."[66]

Enforcement

According to Msgr. Timothy Thorburn, then-Lincoln Diocesan Chancellor, no priest was going to conduct any investigation regarding group membership. Msgr. Thorburn said, "We're not making up lists and making priests or Eucharistic ministers memorize lists of people. The legislation (edict) was set up so that it covered all of them and they know who they are. . . . It's up to them to be honest enough to realize . . . that they have separated themselves from the Catholic Church."[67] Further, he stated, "If a person was recalcitrant and they defied the sanction and received Holy Communion anyway, it would only prove the fact that they had no respect for the authority of the Catholic Church anyway."[68]

Bishop Bruskewitz told a reporter that those members of the twelve organizations who continue to receive communion "are doing something very bad and evil" and he "would question the genuineness of their faith."[69] In a column he published in the *Southern Nebraska Register*, Bishop Bruskewitz compared Call To Action Nebraska members' reception of the Eucharist to the kiss of Judas.[70]

Bishop Bruskewitz's Power to Define

Though the legislation was enacted in part to respond to the establishment of Call To Action Nebraska,[71] Msgr. Thorburn noted that Bishop Bruskewitz had been questioned regarding the Catholic Church's official position on the other listed organizations.[72] The Church did have official positions on groups such as Masonic organizations, but there was no "official" position on Call To Action. While many bishops did not agree with some of the agenda items of CTA, they respected the group's commitment to Catholic social teaching and social justice.

Bishop Bruskewitz seemed to derive much of his information about Call To Action from accounts of the group published by ultra-conservative people and groups. Their take on what was happening at Call To Action gatherings is quite different from the perception of the actual participants.

While Call To Action was educating people about their organization, Bishop Bruskewitz shared his different perspective on CTA. Just a few days after the interdict went into effect, on April 19, 1996, the *Southern Nebraska Register* published an article by Mary Jo Anderson which was reprinted from *Crisis*, an ultra-conservative Roman Catholic periodical. Anderson had attended the 1995 Call To Action conference and in the article she explained her experience and negative impressions. CTAN member Mel Beckman described the article as "particularly long and venomous."[73] Surely, the point of reprinting the article was to inform the Catholics in the Lincoln diocese, from a particular viewpoint, of the dangers and evils of Call To Action. Anderson describes the participants in the following way:

The average participant was a sixty-something ex-nun, ex-priest, social worker, diocesan employee, or academic. They had spent their early careers promoting leftist agendas, liberation theology, and protesting the Vietnam War. The cold war is over, but old habits die hard. Few have a business background, and most are dependent upon parish, diocese, government social programs, or grants for employment.[74]

Though this description is meant to be damning, Anderson identifies attendees who chose to pursue vocations that help others. They have responded to Jesus' exhortation to "seek ye first the Kingdom of God," engage in works of service to others, and to do the work of peacemakers.

When he was Bishop of Lincoln, Bishop Bruskewitz had the ear of many Roman Catholics in his diocese. He had great power to define and assign meaning. One would not likely be surprised to learn that Lincoln Catholics who have had no experience with Call To Action believed Bishop Bruskewitz when he claimed that Call To Action is an anti-Catholic group. Bishop Bruskewitz did not share the fact that members of Call To Action are deeply committed to their Church as manifested in their involvement in their parishes and other organizations that promote the interests of the Roman Catholic Church. Nor did he appear to grant that even if the members of Call to Action Nebraska believe differently than he does, that they act with integrity.

Bishop Bruskewitz's extra-synodal legislation can be viewed as one bishop's attempt to define who is and who is not truly Roman Catholic. Indeed, Bishop Bruskewitz's rhetoric about members of Call To Action escalated to the point that several years after Bishop Bruskewitz promulgated his legislation, he questioned whether those impacted by it "ever were actually Catholics to begin with, or practiced the Catholic faith in any meaningful way."[75]

Bishop Bruskewitz acted swiftly and decisively to attempt to silence the voice and views of Call To Action Nebraska members. His highly unusual legislation shocked Lincoln CTAN members and Catholics around the United States and the world. Perhaps neither Bishop Bruskewitz nor the members of Call To Action Nebraska could have predicted what was to happen next.

Notes Chapter 5

1.   Jim McShane, "Memo to Lincoln Diocese Catholics claiming membership in Call To Action Nebraska," April 3, 1996.

2.   Joan Johnson, letter to Harold Radday, June 8, 1995. To this day, former CALL members continue their once-a-month volunteer night at Matt Talbot Kitchen and Outreach during which they cook and serve meals for Lincoln's hungry. In addition to service work, the group socializes as well. For example, Betty Peterson hosts an annual Epiphany party.

3.   For a more complete history of the dialogue initiative, see Bradford E. Hinze, *Practices of Dialogue in the Roman Catholic Church: Aims and Obstacles, Lessons and Laments* (New York: Continuum, 2006).

4.   Pope Paul VI, *Octogesima Adveniens*, 48, May 14, 1971, http://www.vatican.va/holy_father/paul_vi/apost_letters/documents/hf_p-vi_apl_19710514_octogesima-adveniens_en.html.

5.   Ibid.

6.   Bradford E. Hinze, *Practices of Dialogue in the Roman Catholic Church.*

7.   Darci Smith, "Call To Action," *Superior Catholic Herald*, November 14, 1996.

8.   Bradford E. Hinze, *Practices of Dialogue in the Roman Catholic Church.*

9.   Ibid.

10. Ibid, 84.

11. Ibid, 86.

12. Bob Reeves, "Call to Action Was Praised by Cardinal: Group Now Forbidden by Bishop," *Lincoln Journal Star*, April 21, 1996.

13. Bernard J. Cooke, "Call To Action: Engine of Lay Ministry," in *What's Left?: Liberal American Catholics*, ed. Mary Jo Weaver (Bloomington, IN: Indiana Unviersity Press, 1999).

14. CTA-USA website, http://www.ctaww.org/documents/a_brief_history_of_call_to_action.htm.

15. CTA-USA website, http://www.cta-usa.org/about/history/.

16. Ibid.

17. Bernard J. Cooke (1999). "Call To Action: Engine of Lay Ministry."

18. CTA-USA website, http://www.cta-usa.org/about/history/.

19. CTA-USA website, http://www.ctaww.org/documents/a_brief_history_of_call_to_action.htm.

20. Pamela Schaeffer, "Call to Action draws 4,000 'priestly people,'" *National Catholic Reporter*, November 17, 1995.

21. Letter from Call To Action to those interested in church renewal, April 1990.

22. Pamela Schaeffer, "Call to Action draws…"

23. Joan Johnson, interview with the author.

24. Mel Beckman, interview with the author.

25. Ibid.

26. Mary Jo Bousek, interview with the author.

27. Diana McCown, interview with the author.

28. Teresa Hawk, interview with the author.

29. Mel Beckman, letter to Call To Action Nebraska Steering Committee, February 9, 1996.

30. Lori Darby, interview with the author.

31. Ibid.

32. Letter to the bishops, archbishops and cardinals of the National Conference of Catholic Bishops, from Lincoln diocesan member of CTAN, October 25, 1996.

33. Lori Darby, interview with the author.

34. Msgr. Timothy Thorburn, letter to Fr. Jack McCaslin, February 8, 1996.

35. Julia McCord, "Priest Recalls Bishop Threatened Ouster," *Omaha World Herald*, April 14, 1996.

36. Mel Beckman, letter to Call To Action Nebraska Steering Committee, February 9, 1996.

37. Ibid.

38. CTAN Steering Committee meeting minutes, February 24, 1996.

39. Lori Darby, interview with the author.

40. Joan Johnson, interview with the author.

41. Jim McShane, letter to Msgr. Timothy Thorburn, March 4, 1996.

42. Msgr. Timothy J. Thorburn, letter to Jim McShane, March 7, 1996.

43. Lori Darby, interview with the author.

44. Lori Darby and John Krejci, letter to Bishop Fabian Bruskewitz, March 6, 1996.

45. Archbishop Elden Curtiss, letter to Lori Darby and John Krejci, March 12, 1996.

46. Bishop Fabian Bruskewitz, letter to Lori Darby and John Krejci, March 18, 1996.

47. Bob Reeves, "New Catholic Group Forms Network for Discussion in Nebraska," *Lincoln Journal Star*, March 16, 1996.

48. Julia McCord, "Catholics Seeking Change Start Chapter," *Omaha World Herald*, March 16, 1996.

49. Lori Sharn, "Some Catholics Plan to Disobey Neb. Bishop: Vow to Ignore Communion Ban," *USA Today,* April 15, 1996.

50. Diego Ribadeneira, "Nebraska Catholics Facing Threat of Excommunication for Their Views," *Boston Globe*, March 30, 1996.

51. Rev. Msgr. Timothy Thorburn, "Extra-Synodal Legislation," *Southern Nebraska Register*, March 22, 1996.

52. "Dissipating Ambiguities," *Southern Nebraska Register*, March 22, 1996.

53. "Bishop in Nebraska Threatens Dissidents: He Will Excommunicate Members of Certain Groups," *Kansas City Star*, March 38, 1996.

54. "Bishop threatening excommunication for members of 12 groups," *Los Angeles Times*, March 30, 1996.

55. Jerry Filteau, "Lincoln Bishop Sees His Statement About Groups as a Warning," *Catholic Voice,* April 5, 1996.

56. Leslie Wirpsa, "Bruskewitz Elaborates on Recent Decree," *National Catholic Reporter*, April 12, 1996.

57. James D. Davidson, Andrea S. Williams, Richard A. Lamanna, Jan Stenftenagel, Kathleen Maas Weigert, William J. Whalen, Patriica Witberg, *The Search for Common Ground: What Unites and Divides Catholic Americans,* (Huntington, IN: Our Sunday Visitor Publishing Division, Our Sunday Visitor, Inc., 1997), 65.

58. Frank Newport, "Americans, Including Catholics, Say Birth Control is Morally OK," *Gallup Politics,* May 22, 2012, http://www.gallup.com/poll/154799/americans-including-catholics-say-birth-control-morally.aspx.

59. The Pew Forum on Religion and Public Life, Religion and Attitudes Toward Same-Sex Marriage, February 7, 2012, http://www.pewforum.org/Gay-Marriage-and-Homosexuality/Religion-and-Attitudes-Toward-Same-Sex-Marriage.aspx.

60. The Pew Forum on Religion and Public Life, "U.S. Religious Landscape Survey," 2010, http://religions.pewforum.org/portraits retrieved February 1, 2011.

61. Nolan Zavoral, "Catholics' Call & Response," *Minneapolis Star Tribune*, September 14, 1996.

62. John Carlson, "Catholics Defy Bishop's Order: Members of Lincoln Diocese Confront Excommunication," *Des Moines Register,* July 28, 1997.

63. Dan Morris-Young, "'I Suspect Jesus Was Not All That Popular': Bishop Vasa Reflects on his Time in Baker, Ore., Diocese, *National Catholic Reporter*, March 21, 2011, http://ncronline.org/news/accountability/i-suspect-jesus-was-not-all-popular.

64. Bob Reeves, "Groups Off-Limits for Catholics, Bishop Says," *Lincoln Journal Star*, March 23, 1996.

65. Appendix B of letter sent from Lincoln diocesan members of CTAN to the bishops, archbishops and cardinals of the United States Conference of Catholic Bishops, October 25, 1996.

66. Bob Keeler, "Rebuking Reform: Catholic Bishop Orders Flock to Toe the Doctrinal Line," *Newsday* (New York City Edition), March 26, 1996.

67. Adelle M. Banks, "Bishop Forbids 'Incompatible' Memberships: Says Freemasons, Others may be Excommunicated," *Pioneer Press,* March 26, 1996.

68. Laurie Goodstein, "Excommunication Threat Stuns Catholics: Nebraska Bishop Warns Members of 12 Groups," *Washington Post*, March 29, 1996.

69. Julia McCord, "Lincoln Diocese Completes Synod," *Omaha World Herald,* August 9, 1996.

70. Bishop Fabian Bruskewitz, "An Ordinary Viewpoint: The Kiss of Judas," *Southern Nebraska Register,* April 4, 1997.

71. Bob Reeves, "Groups off-limits for Catholics…"

72. Ibid.

73. Mel Beckman, "Call To Action, Nebraska and the Diocese of Lincoln, Weekly Update," April 23, 1996.

74. Mary Jo Anderson, "Inside Call to Action," *Crisis*, February 1996.

75. Tom Heinen, "Opening Regional Milwaukee Wanderer Forum, Bishop Stresses Historical Significance of Pope," *Milwaukee Journal Sentinel*, November 6, 1999.

CHAPTER 6

Reaction to the Extra-Synodal Legislation

What is happening south of the Platte River, in a heretofore little-known geographically large diocese of about 83,000 Catholics, led by a man who relies on church law and obedience, has been so loud and ugly, has so captured the curiosity of the secular media, has so pitted the traditional concept of church against the reformist one, has brought forth so many charges and countercharges, so many editorials and counter-editorials, that one is tempted to think there is some greater purpose, some unseen hand, at work. Which is only to say God may be writing straight here with crooked lines.[1]—Paul Hendrickson, *Washington Post*, April 12, 1996.

EXCOMMUNICATION OF THE TYPE AND SCALE undertaken by Bishop Bruskewitz was unprecedented in the United States.[2] The action attracted local, national and international attention. Members of CTAN were thrust into the media spotlight.

Bishop Bruskewitz's legislation profoundly impacted a large group of people. To give voice to their thoughts and experiences, throughout this chapter I include the words of members of Call To Action Nebraska as they recalled and reflected on their reaction to the legislation. The words were spoken in the interviews I conducted with them. I include them, in italics, throughout this chapter.

CTA and CTAN's Initial Response to the
Extra-Synodal Legislation[3]

Most members of Call to Action Nebraska were blindsided by Bishop Bruskewitz's extra synodal legislation. Many CTAN members learned of the bishop's move through the local media. CTAN board member, Jim McShane, recalled receiving a phone call from a reporter for the *Lincoln Journal Star*. The reporter called to ask for a comment. McShane recounted this moment in an interview:

> And a guy called me on the phone and said, "How does it feel to be," or, "What are you going to do about the threat of excommunication or about the excommunication policy," or however it was. And I laughed and I said, "I'm not going to do anything about it, it doesn't exist. Nobody would do that." And he said, "No, I'm perfectly serious. It's been announced in the *Southern Nebraska Register*." I said, "You're putting me on. And, I'm a busy man, I got work to do. And it's hardly credible." And he said, "No, I am very serious." And I said, "well then you better send me a copy of the announcement before I'll comment on it.". . . And shortly, on the office fax machine, there came this, this thing. Which I must say was less funny.[4]

Joan Johnson remembered learning about the excommunication by reading the *Southern Nebraska Register*. She said, "Of course, I couldn't believe it. This was such a middle-ages thing to do."[5]

As an official response, CTAN Co-Chairs, Lori Darby and John Krejci, signed a letter to Bishop Bruskewitz dated March 23, 1996 in which they thanked the bishop for clarifying his position regarding Call To Action. In the letter they wrote: "As faithful and committed Catholics we would be open to discussion of the specific issues that caused you to threaten censure."[6] They noted in their letter that they were seeking the input of several canon lawyers.

Both Call To Action Nebraska and the national Call To Action organization issued press releases on March 24, 1996. In the CTAN press release, CTAN members described themselves as perplexed by Bishop Bruskewitz's ecclesiastical sanctions. They cited remarks of theologian Bernard Cooke that "Catholics do not need permission to gather nor should they be sanctioned for doing good."[7] The press release also noted that in June 1995, twelve United States Roman Catholic bishops signed a statement that called for the United States Conference of Catholic Bishops (USCCB) and the Vatican to discuss issues that Call To Action supports. The press release cited surveys of Catholics that showed great support for the ordination of women (almost 65%) and the married priesthood (75%) as well as disagreement with the Church's teaching on birth control (85%). CTAN's statement indicated that "Whereas, Church teaching should not be determined by popular vote, these surveys are an indication that these issues are problematic for Catholics."[8]

The national Call To Action press release quoted Co-Director Sheila Daley as saying, "The intemperate action of threatening Lincoln Diocese Call To Action members with excommunication unless they resign from Call To Action violates the most basic principles of justice." Co-Director Dan Daley continued: "It is precisely because of Bishop Bruskewitz and people like him that Call To Action exists—to proclaim that the Church is not a dictatorship but a community of believers. All Church members are given the gift of the Spirit at baptism and deserve fundamental human respect, communication, and participation in the life of the Church."[9]

CTAN and Lincoln Diocese In the Media Spotlight

Mel Beckman, Archdiocese of Omaha CTAN member:

> *I think I was surprised that they would go to such an extreme measure without even having contact with us, not knowing what we were doing, it seemed incredibly stupid to me to go after us like that and to attract all that publicity.*[10]

If, as indicated by Fr. Gutgsell, Nebraska Catholic leaders hoped to avoid division and tension,[11] then Bishop Bruskewitz was surely disappointed. The diocese of Lincoln was thrust into the local and national media spotlight. Bishop Bruskewitz's legislation was so unusual that it caught the attention and imagination of many Catholics and non-Catholics. Charles M. Wilson, Executive Director of the St. Joseph Foundation, noted in *Christifidelis*, the newsletter of his organization, that to the best of his knowledge, "no act of any individual bishop in North America during the past twentyfive [sic] years has received as much media coverage as has been given to Bishop Bruskewitz's action."[12] Bishop Bruskewitz expressed great surprise that his legislation touched off such a firestorm.[13] The *Lincoln Journal Star* listed this story as its second top story of 1996.[14] Indeed, within a matter of days, the *Lincoln Journal Star* and the *Omaha World Herald* covered the story as well as many other Nebraskan newspapers including the *Kearney Hub*, *Hastings Tribune*, *Plattsmouth Journal*, and the *Grand Island Independent*. News coverage reached well beyond Nebraska as the story was reported nationally and internationally.[15]

The *National Catholic Reporter* (NCR) covered the extra-synodal legislation extensively as its cover story in the April 5, 1996 edition. *NCR* staff writer, Leslie Wirpsa, pointed out that there is a "deep divide among U.S. Catholics, including members of the hierarchy, regarding a basic vision of church. One is open to wide participation by laypeople and discussion of controversial issues; the other relies heavily on church law and unquestioning obedience."[16] In her story, Wirpsa questioned whether Bishop Bruskewitz's thoughts are common among bishops.

Patty Hawk, Lincoln Diocese CTAN member:

Well when I first heard about it, I thought, these are the bravest people I know, and I didn't know them. I saw this stuff on television and I thought, I'm really impressed with these people. Because they're saying what I think. They said, in the interviews I saw on television, things like, "this is my family. You can't ask me to leave my family. I'm staying in this family, I just want it to be better." And I thought "Yes. This is my Catholic family. I can't leave my family. But, I should not have to put up with behavior in my family that I so wholly disagree with." So they spoke to me when I saw that on television.[17]

The discussion played out in the letters to the editor section of news-papers for many weeks after the publication of the legislation including the *Lincoln Journal Star* and the *Omaha World Herald*. On March 27, 1996, each of the thirteen letters to the editor published in the *Lincoln Journal Star* addressed Bishop Bruskewitz's extra-synodal legislation.[18] Some let-ters supported Bishop Bruskewitz. For example, "Thank you, Jesus, for Bishop Bruskewitz. It's about time. . . This is what true Roman Catholics want. . . Frankly, no further discussion or dialogue is needed. Either be in union with the infallible moral teachings of the Pope or find another church, end of story" (Daniel J. Konrady, Lincoln). Others spoke against the legislation. For example, "On many occasions I have heard reference made to the Lincoln Diocese as 'conservative.' Perhaps those were under-statements. Reactionary would seem to be more appropriate. . ." (Joseph J. Stork, Lincoln). And, "[Bishop Bruskewitz's threat of excommunication] will surely further divide the church and encourage others to leave along with the excommunicated" (Kelly O'Neill, Walthill).

Jean Krejci, Lincoln Diocese CTAN member:

> *We had people stumbling over each other coming in and out with tapes and recorders and videos. . . We are nobody. We are here in the middle of Nebraska and I thought, that's kind of neat. Nebraska is in the middle of the country and if Jesus, if God, wants to prove something or choose some-body, he's always chosen insignificant people. Simple people. Insignificant people, unimportant places. . . I keep saying we were naïve. I think we were very naïve, but I'm glad we were because it didn't upset our equilib-rium. But I remember all the press coming in and I thought, "this is good for the church. This is going to educate people."[19]*

As reporters researched Bishop Bruskewitz's extra-synodal legisla-tion, they contacted experts for comment. A number of bishops, canon lawyers and theologians expressed opinions about the legislation and these opinions were published widely.

U.S. Bishops Respond

While it is extremely unusual for United States bishops to publically criticize the actions of their fellow bishops, a number of bishops expressed negative opinions about Bishop Bruskewitz's legislation. Joseph Cardinal Bernardin, Archbishop of Chicago, issued a statement dated March 26, 1996 indicating that while Call To Action holds some positions contrary to Church teaching, it also holds other positions that are in accord with Church teaching. Like Bishop Bruskewitz, Cardinal Bernardin expressed concern that members of CTA would publicly express their positions in opposition to Church teaching as it "often results in confusion and tensions within the Catholic community." However, Bernardin explained that he avoids engaging in conflict with CTA in favor of "moral persuasion and dialogue." He then addressed Bishop Bruskewitz's actions:

> I do not think that cutting off Call to Action's members completely from the Catholic community would serve any good purpose; indeed, it would exacerbate the situation. Moreover, it is important to note that many of those who participate in Call to Action programs do not agree with every position taken by the group but attend because they are concerned about the Church and want to hear the views of others. In other words, we must take into account the fact that there are different levels of commitment to the organization.[20]

Jim McShane, Lincoln Diocese CTAN member:

As . . . [Cardinal Bernardin] pointed out. . . he said you don't excommunicate people because they belong to a group because you don't know why they belong to the group. They may want the newsletter. They may want to see what other people are thinking about one issue or another. You can't make assumptions about the state of their soul by their association. Perfectly reasonable to me. [Bishop Bruskewitz's legislation was] Flagrantly unfair. And shockingly stupid. I thought that now; I've thought so still. On several grounds. A friend of Carol's suggested to her that the guy made a big mistake because he's got a whole lot of arrows in his quiver and one big club. And if you're upset with somebody and you want to effectively modify their behavior, you don't take the biggest club you've got and throw it at them. Because if you miss, you don't have a big club anymore. And the advantage of the big club is always in the threat more than it is in its ineffective execution.[21]

Bishop Raymond Boland of the Diocese of Kansas City-St. Joseph and Archbishop James Keleher of the Archdiocese of Kansas City, Kansas issued statements saying that they would not follow the lead of Bishop Bruskewitz regarding the excommunication.[22] Kansas City-St. Joseph Chancellor George Noonan said, "Bishop Boland is very pastoral and his approach would not be an approach like this. It would not be his style to issue any edict like this."[23]

Colorado Springs Bishop, Richard Hanifen, also publicly stated that he would not follow in Bishop Bruskewitz's footsteps. He reportedly said, "It's not the way I would handle it. We must honor individual conscience... Our job is to challenge the conscience of those people and make sure they have an informed conscience."[24] Another Colorado bishop, Bishop Arthur Tafoya of Pueblo, said he would not enact legislation that would lead to automatic excommunication based on group membership. He prefers to "teach morals and lead people in a correct conscience."[25]

Bishop Raymond Lucker from New Ulm, Minnesota issued a statement in defense of Call To Action: "I am a member of Call to Action. I was invited to speak at their conference last November. It's a wonderful group of people, concerned with social justice in the church and in society."[26] Lucker described CTA members as "very respectful, open and concerned about authentic Catholic teaching."[27] In discussing his experience at the CTA conference, Lucker said, "I came face to face with thousands of very dedicated, active Catholics who are concerned about the church, who love the church and who are interested in church renewal. There are some who I would say would be people with whom I would not agree, but you'd find that at any number of Catholic gatherings. It is worthwhile to talk with them."[28] Another bishop who asked the *National Catholic Reporter* to allow him to remain anonymous remarked on his interactions with members of Call To Action. He said they

> seemed like they were very positive and loved the church and wanted the best for the church. . . When you get a group of laypeople together who are talking about the issues, sometimes it gets messy and it's not orderly like when clerics get together. I think we have to be able to get along with the messiness if we are really going to move ahead in renewing the church. People have to have courage, vision, to be able to see through to the other side.[29]

Charles Kelliher, Grand Island Diocese CTAN member:

> *Well two of the priests of the Grand Island Diocese called me. And I hadn't even seen it, heard about it. They couldn't believe that this man [Bishop Bruskewitz] would do something like that. Anyway, it's a little bit like, I think it's an abuse of authority. . . you have other bishops like Raymond Lucker who is a member of Call To Action who was a professor of mine at St. Paul's Seminary, and others [bishops] who belong to this [Call To Action]. . . Well, you know, they're [Bishop Bruskewitz and his supporters] not using their heads, they're using their emotions, they're using what they feel that they have power over.[30]*

Bishop Kenneth Untener of Saginaw, Michigan said that in addition to placing other bishops in an awkward position, Bishop Bruskewitz's action "raises questions of credibility."[31] He continued, "When do you say to a family member, 'You are no longer part of the family and you can't come to any of our gatherings?'. . . 'this is not just an organizational tightening; you're dealing with people.'"[32]

CTAN member,[33] Grand Island diocese:

> *I think the damage was that it divided people into camps and set up a watch-dog mentality in some areas. And it made loyalty to the bishop more important than loyalty to Jesus.*

Other Catholics Respond Publically

The Archdiocese of Boston's newspaper, the *Pilot*, published an editorial that criticized Bishop Bruskewitz for not consulting with other U.S. bishops before he issued his extra-synodal legislation. The editorial called it "an oversight of some consequence."[34] While the editorial affirmed Bishop Bruskewitz's belief that church teaching is not open for debate, it stated that excommunication should be used as a last resort.

Charles Wilson of the St. Joseph Foundation noted that the canon lawyers on the Foundation's consulting staff agreed that Bishop Bruskewitz's legislation was valid.[35] The action raised many eyebrows among other canon lawyers and theologians, however. The *Omaha World Herald* quotes canon law specialist, Rev. Richard Hill, on the matter of the excommunications. Hill said it was within Bishop Bruskewitz's authority to excommunicate the members of the twelve organizations, "'But it is very rare—very, very rare,' he said. 'In the last 25 to 30 years, I haven't known of any similar instance except one. It's difficult for a Catholic to get excommunicated. It truly is. We want to be able to get people to march with us.'"[36] Hill further explained that excommunicating people is "very, very complex. In the procedure, every effort is supposed to be made to have individuals explain themselves."[37] Canon lawyer, Tim McCarthy, explained that Bishop Bruskewitz's actions were "'extraordinary' because bishops usually try to open a dialogue with a person they consider to be involved in 'delinquent actions.'"[38] Canon law professor, Rev. Thomas Green, is quoted as having said, "He can do it. Whether he should do it is another question. It does seem to be a little bit strange."[39] Green explained that bishops are expected to use restraint in their application of excommunication, "Bishops are not supposed to do this unless there's a really serious issue. Apparently, most of his peers—at least up to the moment—have not seen it to be that kind of issue."[40]

Pat Sullivan, Archdiocese of Omaha CTAN member:

> *I began to realize a bishop really has that kind of power. I mean, I can't believe that this is allowed to continue. Surely they're going to stop this,*

somebody's going to say something. No! This, this won't go on! At first I just denied it, you know. But I couldn't take it too seriously. But then I began to realize, nobody's saying anything. This is being allowed to continue. And then I'm hearing people say, well, under the church, under Canon Law, a bishop has that right in his diocese, and you can't really do anything about it. And I'm going, "Oh boy! This is not the Church that I thought I belonged to!". . . the excommunication was being allowed to stand, and that people were actually feeling this and suffering from it, and nobody was doing anything about it, and the true injustice of it was just really grating on me.[41]

University of Notre Dame theologian, Rev. Richard McBrien, used the word "bizarre" to refer to Bishop Bruskewitz's threat.[42] He believed, "This edict is so irresponsible that no one is bound by it."[43] Further, he opined that the rest of the United States Catholic bishops will not follow suit, "I'm fairly confident that most of the bishops in the U.S.—even the most conservative ones—rolled their eyes and sighed."[44]

Theology professor Daniel Maguire believed that Bishop Bruskewitz "went too far" and that "even if [Bishop Bruskewitz] tried to excommunicate (members of various groups), his attempt would be invalid."[45] William McInerny, Professor of Theology and Religious Studies at Rockhurst College, addressed the issue of the primacy of conscience. He stated that if people have "sincerely informed their conscience" through careful study, prayer and understanding, they can dissent from the teaching. He said, "The bishop of Lincoln is giving the impression that there is one and only one path to follow if you are to be a faithful Catholic."[46]

Jim Orwig, Archdiocese of Omaha CTAN member:

It just doesn't make any sense. I just, I don't know what he was trying to accomplish. It's a grandstanding thing. . . It doesn't accomplish anything, it doesn't mean anything. He can excommunicate all he wants to, but people have to have an awareness that they're doing something wrong and I don't think anybody from Lincoln ever felt like they were doing something wrong or that they had not attempted to enter into a meaningful dialogue.[47]

According to Lincoln diocesan reports, the laity had raised questions about the twelve groups on Bishop Bruskewitz's list, necessitating the extra-synodal legislation. Though Bishop Bruskewitz claimed to have issued this legislation to "dissipate ambiguities," Rev. Thomas Reese, then-senior fellow at Georgetown University's Woodstock Theological Center, expected it to have the opposite effect, to cause confusion: "Every bishop in the country is now going to be asked why he is not excommunicating members of these groups in his diocese. This is the kind of thing the bishops normally don't do—go off on their own like this without consultation and collegial cooperation with other bishops."[48]

Lincoln diocese CTAN member:[49]

I was reading the NCR and some of the letters were very funny. Like, "I'm Catholic and if I fly from California to New York, as I cross Nebraska am I excommunicated for that period of time?" It was hard to take seriously because it was so bizarre and it was medieval. But then there was a kind of sadness about the whole thing, a terrible sadness about it. Also this raw demonstration of power exercised without justice was truly appalling.

Jim McShane, Lincoln Diocese CTAN member:

The only ambiguity that has been addressed by our excommunication, it seems to me, is the ambiguities that arise from the arbitrary abuse of power. And they've been made more complex, not more simple.[50]

Some Catholics wonder how rules can change from diocese to diocese.[51] When asked about this matter, Bishop Bruskewitz responded, "I don't see how legislation which is meant to apply only to Lincoln should cause undue consternation for people who live elsewhere and whom I would urge to follow the legislation that exists in their own diocese."[52]

Sandy Matthews, Archdiocese of Omaha CTAN member:

Nobody will answer me! How can it be a mortal sin on one side of the Platte [River] and not the other? . . . It doesn't make sense! . . . why are you excommunicated and I am not? How can you be excommunicated from an organization that archbishops, priests, bishops, nuns, other people aren't?. . . Plus, when no one speaks against this. When no priest, no bishop speaks against this, either they say, as was said to me. . . "don't give them credence," or "Every bishop is the power, the final word in his own diocese." I don't care. . . It simply doesn't make sense to me. And viewing injustice this way, that they lost credibility. And I don't value their teaching authority if this is what they allow.[53]

Dave McCauley, Executive Director of the Minnesota Catholic Conference, is quoted as having said, "I can't imagine that this is going to catch on. It's a drastic step, not one that's common in the church today."[54] Professor of Church History, Msgr. Robert Tisco, described Bishop Bruskewitz's blanket excommunication as "unique." He said, "I can't think of any historical precedents."[55]

Professor Emeritus of Canon Law at the Catholic University of America, Msgr. Frederick R. McManus, said "It is exceptional because while the general [church] law allows a bishop to do this, it does express pretty strongly that he shouldn't do it except in serious situations."[56] Catholic News Service contacted three canon lawyers who all agreed that Bishop Bruskewitz had the "legal authority" to issue the extra-synodal legislation. However, they all "viewed his action as out of keeping with the revised Code of Canon Law's basic approach to penal legislation" including a reduction of automatic penalties.[57]

James Coriden, Professor of Church Law at Washington Theological Union, directly addressed the use of *latae sententiae* penalties in an opinion[58] on Bishop Bruskewitz's legislation. He explained that the Code of Canon Law was revised to make such penalties very rare. He quoted Canon 1318 which states that:

A legislator is not to threaten *latae sententiae* [automatic] penalties except possibly for certain singularly malicious delicts which either can result in graver scandal or cannot be punished effectively by *ferendae sententiae* penalties; he is not, however, to establish censures, especially excommunication, except with the greatest moderation and only for graver delicts.[59]

Coriden also highlighted Canon 1316, "Insofar as possible, diocesan bishops are to take care that if penal laws must be issued, they are uniform in the same city or region."[60] No other diocese in the region has adopted the same legislation.

Coriden then explained multiple reasons why Catholics in the Lincoln diocese need not hold themselves to this interdict. Such a sanction would require the receiver of the interdict to act with malice as well as have an awareness of the law and penalty. He concludes that

> a law so contrary to the spirit and letter of Canon Law, so sweepingly broad and aimless, so unsupported by evidence of necessity, so intemperate and harsh, and so contemptuous of the precious value of ecclesial communion, is invalid on its face, or at best a doubtful law. Doubtful laws do not oblige (c. 14). They are worse than no law at all, because of the confusion they engender.[61]

When asked whether or not he believed, as Canon 1318 stipulates, the offenses in this case rise to the level of "particularly treacherous," Msgr. Vasa reportedly responded,

> I think they are particularly treacherous in that there are Catholics who are claiming the possibility of believing and holding things which are diametrically opposed to the teaching of the Catholic Church and at the same time saying, "I can be a good and faithful practicing Catholic." Our Lord in the Scriptures was very stern with those who led others astray.[62]

Bishop Bruskewitz said he did not think his action was extreme. He said he believed the situation as it stood was serious, putting the Catholic faith of those involved in jeopardy.[63] Bishop Bruskewitz stated, "I hope what I did, I did out of pastoral love. I had no intention of doing anything that wasn't done in charity and love for my flock."[64]

Patty Hawk, Lincoln Diocese CTAN member:

> *And I also think that there is a genuine desire on the Bishop's part to be a shepherd. I think that's where he sees his role. I also think there's a genuine*

part of him that's extraordinarily ambitious and enjoyed the press and sought it. And that's sad for me.[65]

Vatican officials who spoke under condition of anonymity with a reporter or reporters from Catholic News Service said that the "pastoral and legal ramifications" of Bishop Bruskewitz's legislation were under consideration at the Vatican.[66] While the officials believed Bishop Bruskewitz had a good motive for his action, they believed that the application of the penalty to individuals could prove problematic. In addition, his failure to consult other bishops "raised questions of collegiality." One official commented, "It would be better for such a decision to be agreed upon, at least in the same region."[67] Bishop Pilla, President of the U.S. Conference of Catholic Bishops, stated that variation in penalties "clearly is not a good thing. One would hope for consultation, but clearly we can't demand that."[68] The Vatican officials also explained that they respected Bishop Bruskewitz's resolve to protect the people in his diocese from danger.

Late conservative columnist and practicing Catholic, William F. Buckley, Jr., addressed Bishop Bruskewitz's legislation calling the "short fuse of the bishop of Lincoln. . . something of an embarrassment."[69] Buckley recalled a televised conversation he had with Bishop Fulton Sheen during which Buckley asked Bishop Sheen to list the excommunicable offenses. Sheen's response: "The desecration of the Blessed Sacrament." Buckley concludes his commentary: "Bishop Bruskewitz should pause to consider the fraternal implications of his sortie. If his move was called for in today's circumstances, then the 162 other bishops in America are delinquent."[70]

John Burke, former Lincoln Diocesan CTAN member:

. . . I was just bewildered by the extremity, but I just thought it was, it was just comical. And I thought, "this is going to backfire on you," . . . And I thought, you can push people so far... only so far before the average person is going to, is going to recognize it as extreme. . . Word was out nationally about that pretty quickly, and I know my family and almost all the

Catholic associations they had outside of Lincoln were just dumbfounded. . . You can disagree with someone without going to that extreme. But then of course, what was even more comical, was and I understand this more from being in school administration was once you set your boundary, you've got to be able to enforce it.[71]

In a column in the *Southern Nebraska Register*, Bishop Bruskewitz noted "the profound ignorance" toward religion of "media types."[72] Bishop Bruskewitz continued that he guessed the misinformation conveyed in the media about his extra-synodal legislation "was due about seventy percent to ignorance and thirty percent to malice." Bishop Bruskewitz quoted from a few of the letters of support he received, including one that said, "May the arm of the Almighty strengthen you in your endeavor to cast out those snakes."

Mary Jo Bousek, Lincoln Diocese CALL member:

Well I know a lot of us were very hopeful that things would change, and especially when he said okay, well, you can read [at Mass]. We thought, oh this man is okay. He's going to be okay. So there was hope I thought, but it didn't seem to last too long because he did allow women to read and still does. We'll see how long. But other than that he was pretty, pretty conservative, almost as reactionary as Flavin, but not quite, until his big pronouncement of all these excommunications. That is the biggest farce I've known in my Christian life, in my Catholic life obviously, but that really set him down many pegs from where he should be as a bishop. . . Oh I think it's, one thing, excommunicating CALL people is ridiculous. These are some of the most faith-filled Catholic people in this diocese and yet somehow he's excommunicated them because he doesn't want to talk to us. Because maybe he doesn't agree with everything they want to pursue, which I understood—married priests and women priests, that's like profanity I guess.[73]

Non-Media Response

The Call To Action Nebraska chapter received a great deal of support from the national Call To Action organization. Dan Daley, co-director of CTA-USA, supported CTAN members, in part, by visiting Nebraska multiple times. He attended the first general Call To Action Nebraska meeting to take place after Bishop Bruskewitz published his extra-synodal legislation. The April 27, 1996 meeting in Omaha drew 200 participants. CTA-USA kept other Call To Action members around the country apprised of the situation and requested their members write letters of support to members of CTAN as well as letters to their bishops. CTAN received letters of solidarity from 27 states. One CTAN member from Lincoln received "a check for $10, some small purple and yellow flowers, and a note from a woman in New York. The note said, 'The money and flowers are a gesture of encouragement for Call To Action Nebraska.'"[74] Just after the May 15 excommunication deadline, Call To Action USA published and circulated a document called "Profiles in Courage and Faith." The document highlighted the personal faith stories of Lincoln CTAN members Jim and Carol McShane, Jean and John Krejci, Benedict and Ellen McWhirter, Joan and Jerry Johnson, Rosalind Carr, and Marilyn and Francis Seiker. This CTA-USA publication pointed out that the profiled Catholics raised children in the faith. They had been involved with many types of ministry including leading the rosary before Mass, music ministry, marriage preparation, reading at Mass, altar society, and parish council. They were active in social justice work in their community as well as through volunteering at a soup kitchen and homeless shelters.

Some organizations spread information about the interdict and excommunication to their members and suggested actions their members could take. For example, Catholics Speak Out suggested their members send letters to their bishops as well as the Apostolic Pro-Nuncio, write letters to the editor and join CTAN. One group of thirty-five Catholics from various places in the country wrote to Bishop Bruskewitz and informed him of their pledge to attend Mass one extra day a week during the Easter season in support of CTAN members and in a hope to "restore peace and understanding" in Lincoln.[75]

CTAN members were not the only ones to receive support from outside the diocese. Bishop Bruskewitz reportedly received letters, faxes, calls of support, and bouquets of flowers. According to Bishop Bruskewitz, the support came from all over the country and some of that support came from Protestants and Jewish people.[76] Bishop Bruskewitz reported that, "The negative responses are minimal, and if you discount the usual cranks and eccentrics, they're minuscule."[77] He did, however, report that he "received some letters with a lot of invective and obscenities."[78] Bishop Bruskewitz said the reactions he received ran "hundreds to one in my favor."[79] By May 15, 1996, Bishop Bruskewitz reported he received around 3,500 letters supporting his action and around 100 letters of disagreement[80] and by the five-year anniversary of the excommunication, Bishop Bruskewitz was said to have received over 50,000 "communications of support" and about 300 negative communications.[81] Though no other United States bishop had publicly supported him, he said he had the support of twenty-five US bishops.[82]

President of the conservative Catholic League for Religious and Civil Rights, William Donohue, was among those who commended Bishop Bruskewitz.[83] Franciscan University of Steubenville Professor of Theology, Regis Martin, expressed hope that other bishops would act as did Bishop Bruskewitz.[84] Bishop Bruskewitz reportedly received a standing ovation when he spoke at a gathering of the conservative Institute of Religious Life shortly after the publication of the extra-synodal legislation.[85]

According to a short news piece in *This Rock*, Human Life International organized a petition drive in support of Bishop Bruskewitz's legislation. The letter the signers were asked to endorse said, in part, "We the undersigned salute your courage in staunchly defending the faith" and "We hope and pray that your brother bishops throughout the world will follow your leadership."[86] Fr. Richard Neuhaus wrote, "The prospect of being excommunicated in a month wonderfully concentrates the Catholic mind. It is agreed that Bishop Bruskewitz acted within canon law."[87]

Marilyn Seiker, former Lincoln Diocese, current Archdiocese of Omaha CTAN member:

> *Bruskewitz is a man of vision and a pragmatic politician. He's not cling-ing to the past. He's promoting it. Call To Action was a gift to him. Excommunicating us was his ticket to world notoriety. He's become a dar-ling of the very far right. If he had hopes of promotion, his extremism will keep that from happening. With the appointment of two Lincoln priests to the episcopate, the establishing of an Order of St. Peter's Seminary in the diocese, his status as a frequent guest on Mother Angelica's network, he may be satisfied to stay in Lincoln while propagating his extremism through protégés.*[88]

Many people who might call themselves conservative, orthodox, or traditional Roman Catholics were pleased with Bishop Bruskewitz's extra-synodal legislation and praised his leadership. Some Catholics chose to move to Lincoln specifically to be in this environment. For example, Julie and Alton Davis moved from San Antonio to Lincoln in 1998. Regarding the extra-synodal legislation, Julie Davis told a reporter, "We were really impressed by a man who would exercise such leadership, because it was so unheard of."[89]

In fact, men from other parts of the country choose to become priests in the Lincoln diocese. Just over half of the group entering priestly forma-tion in the Lincoln diocese in the fall of 1996 came from the diocese of Lincoln.[90]

Not all who moved to the Lincoln diocese were pleased with what they found. Before he joined CTAN, John Burke explained that he knew he and his wife might have difficulty being nourished by parish life. He commented,

> It's a tougher row to hoe than you realize. . . when we went to Mass, we were almost on a regular basis just angry, what we heard. . . there's no female participation. . . At first I was thinking, "Thank God I don't have a girl!" But as I thought about it more, I thought it's even worse that we have boys, because this perpetuates to them that this is okay. It's

much easier to move out of victimhood than it is to move out of being an oppressor. And I think that's one of my worries for my boys, is that they're going to see these models presented as the norm.[91]

CTAN Members Decide

On April 15, 1996, the day the interdict went into effect, *Newsday*[92] reported that only two members of Call To Action Nebraska withdrew membership, though they asked to have their names remain on the mailing list. The CTAN membership had grown by around 30 people in the three weeks after the publication of the legislation. Francis and Marilyn Seiker were the two who originally withdrew membership from the organization. They explained that they were worried about being denied communion in front of three of their grandchildren who belonged to their same rural parish. However, after discussing the situation with a bishop friend, they renewed their membership in CTAN.[93] The bishop "suggested that Bruskewitz was using an outdated sixteenth century tactic. 'Does the excommunication trouble you?' he asked. 'If it doesn't, then just ignore the whole thing.'"[94]

After the threat of excommunication, Rosalind Carr, a founding member of CALL, temporarily asked to be an inactive member of Call To Action Nebraska. One of her reasons was that she had just finished lector training and was pleased that she would be able to read scripture during Mass. As the main advocate for women readers in her parish, Carr was also worried that the other women who had trained as lectors would be considered by the pastor to be "guilty by association."[95] In addition, Carr's daughter was planning to be married in the Catholic Church and Carr told a reporter she was worried her membership in CTAN might impact her daughter's wedding plans. She said, "I dropped my membership out of fear, fear of retribution."[96] Not long after, she asked to be reinstated as an active member. Carr explained her thoughts after the excommunication:

It's a power thing. It's a power thing. And it was issued by a man who had no understanding about people who know their faith, who know about their faith, and people who have confidence in God's presence in the church and the Holy Spirit in the church. It's the kind of thing where, it's a management kind of thing. They've no concept that we knew and know what we were doing. We were confident in knowing what we were doing and we were also confident that the Holy Spirit was with us and we had nothing to contradict that from others. I mean, this wasn't just our feeling. We had this confidence from things that were happening outside our little walls.[97]

Lincoln diocesan CTAN member, Joan Johnson, explained how she and her husband, Jerry, decided to retain their membership in CTAN:

[Bishop Bruskewitz] had never made any attempt to speak with us, to try to come to some sort of understanding. [The excommunication] was so harsh and uncalled for. There was a lot of shock and disbelief and uncertainty in the first few days after the pronouncement was made. Each member of the group had to decide for themselves the effect it had personally. We were all torn, I can tell you that. Jerry and I discussed it a lot over the next few days, vacillating over what to do. On Sunday, we went to Mass. We arrived early, still somewhat stunned and not sure what we were going to do, and I know I said a prayer for guidance. About a third of the way through Mass, it became very clear to me, and I turned to Jerry and I said, "I am not leaving. I am going to stay in CTA." And he said, "I am, too." I had asked myself what would it be like if I dropped out of CTA after finally finding my spiritual home after so many years. I knew then that I could not live with myself and at that point it became a matter of conscience. I really feel that the Holy Spirit touched me during that Mass and ended the uncertainty about whether to leave or stay in CTA. It was such a sense of relief.[98]

A Lincoln CTAN member explained how she responded to the news of the extra-synodal legislation:

Disbelief, I just couldn't believe it. And I just thought, I couldn't believe it. And I was so confused, well now what do we do? Do we, because we felt like we were part of, that we were Catholic and we were part of our faith and that we weren't doing anything worthy of excommunication. I don't think Call to Action Nebraska was radical at all. Do you? I don't think people were protesting and doing anything even disrespectful. So I don't understand what prompted the excommunication just because it was people who wanted to have open discussion about what they believed in, or more about those issues that were difficult, trying to decipher what's right and what's wrong or how you can be involved in a just way, I guess.[99]

Not every member of Call To Action Nebraska found the excommunication to be a time of soul searching. John Krejci, then co-chair of CTAN, reflected: "I know sin when I see it and this isn't it. We checked very early on and said, he [Bishop Bruskewitz] technically has the authority to do that, but he's abusing this authority. . . It's invalid, it's a violation of human rights, a violation of us in the church. . . [to] a lot of our members it was crushing and sad and horrible. . ."[100] Lincoln diocesan CTAN member Mary Hawk lived outside Nebraska at the time of the excommunication; she has since moved to the Lincoln diocese. She explained her thoughts about the excommunication:

It was interesting in a sociological way. But I was never afraid of it. I knew that a person, a mandate from a person couldn't change who I was. The way it's changed is how significantly it impacts people around me. My fellow Catholics who are members of Nebraska Call To Action who take the excommunication very seriously. . . They were raised with much more of a church doctrine kind of Catholicism. . . So again, I don't see the Church as being the law. I see the Church as being the community in which I express my faith. And no person can take that way from me. No hierarchy of the Church can take that away from me. But I do know that there are people around me who struggle with it every day.[101]

Charles Kelliher offered a different interpretation of what might have been happening regarding the excommunication:

> If all the truth was known, I think there was a little bit personal that got involved there, more so than doctrinal, in the sense that Bruskewitz and John Krejci went to school together in Rome. They were two years apart. . . And there's, in my estimation, there's more underneath the surface to this excommunication than just a group of people wanting change. I think there is some, almost like a personal vendetta. You know? Two bulls hitting head.[102]

Much had happened by May 15, 1996, the date the excommunication was to come into effect, including a great deal of activity and media attention. Twenty-two prayer services were held on May 14 and 15 to support CTAN members. These services took place from California to New Jersey, from Illinois to Arizona as well as one international service in Ecuador.[103]

Call To Action Nebraska reported that their membership doubled since the extra-synodal legislation was published. They went from 72 to 156 statewide members and from 22 to 33 in the city of Lincoln.[104]

In an Associated Press article on May 15, 1996, Bishop Bruskewitz is quoted as having said that he believed his legislation unmasked "some people who previously had a very questionable relationship with the Catholic Church. They may have been in their heart anti-Catholic, though they externally professed to be Catholic."[105] I can't imagine whom Bishop Bruskewitz had in mind when he wrote that his legislation unmasked some people who in their hearts were anti-Catholic. Bishop Bruskewitz's may have intended to root out people he considered to be "anti-Catholics" from the Catholic Church, but the effects of the legislation were much broader. The bishop may not have foreseen how the effects of his legislation would spiral outward. For example, an interviewee shared the story of a young Catholic woman in the Lincoln diocese married to a non-Catholic who is a Mason. Their daughters belonged to the Rainbow Girls. When the extra-synodal legislation was published, an interviewee told me:

She went to her husband and she said, "I'm going to have to take the girls out of Rainbow Girls because the bishop says that they can't be a member of that." And he said, "If you do that, you can kiss me goodbye because I want to stay a Mason and I want you to be involved and the girls." And so she, it was like, which is the worst of two evils? So she chose excommunication. And she lives by it. She attends Mass regularly; she is a faithful Catholic. She never receives communion.[106]

The interviewee continued, "It's a terrible thing for him [Bishop Bruskewitz] to have caused this woman to be threatened with the loss of her husband." Certainly, something can be said about her husband who acted in such a manner toward his wife. It seems two incompatible demands were placed on this woman and she did what she thought she had to do. She may not be the only person to find herself in such an untenable position. It is possible that Bishop Bruskewitz considers any person who hopes for reforms in the church to be a fraud and it is likely that by issuing his legislation he intended to expose the people he views as anti-Catholic. Others, like the woman described here, however, found themselves in Bishop Bruskewitz's crosshairs.

Lori Darby, former Archdiocese of Omaha CTAN member:

. . . people were being hurt. . . These were some of the most faithful Catholics I had ever known, who loved the church, loved the Roman Catholic church. . . We were prayerful, each one of us, some of the most prayerful people I know. I knew that in whatever way they prayed, they were bringing us to God every day, that they wanted us to be faithful. . . Each of them has a strong history of involvement in the church and in justice. In a way, John and Jean and me, we were not thrill seekers. We were not looking for a fight. We were looking to express our faith. To find a voice that in Nebraska was missing. That, beyond anything, was our strength.[107]

Omaha Archbishop Responds

Archbishop of Omaha, Elden Curtiss, dropped a bomb of his own on April 22, 1996. Archbishop Curtiss wrote "*A Pastoral Letter on Catholic Doctrine and Practice*" in which he addressed many of the issues raised by Bishop Bruskewitz's legislation. Priests of the Archdiocese of Omaha were instructed to read the letter at Sunday Masses, April 28, 1996.[108] The letter was reprinted in the *Southern Nebraska Register*, the Lincoln diocesan paper on May 3, 1996. Archbishop Curtis began the letter by saying he would address issues of Catholic doctrine that had been raised in the public media.

In his letter, Archbishop Curtiss wrote that any Catholic who publically supports abortion, euthanasia, and the ordination of women "may not be in any teaching, liturgical, or ministerial role in this archdiocese, or be a member of any parish or archdiocesan council."[109] He continued to affirm a celibate-only priesthood for the Western Church. Archbishop Curtiss explained that lay people are consulted in the Omaha archdiocese through their participation in parish finance councils, parish pastoral councils and the Archdiocesan Pastoral Council. He dismissed the idea of lay selection of bishops, "Those who promote a popular vote for the selection of bishops[110] either do not understand the present process or they want to assert their own authority over that of the bishops to nominate and even choose their own candidates."[111] Finally, he affirmed the ban on Catholics from active membership in Masonic organizations. He ended his letter by inviting those who wished further dialogue or further information on the issues addressed in the letter to contact him in writing; he promised a response. Bishop Bruskewitz did not comment publicly about Archbishop Curtiss' letter except to call it "admirable."[112]

Archbishop Curtiss' letter indicated that membership alone in a group that espouses opinions contrary to official Catholic Church teaching would not lead to a prohibition from parish participation. Instead, Archbishop Curtiss placed emphasis on public dissent from official church teaching. Omaha Diocesan Chancellor, Fr. Michael Gutsgell, offered examples of what would be considered public dissent: "writing articles or letters, granting interviews or making public statements where they had an audience."[113] Still, this action provoked some confusion. As Omahan CTAN member, Mel Beckman, stated in an interview:

> Who is to decide when public dissent happens and when it's simply loyal opposition or whatever. And is it supposed to be the pastor that decides? Is it the school principal that decides? Is it the archbishop himself? Does it have to be in writing. . . ? It's like a behind the scenes threat. Be careful, at some point you could lose your job as a lector or whatever. Or as a teacher in the school.[114]

The timing of the pastoral letter led members of Call To Action Nebraska to assume concern about whether CTAN prompted Archbishop Curtiss' action. In fact, Lori Darby reported that Omaha Chancellor, Fr. Gutsgell, told CTAN members that Archbishop Curtiss "was under a great deal of pressure" to offer a response to Bishop Bruskewitz's extra-synodal legislation.[115]

CTAN responded in writing to the Archbishop's letter. In its response, CTAN noted that, "While always respectful of the Archbishop's role as teacher and unifier of the Catholic community we must also be responsive to the Holy Spirit who enlivens us and the entire Community of God's People."[116] CTAN sent its written response to Archbishop Curtiss' Pastoral Letter to the Omaha Diocesan paper, the *Catholic Voice*. The editor declined to publish the response.[117]

Call To Action Nebraska co-chair, Lori Darby, told a reporter at the *Omaha World Herald* that she personally had heard from a number of people from Omaha who were concerned with how this new rule would impact their jobs or ministries. One woman told Lori Darby that she planned to resign from her lector ministry.[118] CTAN member from Omaha, Sandy Matthews, reflected, "In Lincoln, the excommunication was like death. In Omaha, it's like divorce. With always, there's always remnants going on. There's always... there's no closure."[119]

Rev. Richard McBrien, Notre Dame professor of theology, said the bishop made a mistake when he linked "life and death issues" like abortion and euthanasia to women's ordination. McBrien said, "If nothing else, the bishop is incredibly insensitive if he doesn't think that the linkage doesn't send a hurtful message to women."[120]

Omaha Chancellor, Fr. Gutsgell, attended the second meeting of Call To Action Nebraska on April 27, 1996. He reportedly received a round of applause when he was introduced at the gathering.[121] Gutsgell told a reporter that dissent has a long history in the Catholic Church and that as long as discussion is approached as a search for understanding and not an "act of defiance," the discussion can be considered healthy. Gutsgell characterized what he observed at the April 27 meeting as falling within "the search for understanding."[122]

Effects of Excommunication

It is not possible to know how Bishop Bruskewitz's legislation impacted everyone. According to one report in the *Lincoln Journal Star*, sixteen people quit their Masonic organizations and about four times that number of Masons left the Catholic Church.[123]

Members of Call To Action Nebraska experienced repercussions in their parishes. For example, Jean Krejci was told she could sit in the front pew and sing with the choir, but she would not be allowed to stand with the choir and face the congregation.[124] Jean Krejci was also told she could no longer attend meetings of the Bishop's Hispanic Advisory Committee, a group she helped found.[125] Jim McShane spoke of being in the parking lot of St. Theresa's Catholic Church, a church where he had been a member for twenty-five years, and having people turn their backs on him.[126] Carol McShane explained that though she never felt "legally excommunicated," the legislation did have a psychological effect:

> But the psychological label of being excommunicated is very real and the word has two different meanings for me now. Excommunicated is a legal term of the church, but excommunicated also has to do with your relationship to community. Even if I was never a major church community person in this diocese, to be told that you can't be part of that community is very isolating. And you, you become somewhat paranoid about things

that happen within the church. Things that happen to you in your life. You wonder if they know that you're excommunicated so you tend not to talk about it. You don't hide it, yet you don't want to talk about it. So, yes, I have felt excommunicated in a social sense.[127]

In my own experience, I never recognized the excommunication as valid; it did and does, however, impact my thoughts. I also understood that though I did not consider myself to be excommunicated, others did. So, for example, when I was approached by a member of my parish and asked to consider teaching CCD, I felt it necessary to explain my unusual situation. Similarly, I was asked by a student to be the faculty sponsor of a Catholic student group, Fellowship of Catholic University Students, at Nebraska Wesleyan University. The student who asked me if I would be willing to serve in this capacity wrote, "naturally I thought of you."[128] He explained that the sponsor could be as involved as he or she wished "but I thought you might enjoy getting involved too." In my response I indicated that I was honored to be considered and that I was willing to serve in the role of sponsor. I also thought I should share that I am a member of Call To Action and, therefore, the bishop, and many of the local priests and laypeople consider me to be excommunicated. I explained that an appeal was under consideration in Rome [see Chapter 7]. I ended by writing, "If you are not comfortable with me as a sponsor (for these reasons), I would understand if you ask someone else. However, I would be willing to do it if you still want me to." The student responded, "I'm sorry to hear about your situation. Since the offering of Mass on campus was made possible by a direct appeal to the Bishop and he continues to indirectly oversee the arrangements, it would probably be best if someone else was the sponsor."

Reflecting on the excommunication, CTAN member John Burke explained, "we became occasions of sin. We became this group that would lead you astray if you even talk to them, even bothered to look at what was going on with them."[129] Though Burke questioned whether people actually accepted that characterization, he said "as long as they had their own status quo things going on, they didn't need to bother with Call To Action."[130]

Dueling Conferences

CTAN co-chairs at the time the extra-synodal legislation was issued, John Krejci and Lori Darby, were scheduled to appear on a panel of Nebraskans at the national Call To Action conference. The panel was to address multiple topics including the media blitz and canonical appeal. A coalition of Catholic organizations, including Ignatius Press, planned a national conference, Call to Holiness, to take place to "counter" the national Call To Action conference in the fall of 1996 in Detroit. The Call to Holiness conference theme was "Show Your Support for the Holy Father and the Magisterium of the Catholic Church."[131] The promotional article in the Lincoln diocesan paper explained that "speakers will address the errors of Call to Action."[132] Included on the speaker list were ultra-conservative figures Mother Angelica, Fr. Joseph Fessio of Ignatius Press, and Donna Steichen. A news report just before the dueling conferences reported that about 5,000 people were expected to attend the Call To Action conference making it the largest CTA national conference to date and the counter conference expected about 1,600.[133] Approximately 2000 persons reportedly attended the counter conference[134] and at about 5000, the turnout for the CTA conference was the largest in the organization's history.[135]

A Call to Holiness conference spokesperson said the organization chose to hold their conference at the same time that the national Call To Action conference was scheduled as a way to "throw down the gauntlet, in effect a call to war between two strikingly different versions of church."[136] One report of the Call to Holiness conference claimed the "Church Militant strikes back."[137] Mother Angelica, the Call to Holiness keynote speaker, reportedly said, "We need great compassion and prayer for those who yell and scream a lot about renewal and freedom . . . hold séances with a candle in the middle, mumble their crazy stuff. . dance around like they're drunk."[138] In contrast, at the neighboring conference, President of Call To Action, Linda Pieczynski, was quoted as saying, "There is room for all of us."[139]

Pro-life organization, Human Life International, published a special report by Fr. Richard Welch and Brian Clowes in which it provided a review of both the Call to Holiness and Call To Action conferences. The report clearly indicated their negative assessment of members of Call To Action. For example, they addressed issues such as "how you can torpedo the dissenters" and "how to expose the church-wreckers."[140]

In addition, Welch quoted from a 1993 *Wanderer* article in which News Editor, Paul Likoudis, asked Cardinal Gagnon, "What is the status of people in the Church—professors, politicians, priests—who claim to be Catholic but who formally, publically dissent from Catholic teaching?" Likoudis reported Cardinal Gagnon's response: "They condemn themselves. We don't have to judge them. They are going to Hell and they are taking others with them."[141]

Call To Action Nebraska organized a conference that would take place May 16 and 17, 1997, in Lincoln, to mark Pentecost as well as the one-year anniversary of the excommunication. The theme of the conference was "It's a Matter of Conscience."

In a press release about the conference, John Krejci said,

> In recent months extremists in the Catholic community have spread false and misleading statements about CTA-Nebraska and the national Call To Action. Whereas CTA-Nebraska does not judge these fallacious statements to be the result of malice or bad will, our group feels a responsibility to protect its good name by affirming publicly what we believe. This conference is one way of accomplishing this goal.[142]

Speakers scheduled for the CTAN conference included Edwina Gately, Sr. Amata Miller, Ray McGovern, Patty Crowley, and Bob McClory. The program for the conference quoted from section 16 of the Vatican II document, *Gaudium et Spes,* Pastoral Constitution on the Church in the Modern World:

> In the depths of his conscience, man detects a law which he does not impose upon himself, but which holds him to obedience. Always summoning him to love good and avoid evil, the voice of conscience when necessary speaks to his heart: do this, shun that. For man has in his heart a law written by God; to obey it is the very dignity of man; according to

it he will be judged. Conscience is the most secret core and sanctuary of a man. There he is alone with God, Whose voice echoes in his depths.[143]

John Krejci, CTAN Chair, wrote a welcome letter that was printed in the conference program. In the letter, Krejci asked attendees to "be respectful of Bishop Bruskewitz if you are approached by the media for comment." Around 200 people from thirteen states attended the CTAN conference.[144] National CTA Co-Director, Dan Daley, spoke briefly at the conference. Once again, the above-mentioned coalition planned a counter Call to Holiness conference in Lincoln for the same weekend, May 17 and 18, 1997 and Dan Daley shared that he had attended the Call to Holiness conference's Holy Hour so that he could pray with his brothers and sisters.[145]

The purpose of the Call to Holiness conference was "to show support for Bishop Fabian Bruskewitz and the authority of the Catholic Church."[146] Joann Weaver, a leader of Call to Holiness in Lincoln said, "We don't like that group (CTA) acting as though they are speaking on behalf of the church. We are called to action in our pursuit of holiness. We are called to worship and obey."[147] About 800 people attended the Call to Holiness conference.[148] Carol McShane told a reporter for the *National Catholic Reporter* that she considered the counter conference to be a positive sign, "Eight hundred of them over there are focused on 200 of us. They can feel our energy. I find that hopeful."[149]

Speakers for the Lincoln Call To Holiness conference included Fr. Joseph Fessio who said in his address that Lincoln was the best diocese in the country.[150] Fessio addressed a recent statement by Head of the Congregation for the Doctrine of the Faith, Cardinal Joseph Ratzinger, before he became Pope Benedict XVI. Cardinal Ratzinger stated in a news conference at the Vatican on January 24, 1997 that Catholics who believe that women could be ordained priests are not necessarily heretics.[151] Ratzinger explained that they are in serious error, but that error was not grounds for excommunication.[152] Fr. Fessio, a speaker at the Lincoln Call to Holiness conference called Cardinal Ratzinger's statement "confusing." He said, "I don't think you can be Catholic and not accept this teaching."[153]

Call to Holiness speaker E. Michael Jones is the founder and editor of two Catholic magazines, *Culture Wars* and *Fidelity*. According to an *Omaha World Herald* reporter, Jones said, "Call to Action evolved from a post-World War II effort of liberal Protestants, Jews and secular humanists to subvert the Catholic Church's teaching on birth control because of their fear of burgeoning Catholic numbers."[154] Speaking of Call To Action, Jones said, "Get thee behind me Satan!"[155] He called CTA members "traitors" and suggested they either repent or leave.[156] The purpose of Jones' presentation was to review the history of the Call To Action movement; he tied the movement to a group at Notre Dame in the 1960s "who wanted to promote contraceptives in the name of 'sexual liberation.'"[157]

In her talk at Call to Holiness, Donna Steichen claimed that Call To Action "is part of a 'conspiracy' to destroy Catholic culture and institutions."[158] Steichen reportedly said, "The Arian heretics led moral personal lives and exhorted their followers to do so. That can't be said of the Call to Action folks."[159] In contrast, CTAN conference attendee from Omaha, Frank Winner, called CTA members "'gentle dissenters' who love the Catholic church and want to preserve it. 'What these people want is a little freedom, a little credit for good sense.'"[160]

Bishop Bruskewitz presided at the closing Mass of the Call to Holiness conference in Lincoln and after that Mass he granted an interview to Peggy Moen from the *Wanderer*. Moen asked Bishop Bruskewitz for his reaction to the claim that membership in Call To Action had grown since he issued his extra-synodal legislation. Lincoln diocesan membership had, in fact, grown from twenty to sixty in the year since the extra-synodal legislation.[161] Bishop Bruskewitz replied, "I would dispute that their membership has grown in Lincoln; I think it has diminished. It may have grown in other places. However I have grave doubts, unless they were to open their membership books for a check. Anyone can make these claims, and they haven't been entirely honest in their claims in the past."[162] Bishop Bruskewitz went on to claim that many of the Call To Action members from Lincoln "are not good Catholics and weren't to begin with." He called Robert McClory, a speaker at the CTAN conference, "a fallen priest. . . it's very difficult for me to have much interest in anything he has to say. . ."[163] McClory was, in fact, laicized in 1971.[164]

Bishop Bruskewitz claimed that Call To Action was a pro-abortion group.[165] In fact, CTA takes no position on this issue. Linda Pieczynski, then-President of the national CTA board stated, "Once you take a stand on [abortion], there's so much noise that nobody hears what you have to say on anything else."[166] Despite CTA's choice not to address the issue, Bishop Bruskewitz continually claimed that CTA is pro-abortion. A group called Collegians Activated to Liberate Life protested outside the CTAN conference in May 1997. Then-President of CTAN, John Krejci, told a reporter, "Most of our members are pro-life. They (the collegians) are just trying to besmirch our good name."[167]

About two weeks after the two conferences, Fr. Frank Cordaro, a priest from Iowa who celebrated Mass at the Call To Action conference, received a letter from Msgr. Timothy Thorburn. The letter stated that Bishop Bruskewitz asked Msgr. Thorburn to communicate that:

> You have no faculties to celebrate or perform any liturgical or ecclesias-
> tical acts or functions in the Diocese of Lincoln, including the celebra-
> tion of Holy Mass, the hearing of confessions, and preaching. You are
> forbidden to celebrate or perform any liturgical or ecclesiastical acts or
> functions in the Diocese of Lincoln, and this prohibition is in perpetu-
> ity. This communication is also a canonical warning. Any violation of
> this prohibition will be punished with a decree of excommunication.[168]

Fr. Cordaro's bishop, Bishop Joseph Charron, also received a copy of this letter. In a statement about Fr. Cordaro, the Lincoln Diocese wrote "Rev. Cordaro disrespected canonical propriety as well as disregarded common courtesy by accommodating this anti-Catholic organization."[169] Cordaro was reportedly told by his bishop that he would lose his position in Iowa if Bishop Bruskewitz excommunicated him.[170]

After the two conferences, *The Southern Nebraska Register* published an opinion piece called "Overheard at the Call to Holiness Conference."[171] The column was a fictional account of an interaction that the writer imag-
ined might have happened if a CTA supporter registered at the Call to

Holiness conference by mistake. Though, presumably intended to be humorous, CTA members are portrayed as elderly, ignorant about the church, (the fictional woman asks, "What is a Magisterium?") and celebrating excommunication (not protesting it). The fictional CTA woman tells a young woman, with a baby, "My first husband was a priest."

Call To Action Nebraska received a copy of a letter sent to Call to Holiness speaker, E. Michael Jones, by Omaha resident, Robert Ruetz. CTAN published a copy of this letter in its newsletter, *Voices of Nebraska Catholics*.[172] In his letter, Ruetz explained that he did not support either Call To Action or Call to Holiness, but he felt he must respond to the *Omaha World Herald* report of the talk Mr. Jones's gave at Call to Holiness. Ruetz wrote that, if the report was accurate, "there seems to be a gross distortion of facts and inflammatory rhetoric involved in your comments."[173] Ruetz explained:

> Over the past year, I have searched for some hard facts about the historical foundation of Call to Action because of numerous tales and fables, much like yours, which have been floating around Nebraska, triggered by Bishop Bruskewitz's "excommunication" of the Lincoln Diocese's Call to Action participants. These subjective fabrications made me highly suspicious of their credibility. Your recent appearance in Lincoln substantiated my initial reaction and led me to believe that for some unknown reason, opponents of Call to Action seem to be frightened to death of the movement's current quest for dialogue on some crucial Church issues.[174]

Mr. Ruetz addressed the roots of Call To Action in the United States bishops' initiative that culminated in the 1976 conference in Detroit. Reutz observed,

> As an objective observer of the current travesty playing itself out in public in Nebraska, it appears to me that some powerful representatives of the Catholic bureaucracy are not being aboveboard with their constituents and are either unknowingly or perhaps surreptitiously linking Call to Action with the Masons and even the pro-abortion movement.[175]

John and Jean Krejci reflected on the simultaneous Call To Action Nebraska and Call to Holiness conferences in a commentary published in the *Lincoln Journal Star*.[176] Quoting Cardinal Bernardin, "Life is too short for acrimony," the Krejci's wrote that it is possible to disagree and still treat each other kindly.

A Lot for a New Organization to Handle

Clearly, for such a new organization, Call To Action Nebraska had much to address. Members in both Lincoln and Omaha had to consider the responses from their two bishops. The fledgling organization had been immediately thrown into the media spotlight and members faced a great deal of turmoil even before the organization had an established structure.

CTAN Co-Chair, Lori Darby, recalled in an interview what it was like to lead the Steering Committee during this time. She said, "I would put the phone down after talking to somebody and there would be four or five messages waiting for me from other people, other news agencies and the Lincoln paper, the Omaha paper." Darby continued:

> We thought we were just putting our name out there to gather like-minded folk to us. Since then I think I've learned a whole lot. We should have waited. We really should have cohesed [sic] more as a group before we put ourselves out there publicly, but we really, there was no precedent for what Bruskewitz did. And still is no precedent. There has never been a bishop since then to do what he did. And it just all ballooned from there. Dan Daley [Co-Chair of Call To Action-USA] took notice of us. *NCR* [the *National Catholic Reporter*] took notice of us. We were, we had several front-page articles about this bishop in Lincoln and several emergency meetings. What do we do? I don't, I, none of us, I think, really had a lot of experience with the press. . . And we relied on Dan Daley and his expertise quite a bit. He spent a lot of time here. He spent a lot of time in Lincoln because obviously the Lincoln Diocese was where the ax was falling.[177]

During this time Lori Darby received a death threat. She explained what happened:

> I was at the meeting in May [1996]. A gentleman came to the front of the building of the First United Methodist Church and asked to see me by name, "I'm here to see Lori Darby." So they came and got me. I went up to this guy, knew instantly I had no idea who he was, and he handed me a letter that could be considered more or less of a death threat and if he'd had a gun I think he could have probably done some damage. And that was really the only serious encounter we had. We filed a police report. The letter was very cryptic in what it said, but what it basically said was that what he hoped would happen to me is what happened to Jezebel. . . And he very clearly said that, this is what's going to happen to you if you keep on this way. And I thanked him. I was so stupid. I thanked him for coming and told him I appreciated it and he said he was going to be praying for us while we met and he left. Thank God.[178]

Lori Darby attempted to participate in her parish but was "pretty well shut out." Darby's church had a book in which people could write petitions. This book was brought forward each week at Mass during the prayers of the faithful. Someone brought to Darby's attention that a person had written "For Lori Darby, that she will change her mind and come back to the faith." Darby commented,

> And every Sunday that was brought to the church, brought to the altar. When a person noticed it, who was my friend and who was fairly powerful at the church, the book was removed. That was among the last straws, some of them are too personal for me to tell you about. But that was one of the last straws because it seemed a very insidious way to use that book and to use prayer.[179]

In August 1996 Lori Darby wrote to the members of the CTAN Steering Committee to inform them that she would no longer be involved as a member of the CTAN leadership. Darby explained that she believed it was the best decision for her and for her family. "It was the Spirit that called me to put my efforts into Call to Action, Nebraska throughout the past year and a half. I believe it is this same Spirit calling me now to end my association with this group at the leadership level."[180]

Writing for the Catholic Women's Network, Darby called her experience co-chairing CTAN at the time of Bishop Bruskewitz's extra-synodal legislation and Archbishop Curtiss' pastoral letter "tumultuous and wrenching."[181] Besides having her beliefs "examined under the glare of public attention," Darby addressed the difficulty of explaining what was happening to her daughters as well as the pain of being forced to become a "Sunday Catholic" with no role other than donating money to the church. She mentioned the death threat and said it came from a man "who informed me he had been 'sent by the big boss to tell me not to mock God.'"[182] Darby raised a number of questions:

- Where is the justice in baptizing and confirming people and calling them to be prayerful disciples of Jesus Christ if it all just comes down to doing what the bishop says anyway?

- What would be the point of being involved in a Christian community where the Spirit reveals the truth to only one class of people and any other revelation is suspect?

- What do I do when the truth revealed to me in my own inner life and prayer is at odds with the obedience demanded by church leaders?

- What do I do when, in order to be obedient to the bishop, I must reject the truth as I am given the grace to know it?[183]

Darby acknowledged that the bishop would respond, "in obedience there is peace." She cited the gospel, "You shall know the truth and the truth shall set you free."

Lori Darby eventually joined the Methodist church. She told of her experience when her family attended a service on a communion Sunday. She recalled how powerful it was to hear the words, "This is the Lord's table and the Lord makes you welcome and the Lord gives you power." "I about lost it because I had spent the last year, this was [about a year after the excommunication], I spent the last year feeling very much unwelcome. Told that I was unwelcome. . . And so those words were just overwhelming to me."[184]

Lori Darby, former Archdiocese of Omaha CTAN member:

What comes after excommunication? What do we do for an encore? What's next?[185]

Notes Chapter 6

1.   Paul Hendrickson, "Questions of Faith: They Say They're Good Catholics. But their Bishop is Threatening Excommunication," *Washington Post*, April 12, 1996.

2.   Bob Reeves, "Groups Off-Limits for Catholics, Bishop Says," *Lincoln Journal Star*, March 23, 1996.

3.   Bob Reeves, reporter for the *Lincoln Journal Star,* contacted many of the leaders of the twelve organizations Bishop Bruskewitz named in his legislation and they initially responded in different ways. His article, "Groups Off-Limits for Catholics, Bishop Says," (March 23, 1996) reported that the President of the Hemlock Society expressed his belief that the legislation would have little or no effect on his organization stating that he did not believe there were any Catholic members of the Hemlock Society. In contrast, Randy Moody, a Catholic on the board of Planned Parenthood, stated that Planned Parenthood had support from many Catholics and he called the bishop's statement "totally ridiculous." Noting the joint dinner-dance sponsored every spring by the Shriners, a Masonic organization, and the Knights of Columbus, a Catholic organization, Bob Metcalf, Grand Potentate of the Lincoln Sesostris Shrine, expressed his shock at the inclusion of Masonic organizations in the bishop's legislation. In an article, "Pius X Society Defies Effort of Excommunication," published by the *Lincoln Journal Star* three days later, Reeves reported that though Society of St. Pius X member, Stuart Neri, agreed with the bishop that the other groups on Bishop Bruskewitz's list are dangerous to the Catholic faith, he did not agree that his own group should have been included on that list.

4.   Jim McShane, interview with the author.

5.   Joan Johnson, interview with the author.

6.   Lori Darby and John Krejci, letter to Bishop Fabian Bruskewitz, March 23, 1996.

7.   Call To Action Nebraska press release, March 24, 1996.

8.   Ibid.

9.   Call To Action, press release, March 24, 1996.

10. Mel Beckman, interview with the author.

11. Bob Reeves, "Groups off-limits for Catholics…"

12. Charles M. Wilson, "Finally, someone does something," *Christifidelis, 14*, no 3, March 10, 2011, http://www.ewtn.com/library/CANONLAW/FINALLY.htm.

13. Fabian Bruskewitz, "An Ordinary Viewpoint: Responses II," *Southern Nebraska Register,* September 27, 1996.

14. John Barrette, "Merger between Lincoln General and Bryan is top story of 1996," *Lincoln Journal Star*, December 28, 1996.

15. *The New York Times* (March 26, 1996), *St. Paul Pioneer Press* (March 26, 1996), *Newsday*, Long Island and NYC editions (March 26, 1996, April 15, 1996), *Minneapolis Star Tribune* (March 27, 1996), *Electronic Telegraph* (United Kingdom, March 27, 1996), *Kansas City Star* (March 28, 1996), *Arizona Republic* (March 28, 1996), *Washington Post* (March 29, 1996 and April 12, 1996), *Los Angeles Times* (March 30, 1996), *Boston Globe* (March 30, 1996), *News Press* (St. Joseph, MO, April 4, 1996), *Palm Beach Post* (April 12, 1996), *USA Today* (April 15, 1996), *Traverse City Record-Eagle* (April 18, 1996), *Times of London* (May 18, 1996), *Time Magazine* (May 27, 1996), CBS Evening News, Today Show, NBC Nightly News, National Public Radio, and *"As It Happens,"* a Canadian Broadcast Corporation show, and *NBC Dateline*.

16. Leslie Wirpsa, "Excommunication Decree Sows Confusion: Three Bishops Belong to Condemned Group," *National Catholic Reporter*, April 5, 1996.

17. Patty Hawk, interview with the author.

18. There were also letters that spoke of the good done by members of some of the organizations targeted by Bishop Bruskewitz. For example, "As a daughter, wife, and mother of Masonics, please don't knock these organizations unless you know what you are talking about" (Delores Penkava, Table Rock). And, "Job's Daughters is in no way a danger or a risk to a young girl. Actually, it is probably one of the most important organizations parents could get their daughters involved in beside their own church youth organizations." (Beverly J. Nelson, Lincoln).

19. Jean Krejci, interview with the author.

20. Joseph Cardinal Bernardin, statement RE: Call to Action group, March 26, 1996.

21. Jim McShane, interview with the author.

22. Mary Sanchez, "KC's Bishops Vow Not to Threaten Excommunication: They Differ with Nebraska Cleric who Warned Those who Disagree with Doctrine," *Kansas City Star*, March 29, 1996.

23. Ibid.

24. Dennis Huspenl, "Springs Bishop Would Rather Teach than Excommunicate," *Colorado Springs Gazette Telegraph*, March 29, 1996.

25. Teresa Malcolm, "Bruskewitz Criticized in Boston. . . and Coloradans Reject His Tactics," *National Catholic Reporter,* April 19, 1996.

26. Leslie Wirpsa, "Excommunication Decree Sows Confusion: Three Bishops Belong to Condemned Group," *National Catholic Reporter,* April 5, 1996.

27. Ibid.

28. Ibid.

29. Ibid.

30. Charles Kelliher, interview with the author.

31. Leslie Wirpsa, "Excommunication Decree Sows Confusion…"

32. Ibid.

33. CTAN member from the Grand Island diocese who asked to remain anonymous, interview with the author.

34. Diego Ribadeneira, "Archbishop Faults Neb. Bishop's Threat: Editorial Says Consultation Required," *Boston Globe,* April 15, 1996.

35. Charles M. Wilson, "Finally, someone does something."

36. Julia McCord, "Scope of Bishop's Threat Puzzles Group," *Omaha World Herald,* March 26, 1996.

37. Ibid.

38. Virginia Culver, "Threat of Ban Stirs Passion for Catholics," *Denver Post,* March 26, 1996.

39. "Catholics Warned to Leave Causes," *Kearney Hub,* March 26, 1996.

40. Bob Keeler, "Rebuking Reform: Catholic Bishop Orders Flock to Toe the Doctrinal Line," *Newsday* (New York City Edition), March 26, 1996.

41. Pat Sullivan, interview with the author.

42. Dirk Johnson, "Catholic Bishop Threatens to Expel Dissenters," *New York Times National,* March 26, 1996.

43. Jeff Zeleny, "Catholics Struggle with Conscience," *Hastings Tribune,* March 26, 1996.

44. Ibid.

45. Bob Reeves, "Canon Law Experts Differ on How Far Bishop Can Go," *Lincoln Journal Star,* March 27, 1996.

46. Mary Sanchez, "KC's Bishops Vow not to Threaten…"

47. Jim Orwig, interview with the author.

48. Adelle M. Banks, "Bishop Forbids 'Incompatible' Memberships: Says Freemasons, Others May Be Excommunicated," *Pioneer Press*, March 26, 1996.

49. Interview with the author, name withheld at interviewee's request.

50. Jim McShane, interview with the author.

51. Cheryl Wittenauer, "New talk of Excommunication Puzzles Catholics, Masons," *St. Joseph News Press*. April 6, 1996.

52. Paul Likoudis, "An Interview with Bishop Fabian Bruskewitz," *Wanderer*, April 18, 1996, http://www.ewtn.com/library/ISSUES/BRUSKEWI.TXT.

53. Sandy Matthews, interview with the author.

54. Rosalind Bentley, "Nebraska Bishop's Threat of Excommunication is Called Drastic: While Twin Cities' Archbishop Flynn Emphasizes Unity, Lincoln Diocese Head Lists Groups Forbidden to Catholics," *Minneapolis Star Tribune*, March 27, 1996.

55. Larry B. Stammer, "The Edict that Split Believers," *Lost Angeles Times*, May 15, 1996.

56. Laurie Goodstein, "Excommunication Threat Stuns Catholics: Nebraska Bishop Warns Members of 12 Groups," *Washington Post*, March 29, 1996.

57. Jerry Filteau, "Lincoln Bishop Sees His Statement about Groups as a Warning," *Catholic Voice*, April 5, 1996.

58. James A. Coriden, "Even in Lincoln, Doubtful Laws Don't Apply, " *Commonweal*, April 19, 1996. http://findarticles.com/p/articles/mi_m1252/is_n8_v123/ai_18221780/.

59. Code of Canon Law, 1318, http://www.vatican.va/archive/ENG1104/__P4V.HTM.

60. Code of Canon Law, 1316 http://www.vatican.va/archive/ENG1104/__P4V.HTM.

61. James A. Coriden, "Even in Lincoln, Doubtful Laws…"

62. Paul Hendrickson, "Questions of Faith: They Say they're Good Catholics. But their Bishop is Threatening Excommunication," *Washington Post*, April 12, 1996.

63. Paul Likoudis, "An Interview With Bishop Fabian Bruskewitz."

64. Bob Reeves, "Telegrams, Faxes Show Support for Catholic Bishop," *Lincoln Journal Star*, March 30, 1996.

65. Patty Hawk, interview with the author.

66. John Thavis, "Vatican Studying Lincoln Bishop's Actions: Bishop Bruskewitz's Rights Defended, but Potential Problems Cited," *Catholic Spirit,* May 2, 1996.

67. Ibid.

68. Ibid.

69. William F. Buckley, Jr., "Situation in Lincoln Calls for Mediation," *Omaha World Herald*, April 3, 1996.

70. Ibid.

71. John Burke, interview with the author.

72. Bishop Fabian Bruskewitz, "An Ordinary Viewpoint: Responses II," *Southern Nebraska Register*, September 27, 1996.

73. Mary Jo Boesek, interview with the author.

74. Mel Beckman, "Call To Action, Nebraska and the diocese of Lincoln, Weekly Update," April 23, 1996.

75. James Orgren, letter to Bishop Fabian Bruskewitz, May 2, 1996.

76. Bob Reeves, "Telegrams, Faxes Show Support…"

77. Ibid.

78. Paul Likoudis, "An Interview with Bishop Fabian Bruskewitz."

79. Leslie Wirpsa, "Bruskewitz Elaborates on Recent Decree, "*National Catholic Reporter*, April 12, 1996.

80. "Deadline for Catholics in Nebraska: Lincoln Bishop Orders Mass Excommunication," *San Francisco Chronicle*, May 17, 1996.

81. "Another anniversary," *Southern Nebraska Register*, March 16, 2001.

82. Jeff Zeleny, print of untitled Associated Press article dated May 15, 1996, REF5606.

83. Leslie Wirpsa, "Excommunication Decree Sows Confusion…"

84. Ibid.

85. Timothy Unsworth, "Bruskewitz Event as an Emotional Physic: Clerics Chortle, Exult that their Own Bishop Plays with a Full Deck," *National Catholic Reporter*, May 17, 1996.

86. "Following the lead of dissident Catholics…" *This Rock*, April 1996.

87. Richard Neuhaus, "Concentrating the Catholic Mind," *Southern Nebraska Register*, August 2, 1996.

88. Marilyn Seiker, interview with the author.

89. Bob Reeves and Joel Gehringer, "A Beacon of Orthodoxy: Lincoln Diocese Attracts Conservative Catholics," *Lincoln Journal Star*, November 17, 2006.

90. Appendix B of letter to United States Catholic bishops, archbishops and cardinals of the National Conference of Catholic Bishops, dated October 25, 1996. Numbers published in *Southern Nebraska Register*, May 17, 1996 and September 14, 1996.

91. John Burke, interview with the author.

92. Mary Voboril, "Standoff in the Corn Belt: Where Catholics Face Excommunication for 'Disrespect and Disobedience' if they Belong to Organizations the Bishop has Deemed Unworthy," *Newsday*, April 15, 1996.

93. CTA-USA, "Profiles in Faith and Courage," 1996.

94. Marilyn Seiker, interview with the author.

95. CTA-USA, "Profiles in Courage and Faith."

96. Mary Voboril, "Standoff in the Corn Belt...."

97. Rosalind Carr, interview with the author.

98. Joan Johnson, interview with the author.

99. Name withheld at interviewee's request, interview with the author.

100. John Krejci, interview with the author.

101. Mary Hawk, interview with the author.

102. Charles Kelliher, interview with the author.

103. Call To Action USA press release, May 15, 1996.

104. CTAN Press Release, May 16, 1996.

105. Jeff Zeleny, print of untitled Associated Press article dated May 15, 1996, REF5606.

106. Interviewee's name withheld to protect the identity of the woman in the story.

107. Lori Darby, interview with the author.

108. Stephen Buttry, "Curtiss Posts Price of Public Dissent," *Omaha World Herald*, April 25, 1996.

109. Bishop Elden F. Curtiss, "A Pastoral Letter on Catholic Doctrine and Practice," April 22, 1996.

110. While CTA desires lay consultation in the selection of bishops, CTA does not advocate a popular vote.

111. Ibid.

112. Bob Reeves, "Omaha Catholics to Receive Warning," *Lincoln Journal Star*, April 26, 1996.

113. Stephen Buttry, "Curtiss posts price of public dissent."

114. Mel Beckman, interview with the author.

115. Leslie Wirpsa, "Bruskewitz Turns Down Call to Action Appeal," *National Catholic Reporter*, May 3, 1996.

116. CTAN, letter to Archbishop Curtiss, May 4, 1996. A response from Call To Action, Nebraska to the Pastoral Letter [of April 22, 1996, the Pastoral Letter on Catholic doctrine and practice written by Archbishop Elden F. Curtiss to the Catholic people of Northeastern Nebraska].

117. Stephen M. Kent, letter to Lori Darby, July 12, 1996.

118. Stephen Buttry, "Curtiss posts price of public dissent."

119. Sandy Matthews, interview with the author.

120. "Curtiss Issues Second Catholic Warning," *Daily Nebraskan*, April 29, 1996.

121. Stephen Buttry, "160 Catholics 'Speak in the Light,'" *Omaha World Herald*, April 28, 1996.

122. Stephen Buttry, "Catholic Dissenters Look to Centuries of Precedent," *Omaha World Herald*, April 28, 1996.

123. Joe Ruff, J. "Excommunication Numbers Not Known," *Lincoln Journal Star*, March 22, 1997.

124. Stephen Buttry, "Excommunicated Catholics Invite Allies to Lincoln," *Omaha World Herald*, November 17, 1996.

125. Rosemary Radford Ruether, "Thought Control Extends its Reach in Lincoln," *National Catholic Reporter*, March 31, 2000.

126. Bob Reeves, "Catholics Disagree on Role of Church," *Lincoln Journal Star*, May 18, 1997.

127. Carol McShane, interview with the author.

128. Personal email from NWU student to the author, Summer 1999.

129. John Burke, interview with the author.

130. Ibid.

131. Stephanie Block, "Detroit Conference to Counter 'Call to Action,'" *Southern Nebraska Register*, October 25, 1996.

132. Ibid.

133. Joe Ruff, "Dissident Catholics Meeting in Michigan," *Lincoln Journal Star*, November 15, 1996.

134. Stephen Buttry, "Excommunicated Catholics Invite Allies...."

135. Bob Reeves, "Call To Action Expects Large May Meeting," *Lincoln Journal Star*, November 19, 1996.

136. "Call to Action, Call to Holiness Hold Simultaneous Conventions," *Catholic Women's NETWORK*, January/February 1997.

137. Fr. Richard Welch and Brian Clowes, "Special Report No. 145, " *Human Life International*, January 1997.

138. "Call to Action, Call to Holiness hold simultaneous conventions."

139. "Ibid.

140. Fr. Richard Welch and Brian Clowes, "Special Report.."

141. Ibid.

142. CTAN Press Release, May 5, 1997.

143. *Gaudium et Spes,* section 16, http://www.vatican.va/archive/hist_councils/ii_vatican_council/documents/vat-ii_cons_19651207_gaudium-et-spes_en.html.

144. Pamela Schaeffer, "Dueling Catholic Conferences Enliven Lincoln," *National Catholic Reporter*, May 30, 1997.

145. Pat Clossey, "Reflections on Lincoln," *Call To Action New Jersey newsletter,* September 1997.

146. "Call to Holiness to Celebrate Catholic Faith," *Southern Nebraska Register*, March 21, 1997.

147. Bob Reeves, "Dueling Catholic Conferences Illustrate Inner-Church Division," *Lincoln Journal Star*, May 12, 1997.

148. Bob Reeves, "Catholics disagree on role of church," *Lincoln Journal Star*, May 18, 1997.

149. Pamela Schaeffer, "Dueling Catholic Conferences…"

150. Peggy Moen, "The *Wanderer* Interviews Bishop Fabian W. Bruskewitz." *Wanderer*, May 29, 1997.

151. John Thavis, "Ratzinger—Priesthood: Supporting Women's Ordination Called Serious Error but not Heresy," *Catholic News Service*, January 24, 1997.

152. Ibid.

153. Pamela Schaeffer, "Dueling Catholic Conferences…"

154. Julia McCord, "Competing Catholics Make Stand," *Omaha World Herald,* May 18, 1997.

155. Bob Reeves, "Catholics Disagree on Role of Church," *Lincoln Journal Star*, May 18, 1997.

156. Ibid.

157. Ibid.

158. Ibid.

159. Call To Action-USA, letter to its membership, June 15, 1997.

160. Bob Reeves, "Catholics Disagree on Role...."

161. Pamela Schaeffer, "Dueling Catholic conferences enliven Lincoln," *National Catholic Reporter*, May 30, 1997.

162. Peggy Moen, "The *Wanderer* Interviews Bishop...."

163. Ibid.

164. John Burger, "Celibacy isn't the Problem—it's the Answer, Say Priests," *National Catholic Register*, May 19 – 25, 2002. http://www.ncregister.com/site/print_article/12958/.

165. Joe Ruff, "Several Catholics Ignoring Censure," *Lincoln Journal Star*, March 22, 1997.

166. Nolan Zavoral, "Catholics' Call and Response," *Minneapolis Star Tribune*, September 14, 1996.

167. Julia McCord, "Competing Catholics make stand."

168. Msgr. Timothy Thorburn, letter to Rev. Frank Cordaro, May 30, 1997.

169. John Carlson, "Priest's Actions Upset Catholic Church Officials," *Des Moines Register*, July 16, 1997.

170. "Lincoln mass may bring excommunication," *Lincoln Journal Star*, July 17, 1997.

171. "Overheard at the call to holiness conference," *Southern Nebraska Register*, May 1997.

172. Robert Ruetz, "A response to Dr. E. Michael Jones—'Call To Holiness' Conference Presenter," *VOICES of Nebraska Catholics*, June 1997.

173. Robert Ruetz, letter to E. Michael Jones, May 31, 1997.

174. Ibid.

175. Ibid.

176. John Krejci and Jean Krejci, "Diversity no Stranger to Church," *Lincoln Journal Star*, June 4, 1997.

177. Lori Darby, interview with the author.

178. Ibid.

179. Ibid.

180. Lori Darby, letter to CTAN Steering Committee, August 12, 1996.

181. Lori Darby, "Freedom and Obedience Reflections from Nebraska," *Catholic Women's NETWORK*, July/August 1996.

182. Ibid.

183. Ibid.

184. Lori Darby, interview with the author.

185. Ibid.

CHAPTER 7

Appeal

We are spending an awful lot of our time. Not accomplishing much. To diffuse a situation we never should have been presented with. And that's too bad. What we're doing is very important work. It is important for us and it is important for the church in the Midwest and the church of the Americas and the church of the world—to realize that you do not have to accept the coercions of authority. You don't have to. You can stand up and say "No. That is not the way things are. That is not acceptable behavior and we will not accept it."[1]—Jim McShane

THOUGH I VIEWED BISHOP BRUSKEWITZ'S extra-synodal legislation as invalid, I held out hope for redress. I naively believed that if the proper Vatican officials understood what was happening to us in Lincoln, they would have no choice but to support us. I was wrong. I was voiceless in my own church and that situation raises important questions about power and church structure. The organizational structure of the Catholic Church offers no authority to any local body to act. The authority rests with the local bishop and the Vatican.

In this chapter, I describe the ten years of efforts of members of Call To Action Nebraska to appeal the extra-synodal legislation. While each member of Call To Action Nebraska was touched in some way by Bishop Bruskewitz's extra-synodal legislation and the resulting excommunication of Lincoln members, one might argue that they had as big an impact on Jim McShane as anyone else in the organization. This impact may have been the reason Jim McShane took the lead in the appeal process, the result of having taken the lead, or a combination of both.

On the day the *Southern Nebraska Register* published the extra-synodal legislation, Jim McShane wrote a letter to Msgr. Thorburn in which he stated: "...I have read the warning posted in the *Southern Nebraska Register*. It is a startling communication indeed. I am trying to figure out what it means and what my situation is."[2] McShane requested that Lincoln Chancellor, Msgr. Thorburn, send him the specific Canon or Canons on which Bishop Bruskewitz relied when issuing the legislation. Having not received a response from Msgr. Thorburn six days later, McShane sent another letter to the Chancellor dated March 28, 1996. In this letter, McShane again asked for the specific Canon or Canons on which Bishop Bruskewitz based his legislation. He concluded his letter, "Please respond. Delay makes it impossible for me to understand my situation and so interferes with the exercise of whatever rights I may have under Canon Law."[3]

McShane received a response dated April 1, 1996. In this letter, Msgr. Thorburn listed twenty-nine Canons which he said, "apply to the various organizations which have been listed in the Extra-Synodal Legislation."[4]

Two days later, Jim McShane sent a memo to the Lincoln diocesan members of Call To Action Nebraska. He explained that he had received the list of Canons as well as "uncited parts of the Vatican II documents and Apostolic Tradition" and proposed a next step. McShane reported that he had consulted with four canonists and the first step should be to contact Bishop Bruskewitz that very week to ask him "to rescind or emend his legislation."[5] McShane offered an opportunity to the Lincoln diocesan members affected by the legislation to sign the letter after they had a chance to read it. McShane explained:

> The letter will not attempt to present the bishop with elaborate arguments on all issues. Rather it will present a reasoned appeal on several grounds, asking him to rescind or emend the legislation. It will also ask him to suspend its effects pending the resolution of our request. Our purpose will be to continue the dialogue, hoping for a favorable

hearing. Failing that, we will at least be able to say that we have made a good faith effort to resolve this on the local level—which will surely be expected if we have later to seek outside recourse. It is my belief that we owe it to ourselves and to the church at large to try to have this legislation changed. Failing that, we must seek to have it fully tested so as to protect all from arbitrary condemnation.[6]

First Appeal

Call To Action Nebraska submitted a first appeal of the extra-synodal legislation in the form of a letter to Bishop Fabian Bruskewitz dated April 4, 1996.[7] The group acted on the advice of canon law professor, Fr. James Coriden.[8] Fr. Coriden cited canon 1737: "Before proposing recourse a person must seek the revocation or emendation of the degree in writing from its author. When this petition is proposed, by that very fact suspension of the execution of the decree is also understood to be requested."[9] Though Coriden believed the legislation was invalid, he encouraged CTAN members to appeal because even the act of publishing the legislation was injurious to CTAN members.[10]

The letter signers made two requests and offered thirteen supporting points for their requests. First, they asked to meet with Bishop Bruskewitz along with "common counsel" to find an "equitable solution." Second, if the bishop was unwilling to meet with them and a common counsel, they requested that he rescind the legislation or emend it to be more clear and just as well as "less punitive and liable to give scandal." Failing even that, the signers asked for a suspension of the legislation while the bishop could consider their supporting arguments. The letter explained, "We make these requests not challenging your Episcopal authority but recognizing it; we write not with the tight hand of a legal brief but with the open hand of one who [is] seeking redress from benevolent authority."[11]

Some examples of supporting points in the letter include, first, the punishment does not fit the crime. Second, one cannot assume that members of Call To Action hold beliefs contrary to the Catholic faith as membership in Call To Action does not require any particular belief. Rather, membership is based on a monetary contribution. Third, Canon 1318 holds that excommunication is to be used "with greatest moderation." Fourth, automatic penalties are reserved for that which is "particularly treacherous." Certainly what is meant by membership in an organization is unclear and, therefore, cannot be considered particularly treacherous. Fifth, the national Call To Action group has taken positions on matters of church discipline, not matters of creed. Sixth, a penalty so severe ought to take place after interaction with those impacted, but this did not occur. Finally, the other bishops in Nebraska did follow suit; should not such a severe penalty call for uniformity of support?

On April 9, 1996, five days after this appeal letter was sent to Bishop Bruskewitz, Jim McShane wrote to the two other Nebraska bishops, the president of the National Conference of Catholic Bishops as well as the Archbishops of Chicago, Boston and New York and the Apostolic Pro Nuncio, the Vatican's ambassador to the United States. In this letter, McShane addressed the extra-synodal legislation and the request by Call To Action Nebraska members for a meeting with Bishop Bruskewitz or for Bishop Bruskewitz to rescind or suspend the legislation. McShane further highlighted how this action would be best not only for the members of CTAN but also for the whole church. The purpose of the letter was to generate some "outside encouragement." The letter concludes, "We do not look to see our Bishop humiliated, and we understand that pacific intervention requires delicate diplomacy. So it may be that you cannot consult with us, or even formally respond to this request."[12]

Two bishops responded rather quickly to McShane's letter. First, Cardinal Joseph Bernardin asked his Chief of Staff, Sr. Mary Brian Costello, to write to McShane to acknowledge receipt of the letter and express his regret at "the pain the hurt this present situation has caused."[13] He also asked Sr. Costello to include a copy of his statement regarding Call To Action which was widely quoted in media outlets. The second response came from the President of the National Conference of Catholic Bishops, Bishop Anthony Pilla of Cleveland. Bishop Pilla reaffirmed each bishop's authority to safeguard church teaching and practice through sanctions or other pastoral means as he sees fit.[14]

Face-to-Face with Bishop Bruskewitz

At this point Bishop Bruskewitz agreed to meet with Jim McShane and the two met on April 11, 1996. After that meeting, McShane recorded his memories and interpretations of the event. He sent his record of the meeting to some members of CTAN. In a preface to the description of the events of the meeting, McShane wrote that his record of the event was "carefully drawn up and is a good faith effort to recollect a meeting sometimes tense, sometimes intimidating, sometimes confusing."[15] McShane later learned from talking to a reporter that Bishop Bruskewitz had discussed his own perceptions of their meeting and that their perceptions differed substantially from one another.

The meeting between Bishop Bruskewitz and Jim McShane began and ended with prayer. Among the many topics of discussion, McShane wanted to address the extra-synodal legislation in the hopes that Bishop Bruskewitz would prevent its implementation through rescinding, emending or suspending it. After the meeting, McShane felt certain that none of those hopes would come to pass.

In discussing the documents of Vatican II, McShane told Bishop Bruskewitz that he had read them "thirty years ago, but had had little reason to read them since so I could not claim familiarity." Bishop Bruskewitz emphasized the need to accept the documents "in their fullness, and that included the authority of the bishop." McShane felt that Bishop Bruskewitz "was disappointed when I did not claim proficiency. It was as if he had wanted to use John XXIII and the Council to trump my play."

Bishop Bruskewitz expressed concern with the affirmation used at the Call To Action Nebraska liturgy that took place at the founding meeting at Mahoney State Park on February 3, 1996. McShane explained that the liturgy was a weekday Mass and, therefore, no Creed was required. He considered the prayer of affirmation that was used to be a prayer of the faithful, not a substitute for a Creed. McShane noted, "When I put an interpretation on what he called 'a creed' that was less damning than he had been claiming, he seemed more deflated than elated." At this point

McShane came to the conclusion that he should be careful, "'It looks like he is trying to develop information he can use after the fact to justify the penalties. We are not exploring for cooperative ways to ease the crisis.'"

McShane reported that the bishop seemed to want to prove that CTAN members "could not be trusted." The bishop felt that if CTAN members themselves were not heretics, then they allied with heretics. He said some of our allies "were ex-priests who were using the rest of us in self-serving ways."

Bishop Bruskewitz gave Jim McShane the Pope's address in the event the group wanted to appeal to Rome and even provided a list of ten bodies to whom the appeal might be sent. He expressed his great love for the city of Rome and said if he was instructed by the Vatican to rescind the legislation, "he hopes he would have the humility to do so gracefully." McShane continued, "I felt much of this, I must say, as an ill-disguised attempt to be intimidating."

Bishop Bruskewitz discussed the lifting of the penalty through "obedience and repentance," stating that the interdict and excommunication could only be lifted by the bishop. Bishop Bruskewitz confirmed that Christian burial could prove a problem.

Bishop Bruskewitz asked Jim McShane if all of the sixteen signers of the appeal letter had also been members of Catholics for Active Liturgical Life. McShane believed about half were.

Jim McShane listed a number of things he labeled "What I saw that he may not have intended to show." First, Bishop Bruskewitz is distrusting. Second, he is interested in numbers. He mentioned time and again how much support he received in the form of letters, flowers, and calls on the matter of the legislation. He said he received almost no negative comments. McShane commented, "I suggested to him that having threatened excommunication for dissent he could hardly expect many letters of opposition." Third, he had read that the Lincoln priests were fearful and he disputed that by saying when he mentioned it to the priests at the Chrism Mass, they laughed. Fourth, he is anxious. He wanted to be clear he was not apologizing.

Bishop Bruskewitz claimed "he had no choice other than to issue his legislation." Jim McShane explained, "He seems to feel besieged by liberals, especially by the liberal press." He felt the climate limited his choices. That is, he wanted his response to be taken in the serious manner in which it was intended, not as "just an opinion."

McShane noted that Bishop Bruskewitz:

> acknowledges his responsibility to exercise pastoral love, but manifestations of it faded as the conversation progressed. At the same time he seemed to be satisfied to be in a position where he held all the cards; and, where he did not, he certainly was not going to let on. In his early citations of John XXIII and Vatican II, in his encouragement that [we] write directly to the Pope, and elsewhere in the conversation and in communications from the Chancery, I felt almost a tone of swagger. It is a tone that makes one guarded in speech and that makes charity difficult to maintain. It discourages frankness and dampens that sense of shared hope necessary for shared endeavor.

McShane concluded, "I bristled, perhaps unfairly, when—as I left— he bid me to take care of my heart. I left the meeting very drained, very tired and deeply disappointed. I found myself very sad, and—upon reflection—quite angry. I look forward with foreboding to returning."

As indicated above, Bishop Bruskewitz discussed his perception of the meeting with the media and his report of the meeting[16] did not match Jim McShane's account. Bishop Bruskewitz told a Catholic News Service reporter that McShane told him that Call To Action Nebraska members do not accept Pope John Paul II's letter *Ordinatio Sacerdotalis* in which the pope wrote that the church cannot ordain women and declared this to be definitive Catholic teaching. In contrast, in McShane's recollection of that conversation McShane explained to Bishop Bruskewitz that as CTAN had just formed, the group had yet to take any positions on any issue; he could only speak for himself and not the group. McShane said in their discussion he addressed Pope John Paul II's letter on the level of authority not content, "I told [Bishop Bruskewitz] I had some doubts about whether *Ordinatio Sacerdotalis* was infallible teaching."[17]

After the Catholic News Service reporter informed Jim McShane of Bishop Bruskewitz's statements about their meeting, McShane wrote to Bishop Bruskewitz. In a letter dated April 17, 1996, McShane reiterated that, as of that time, CTAN had not taken any positions. He continued, "I did tell you of my own puzzlement as to the process whereby *Ordinatio Sacerdotalis* had achieved the status of an infallible teaching: I did not understand how such a stature could later be attributed to a document that did not itself lay claim to it."[18]

McShane also learned from the Catholic News Service reporter that Bishop Bruskewitz had told the reporter that CTAN "displaced the Nicene Creed with a perhaps blasphemous creed" at their founding meeting on February 3rd at Mahoney State Park.[19] Further, Bishop Bruskewitz mentioned this matter in an interview with a reporter from the *Wanderer*. Bishop Bruskewitz reportedly said, "[CTAN] recited a creed which was at variance with the Creed of the Catholic Church, and which bore little or no resemblance to what Catholics recite or believe."[20] McShane reiterated in writing: "The affirmation in question was offered by someone at the time of the prayers of the faithful and I accepted it as such. As is often the case in my experience, the language of such prayers is not subject to prior vetting and we usually affirm others' petitions."[21] At their meeting Bishop Bruskewitz asked McShane who had written the affirmation and McShane did not know. He later learned that the author was Martin Luther King, Jr. and he shared that information with Bishop Bruskewitz.

Response to the First Appeal

In an article in the *Lincoln Journal Star*,[22] Msgr. Thorburn reportedly said the interdict was lifted for the sixteen people who signed the April 4, 1996 appeal letter to Bishop Bruskewitz. When Call To Action Nebraska members read this, they thought the appeal had been accepted but the reprieve only impacted those who had signed the appeal letter. Jim McShane called Bob Reeves, the reporter who wrote the story, to clarify the situation. He learned that the interdict had not been lifted, it had been put in abeyance while Bishop Bruskewitz decided whether or not the appeal would be accepted.[23] Msgr. Thorburn told Jim McShane that any person who wanted to add his or her name to the appeal letter could do so by signing a note that said as much.[24]

As it turns out, jotting that note would not have made any difference because even before the note would have likely reached the chancery, Jim McShane received a response from Bishop Bruskewitz.[25] The letter, dated April 24, 1996, was said to be a response to the April 4 letter as well as to the meeting between the two that occurred on April 11, 1996. Bishop Bruskewitz first reported that he had happily received "an overwhelming avalanche of support for me from all over our Diocese as well as from the entire United States and abroad." He then stated that the extra-synodal legislation would remain unaltered.

Bishop Bruskewitz took issue with the communication Call To Action Nebraska had with the media. He quoted Pope John Paul II, *Veritatis Splendor*, n. 113: "Dissent, in the form of carefully orchestrated protests and polemic carried on in the media, is opposed to ecclesial communion and to a correct understanding of the hierarchical constitution of the People of God. Opposition to the teaching of the Church's pastors cannot be seen as a legitimate expression either of Christian freedom or of the diversity of the Spirit's gifts."[26] Bishop Bruskewitz expressed his belief that the members of CTAN have acted in ways "opposed to ecclesial communion and to a correct understanding of the hierarchical constitution of the People of God." To put it bluntly, they don't know their place: the bottom of the hierarchy. Bishop Bruskewitz went on to quote *Lumen Gentium* (n. 25) which states that "In matters of faith and morals, the Bishops speak in the name of Christ and the faithful are to accept their teaching and adhere to it with a religious assent of the soul. This religious submission of will and of mind must be shown in a special way to the authentic teaching authority of the Roman Pontiff, even when he is not speaking *ex cathedra*."[27] Bishop Bruskewitz continued to quote *Lumen Gentium* (n. 27) and the "right and duty" of the bishops to "make laws for their subjects, to pass judgment on them, and to moderate everything pertaining to the ordering of worship and the apostolate." The bishop then recalled hearing Pope John XXIII speaking informally about obedience leading to "true interior peace." He stated that he was convinced that obediently terminating membership in Call To Action Nebraska would bring peace to current CTAN members from Lincoln.

Bishop Bruskewitz stated that the letter he received from CTAN members did not incline him to rescind or amend the legislation. Mindful of authority, he stated, "I would gladly do so, however, if so ordered by our Holy Father, to whom you have every right to appeal."

Bishop Bruskewitz wrote that the supporting reasons listed in the letter he received from Lincoln CTAN members could not be distinguished "from the frivolous and contemptuous." He continued, "I gladly forgive you, however, if that is what you intend in my regard, just as I forgive the personal insults hurled at me by your associates, both in the media and in their correspondence, but I hope that you are acquainted with Canon 1369."[28]

Bishop Bruskewitz then stated that the Mass that took place at the meeting at Mahoney State Park was illicit and anti-rubrical. Bishop Bruskewitz called into question the point that CTAN has not taken any positions. He drew attention to Lori Darby's quote in the *Omaha World Herald*[29] that CTAN "will parallel the parent group."

Bishop Bruskewitz went on to address the two young people who were sent by him to the first CTAN Steering Committee meeting at Mahoney State Park. Bishop Bruskewitz wrote:

> It is regrettable that you expelled from one of your group's meetings at Mahoney State Park, the well-informed Catholic people that I sent to attend in order to report to me about your activities. As I understand it, that woman and man were simply observers and caused no disruption, but they were expelled by you because of your desire for secrecy concerning your group's activities and plots.

Bishop Bruskewitz continued, I "exhort you, once again, to take a different path from the one on which you have set out, that of disobedience and aggressive rebellion." He claimed "all the scandal in these matters is entirely due to you and your associates" and "you are the sole cause" of any psychological, communal, and spiritual damages.

Bishop Bruskewitz ended this letter on a surprisingly positive note: "As Saint Thomas More said to the judge who sentenced him to beheading, 'As Saul did hold the cloaks of them that did stone Stephen, yet the twain are together now merry saints in heaven, so prayest thou for me as I shall for thee, that together we might make merry in heaven.'"

Jim McShane responded to Bishop Bruskewitz's letter denying the CTAN appeal in a letter dated May 8, 1996. In the letter McShane stated, "We regret you declined to address any of our fourteen points, believing them to be frivolous or contemptuous. We intended them to be neither."[30] McShane noted in the letter that Bishop Bruskewitz had not officially responded to the request to meet with members of CTAN along with "common counsel."

Though Bishop Bruskewitz wrote that he took issue with Call To Action Nebraska's communication with the media, he or his staff were the initiators of interaction with the media on these matters. In his letter, Jim McShane explained that he released Bishop Bruskewitz's letter in which the bishop rejected CTAN'S appeal to the *Lincoln Journal Star* reporter, Bob Reeves, after McShane learned that someone from the chancery told Reeves he could acquire a copy of the letter from McShane. McShane noted that the chancery's call to Reeves occurred before McShane had even received the letter in the mail. Bishop Bruskewitz responded to Jim McShane's letter on May 9, 1996:

> Notwithstanding the irrelevance of your inquiry, I assure you that I am always ready to engage in dialogue and conversation, provided agreement can be reached on such points as time, place, participants, and agenda. If you have any proposals in these areas, please present them for my consideration. However, it should be clear to you that if your group contests the validity of the general diocesan legislation mentioned above, there would be very little to dialogue or converse about. Furthermore, repeated defiance and exhortations for others toward defiance in the media would nullify any hoped for success in dialogue and conversation.[31]

CTAN Co-Chair John Krejci wrote to Bishop Bruskewitz several months later to request the opportunity to meet informally and in a neutral setting to seek greater understanding. Krejci suggested "we put aside for the moment the controversial issues that have put us at odds and escalated the rhetoric to a level where volume has drowned out substance. This can be an opportunity to reflect on central issues like charity, kindness, the needs of the church, pain of the faithful, what we hold in common, and our vision for the Church in the 21st century."[32] Bishop Bruskewitz responded that he would meet with Krejci "after you regularize your situation with the Church. To hold such a meeting before that might imply that I am indifferent to the ecclesiastical censures which you have incurred, to your sacrilegious reception of Holy Communion about which you have publically boasted, and to your anti-Catholic activities."[33]

As of April 26, 1996 Call To Action Nebraska was the only group to appeal Bishop Bruskewitz's legislation.[34]

Options for Moving Forward:
A Preference for Subsidiarity

With the appeal to Bishop Bruskewitz rejected, members of Call To Action Nebraska carefully considered their options. They believed they had a fifteen working-day appeal period. Carol McShane noted in an interview with the *Lincoln Journal Star* that the appeal process in the Catholic Church is not clearly articulated so CTAN members "have to make our own path."[35]

Members of CTAN considered a variety of non-appeal options, including accepting the validity of the legislation through dropping out of CTA.[36] Though there might be some "peace that comes from obedience," if the group conceded to the bishop, it would appear that the group believed the legislation to be just and valid. Further, this option would encourage the "bullying" behavior of Bishop Bruskewitz. A second non-appeal option under consideration was to accept the sentence even though it was considered to be unjust. The advantage of this approach was that it both accepted the "legitimate authority" of the bishop while acknowledging that there is "real suffering that continues in Lincoln." Finally, CTAN members could ignore the legislation and act as if it did not exist; treat it as "bad law or ambiguous law which does not bind." If CTAN members adopted this option, they would continue to receive the sacraments and "act as if we are in good standing."

The next several response options involved further utilizing the appeals process. The first appeal option listed involved seeking a "brokered solution." One type of brokered solution would involve appealing to the Lincoln Diocesan Tribunal with the request that should the members of the tribunal feel too close to people or the situation, they would refer the matter to an appropriate authority in another diocese. The Diocesan Tribunal is made up of thirteen priests and three lay females.[37] A second option involved sending a formal request to the other Nebraska bishops to ask for their help in the matter. Third, CTAN considered appealing to the regional bishops as organized through the USCCB. Fourth, they could initiate a conciliation and arbitration process through the National Conference of Catholic Bishops. As former members of CALL well knew, for this to occur, both sides must agree to participate. Fifth, CTAN considered requesting that the issue be raised with the entire body of national bishops.

The CTAN document argued that the brokered appeal option that involves the local diocesan tribunal followed the principle of subsidiarity. That is, the people closest to the controversy would deal with the matter at the lowest possible level. According to the document, this option would "encourage deliberation." Further, "it follows a model of church which is collegial rather than simply legal, mutually supportive rather than top-down or adversarial." This option also had a number of disadvantages. The process could be drawn out, uncertain, and messy. In addition, the process might "create anxieties for the priests on the Tribunal or local bishops." The document noted that Msgr. Vasa chaired the Diocesan Tribunal and, therefore, might have a conflict of interest.

A final category of action under consideration involved appealing directly to the Vatican. The appeal could be sent to Bishop Bruskewitz with the request that it be forwarded to the appropriate Roman office

or the appeal could be sent directly to the Roman office most likely to
offer help in the matter. CTAN could then ask that the matter be brought
before the Pope after an appropriate amount of time passed for the process to occur.

One advantage of the direct appeal to the Vatican was that Bishop
Bruskewitz himself suggested this option. The document noted that
Bishop Bruskewitz likely knew which Roman tribunal should receive
the appeal. Further, this option could lead to a "clean and unambiguous
response." However, this route "manifests a model of church that is top-
down authoritarian and bottom-up adversarial." This approach might
also lead to a ruling that might not reflect the time necessary to deliberate
on such difficult matters. In addition, a definitive statement from Rome
could force other bishops to issue similar legislation.[38] The reach of that
action would be enormous.

Diocesan leaders appeared to want CTAN members to appeal directly
to the Vatican. Lincoln Chancellor, Msgr. Thorburn, said an appeal to
higher authority was the only way to determine whether or not Bishop
Bruskewitz's actions were just. Thorburn told a reporter, "If they are truly
believing Catholics, they would seek a judgment on whether the law is
just or not."[39]

When members of Call To Action Nebraska signed the original
appeal letter to Bishop Bruskewitz, CTAN co-chair, John Krejci and his
wife, Jean Krejci, were not in Lincoln. The Krejci's never added their
names to the list of those who appealed because they believed the legislation was unjust and, therefore, did not need to be obeyed.[40] In a letter
to John Krejci in which he refers to Krejci's "primitive understanding of
Catholicism," Msgr. Thorburn reaffirmed his stance on appeal: "If you
possessed a true belief in the Catholic Faith and in the system it provides
for appeal, you would appeal. Fear of the result of such an appeal seems
to be preventing 'Call to Action' members from seeking a further judge-
ment [sic]. The decision of the Vicar of Christ is of no interest to your
non-Catholic group, it seems."[41]

John Krejci provided a media statement on the day the excommunications were scheduled to take effect, May 15, 1996. Krejci said he

believed the law required civil disobedience, "To obey it is to be silent in the face of oppression. To obey it one would lose something of his or her humanity."[42]

On May 14, 1996, Bishop Bruskewitz appeared on the television program *Dateline NBC*. During that program he indicated, as he had before, that he would rescind or amend his extra-synodal legislation if the pope told him to do it. When asked if he expected it to happen, Bishop Bruskewitz answered, "no."[43]

Moving Forward

On the evening of the day the excommunications were to take effect, May 15, 1996, nineteen Lincoln diocesan CTAN members met to discuss their next steps. The meeting included prayer, reflection, and discussion. The group unanimously agreed that Bishop Bruskewitz's legislation was "unjust, ambiguous and without substance."[44] Attendees embraced a vision of a church that is bigger than only their bishop and the pope; their vision includes the clergy and lay people who should have a voice in the church. Because of this vision, the Lincoln CTAN members in attendance developed an appeal plan that afforded "others in the church with the opportunity to exercise their responsibility to influence the church to act with justice, restraint, and compassion."[45] Accordingly, those gathered, while recognizing that these groups hold "no actual coercive authority"[46] decided to first ask the Lincoln Diocesan Tribunal and the Lincoln Pastoral Council for a hearing with the hope that the hearing would be moved out of the diocese should those involved believe the matter could not be fairly heard.[47] The appealers further decided that should they fail in this effort, they would seek other "forums of discussion."[48]

In their press release, the Lincoln appealers further explained their decision regarding their appeal: "We acknowledge that Bishop Bruskewitz has said that only the Pope can force him to change his mind. Without contesting that view, we are trying to get beyond a process that is merely coercive. Our view of the church is more collegial and pastoral. It permits the slow maturation of opinion, and allows ample opportunity for the work of the Holy Spirit."[49] This approach seems not to have swayed Msgr. Thorburn who told a reporter at the *Lincoln Journal Star* that appealing to the Diocesan Tribunal was a waste of time because the tribunal has no authority in the matter.[50] Msgr. Thorburn also told the reporter that the Lincoln diocese is not required to have a Pastoral Council and it did not have one. Further, he said, even if a Pastoral Council existed, it also would have no authority in this matter.

Fifteen Lincoln members of Call To Action Nebraska signed a letter asking Msgr. Thorburn on July 8, 1996 to establish a body that might consider their request.[51] The letter cited the lack of response to any of the thirteen grounds for challenge of the legislation, save Bishop Bruskewitz's opinion that they were "indistinguishable from the frivolous or contemptuous." The letter concludes, "We ask members of the identified body to consider whether automatic and immediate excommunication is the appropriate first step in response to our existence. If it believes that it is not, we would ask it to communicate that judgment to the bishop. If that group believes that such extreme action was not warranted, we ask them to communicate that judgment to the Bishop." In his reply to this request, Msgr. Thorburn wrote, "I do not know of an organization within the diocese of Lincoln which would be in any position, official or unofficial, to consider your appeal against what you call 'extreme action.'"[52] Msgr. Thorburn concludes his response:

> My prayer is that this situation will be resolved, not by a change in the legislation, but by the conversion of you and those who have likewise embraced a man-made organization which has no power to provide for the salvation of your souls, while rejecting the authority and teachings of the Church instituted by Jesus Christ through which alone "is the universal help towards salvation." (U.R. 3; See also L.G. 14)

Fifteen CTAN members from the diocese of Lincoln also wrote to Msgr. Robert Vasa, Chair of the Lincoln Diocesan Tribunal on July 8, 1996. The signers asked Msgr. Vasa for the Tribunal to intervene unofficially with Bishop Bruskewitz by asking him to lift the penalty of excommunication.[53] The writers acknowledged that their request asked the Tribunal to step outside its official duties. However, they explained that they believe the church "is better served when. . . decisions are made in the arena closest to those whom they affect," "when it depends less on coercive authority," and when decision makers consider the "advice of a broad cross section of informed members of the ecclesial community."

Msgr. Vasa passed the letter on to Fr. Daniel Seiker who was appointed Judicial Vicar effective June 17, 1996. Fr. Seiker wrote, "I wish to inform you that Bishop Bruskewitz has reserved the adjudication of any cases relative to his Extra Synodal Legislation (March 19, 1996) to himself personally."[54] Fr. Seiker concludes, "May I suggest that if peace and right order is to be established in these matters it will come from a change of heart in you." Jim McShane told a reporter he was frustrated by the responses he received from Msgr. Thorburn and Fr. Seiker. He said, "What we have to do is broaden the scope of people who might talk to the bishop about these matters."[55]

Reaching out Locally and Nationally

Still hopeful to avoid appealing to the Vatican, members of CTAN in Lincoln sent a letter to all Lincoln diocesan priests. In the letter they asked the priests to either directly or through the Priests' Senate ask Bishop Bruskewitz to rescind the extra-synodal legislation. The letter stated that the signers understood that they could appeal to the Vatican, but "consistent with our view of the Church, we have decided not to go immediately to Rome."[56] A similar letter was sent to selected Catholic lay leaders in the Lincoln Diocese. In addition, Lincoln diocesan members of CTAN also sent the bishops, archbishops and cardinals of the National Conference of Catholic Bishops a letter and supporting material requesting their intervention.[57]

Among the materials that supported their request, the signers included an appendix that detailed their responses to the challenges against them as well as the extra-synodal legislation. The signers addressed the danger of the abuse of legitimate authority. Recognizing that some positions of the church have changed (e.g., on the morality of slavery), the signers note that some dissent is permitted. They also note that Church law helps reduce the abuse of authority. For example, Canon 753 calls for collegiality among bishops and Canon 1316 requires penal laws be uniform in cities or regions. In addition, Canon 1317 requires that the penalties be "truly necessary" and Canon 1318 reserves automatic penalties for "particularly treacherous offenses."

The Appendix noted that there are two kinds of penalties in the church: imposed and automatic. Bishop Bruskewitz's extra-synodal legislation dealt in automatic penalties. Those who receive imposed penalties have the option to ask for a hearing, to appeal or to have common counsel. No such options are available for automatic penalties. The signers write:

> Canon Law sees legislated automatic penalties so rarely invoked, and then against such heinous crimes, that it does not devote a great deal of space to the topic. However, where the Law is silent or obscure, Canon 17 permits the transfer of analogous provisions from parallel sections of the Code. Canon Law expects that, except in the especially treacherous cases mentioned above, penalties will not be in effect until they have been imposed after due process, i.e., after notification of the accused, appointment of a defense counsel, the opportunity for a defense, etc. (See Canon 171 ff.) [58]

They noted this is one reason automatic penalties are used so rarely.

The letter signers then turned their attention to the features of Bishop Bruskewitz's extra-synodal legislation. They indicated that the law applies to membership. "The law applies to individuals only as those individuals are part of the organizations named in it. Consequently, no particular accusation against any particular member is relevant to the excommunication in question, except that of disobedience to the order to get out of the organization." The charge against these organizations is that membership in them "is always perilous to the Catholic Faith and most often totally incompatible with the Catholic Faith."[59]

Next, the signers addressed the validity of the legislation. They reasoned that the validity of the law can be tested in two ways. One, are the charges "clear and grounded in fact?" They explain, "Facts that are alleged on the basis of error, rash judgment or calumny do not offer a sound basis for a conclusion, and so legislation based on such a conclusion can have no logical validity." Two, "Does the law represent sound use of the Bishop's legitimate authority?"[60]

Starting with the first test of validity, the signers declared their belief that the legislation was not based on fact. They examined the specific accusations. First, Bishop Bruskewitz wrote to then-CTAN Co-Chairs Lori Darby and John Krejci that Call To Action is, "intrinsically incoherent and fundamentally divisive. It is inimical to the Catholic Faith, subversive of Church order, destructive of the Catholic Church discipline, contrary to the teaching of the Second Vatican Council, and an impediment to evangelization." The signers note, "If these are to be regarded as serious charges rather than as a string of judgmental invective or an announcement of fears, they must at least be backed up by some specific allegations tied to facts."[61] Moreover, the legislation covers a diverse group of organizations. The accompanying editorial used vague language such as "most often," "most of the time," "frequently," "some of their members and leaders," and "they sometimes give the impression." The reasoning behind the legislation lacks clarity, though that is the written purpose behind the legislation. They explain that "Bishop Bruskewitz has ascribed various damaging effects to CTA-N [CTAN] but he has not connected those alleged effects to particular actions."[62]

The signers turned their attention, then, to some particular charges made against CTAN in the April 24, 1996 letter Bishop Bruskewitz wrote denying their appeal. One difficulty with this letter was that it was hard to determine which charges were levied against Jim McShane and which were levied at the entire group. Personal charges would not be relevant in condemning an entire group.

First, the bishop charged the group with "expelling from one of your group's meetings at Mahoney State Park, the well-informed Catholic people" sent by him. The signers provide context. First, the two people in question, undergraduate students at the University of Nebraska, Lincoln, attended the public meeting on February 3, 1996. They chose to leave before the closing liturgy. Noting their youth, an attendee asked them about their plans to which they responded that they would report "what they had seen and heard" to Msgr. Timothy Thorburn, the Lincoln diocesan Chancellor. The same two attempted to attend the first meeting of the newly-elected Steering Committee on February 24, 1996. They were asked why they were there and "they again frankly acknowledged that they were there to report on events to Msgr. Thorburn." The committee asked them to wait while they deliberated on whether or not the meeting should be considered "open." Bishop Bruskewitz accused CTAN members of wanting to conceal their "activities and plots." The signers explain there was no "plot" to conceal. As described in an earlier chapter, two members of the newly-elected board met with the students, explained the complicated situation to them and then asked them if they still wished to attend the meeting. If they did, the committee would vote on the matter. After a private discussion, the two decided to leave. They did ask for a copy of the meeting agenda and it was provided to them.[63]

Second, Bishop Bruskewitz claimed that CTAN used "a non-Catholic creed" in their liturgy at their February 3, 1996 meeting. The text of the prayer was provided for examination. The bishop makes three charges regarding the prayer. First, he charges that the prayer reflects unorthodox belief. Bishop Bruskewitz claimed that God was omitted from the prayer. The signers point out that the prayer refers to Jesus and "His Father." Though the word "God" was not specifically used, "the assumption of divinity is evident" just as in the Apostles Creed, the Holy Spirit is not specifically called "God."[64]

The bishop also took issue with the phrase, "I believe in people," claiming it represented a "new age" perspective. In his meeting with the bishop, Jim McShane explained that the phrase refers to the dignity of all people, "that individuals are each created by God, endowed by him with a soul; they are therefore possessed of inherent dignity and entitled to respect."[65]

The last line of prayer stated, "And I believe in the resurrection—whatever it means." The bishop read that line as if the intent is "contemptuous or thoughtless" such as "I believe in the resurrection or whatever" or "I believe in the resurrection—whatever *that* means." The signers indicate that the faithful people in attendance at the meeting did not have that attitude. In fact, to them the statement was an affirmation of "the mystery of the resurrection of the body, even though the form taken by the body at the resurrection is mysterious and unknown to us all."[66]

Finally, the signers cited rubrics, or laws, to defend themselves when they were accused of refusing to recite the Nicene Creed at their liturgy. The rubrics do not require the recitation of a creed at a weekday Mass. The prayer was not a creed so it did not demonstrate a rejection of Catholic belief.[67]

The signers point out that Bishop Bruskewitz chose to use inconsistent and escalating language. Bishop Bruskewitz first claimed in a *National Catholic Reporter* article on April 12, 1996 that the creed "had no relationship that I could perceive to any historical creed of the Catholic church." On April 24, 1996, Bishop Bruskewitz called it a "non-Catholic creed," a very different matter indeed. The signers wrote,

> Again, we feel constrained to notice the unsustainable excess in the framing of charges. At each step in the process the same material gets framed to make us out to be guilty of ever more abhorrent crimes—and in each inflated case the charge becomes even more substantial than the facts warrant. For people who have proudly and devoutly recited the creeds of the church for decades, this is very hurtful and deeply felt.[68]

Bishop Bruskewitz claimed that at their organizational meeting on February 3, 1996, Call To Action Nebraska "undertook an illicit Mass in this Diocese of Lincoln, which was not only non-rubrical but anti-rubrical." The signers acknowledge and admit regret that an unauthorized text was used for the Eucharistic Prayer. However, they explain that as the gathering was the first meeting of CTAN, those present had no idea what the liturgy would entail. The liturgy was planned by a small "subset of persons from various parts of the State and was certainly *made prior* to the group's formation and *without group approval*" [emphasis in original].

The intent of those present, the signers explain, was not to dismiss ecclesial authority but to "celebrate our unity with one another in Christ, the Christ of Word and Eucharist." Therefore, the mistake is one "more suited to what Canon Law calls fraternal counsel than of the ultimate punishment." In addition, the signers note that the group has no plans to use unauthorized texts in the future.[69]

Another accusation leveled by Bishop Bruskewitz against Call To Action Nebraska is that the organization has "orchestrated protests and polemics carried on in the media." Msgr. Vasa was quoted by a reporter as having said that CTAN violated Canon 1369: "A person who in a public show or speech, in published writing, or in other uses of the instruments of social communication utters blasphemy, gravely injures good morals, expresses insults, or excites hatred or contempt against religion or the Church is to be punished with a just penalty."[70]

CTAN letter signers note that the idea that CTAN is responsible for and orchestrated the media attention demonstrates a lack of understanding of the way excommunication captures the imagination of the Catholic and non-Catholic public.[71] Catholics are likely to assume that excommunication happens to people who have committed "particularly dreadful offenses and only after the most careful investigation and punctiliously fair hearings." The response by many Catholics when they learn that this is not, in fact, true, is shock and a feeling of betrayal. Protestants have told CTAN members that this action raises a distrust of Rome. Non-Christians find the action "bizarre." On the National Public Radio program, *Weekend Edition*, on June 30, 1996, Msgr. Thorburn explained that the excommunication was medicinal and could be beneficial for the discussion it has prompted. Signers note the irony that the excommunication was issued because CTAN members had already asked for such discussion. Furthermore, CTAN does not have the ability to influence five of the top ten United States newspapers to cover the story of the extrasynodal legislation; those newspaper editors found Bishop Bruskewitz's actions newsworthy.[72]

The signers explained that if the media had been provoked, such provocation came from the chancery, not Call To Action Nebraska.

They provide as evidence of this statement the fact that the Chancery faxed a copy of the extra-synodal legislation to the *Lincoln Journal Star*; many members of CTAN originally heard about the legislation from the Lincoln newspaper. Catholic News Service (CNS) asked members of CTAN for a copy of their appeal to Bishop Bruskewitz. CTAN referred them to the Chancery where CNS was told by the bishop that the bishop did not mind if CTAN released the appeal to CNS. After Jim McShane met privately with Bishop Bruskewitz, he only told the media that "the meeting had not led to change." In contrast, Bishop Bruskewitz discussed his perceptions of the meeting with the reporter. Just forty-five minutes after receiving Bishop Bruskewitz's letter rejecting the appeal of the legislation, a reporter from the *Lincoln Journal Star* called to ask about the letter. McShane had not even had time to inform the members of the Steering Committee and those who signed the letter of the bishop's response. The *Lincoln Journal Star* reporter told McShane he knew about the letter because someone from the Chancery had called and left him a message earlier that morning. Call To Action Nebraska members from Lincoln who were approached by major news outlets asked whether or not the bishop would be interviewed and were told in each case that the interview with the bishop had already been arranged. Lastly, members of CTAN had been careful not to allow their attendance at Mass to be a media event. In contrast, Bishop Bruskewitz had been both photographed and televised during Mass.[73]

Bishop Bruskewitz accused members of Call To Action Nebraska of being defiant and urging defiance in others. In response, the signers note that they acknowledged the right of Bishop Bruskewitz to legislate. They note, though, that they consider the extra-synodal legislation to be an unjust law to which he cannot expect "docile obedience."[74] Some Lincoln diocesan members of CTAN chose not to obey the law. While they acknowledged this, they had not been loud or disruptive in their response. Other Lincoln diocesan members accepted the legislation and stopped receiving the sacraments. No one had been urged to accept or change his/her response to the legislation. They concluded, "The unjust denial or threatening of one's access to the sacraments is deeply unsettling and profoundly disturbing. It cries out for redress. It is not defiant to say so."[75]

Call To Action Nebraska has been described as being pro-abortion and advancing homosexual practices. In a letter denying an appeal for help, Msgr. Thorburn wrote, "Your organization sees no evil in the choice to cruelly murder innocent children in their mothers' wombs, and condemn those mothers to a psychological hell on earth. Is that justice?"[76] Call To Action USA and Call To Action Nebraska did not adopt this position. The only position taken on abortion by CTA is to call "for civility in the public debate." Msgr. Thorburn justified these claims by explaining that Call To Action affiliates with organizations that hold pro-choice positions. This, however, is a red herring. As the signers note, by this standard, "the US Catholic Conference could be condemned as pro-choice because it joined forces with the National Abortion Rights Action League (NARAL) in an umbrella coalition to lobby Congress against certain proposals for welfare reform."[77]

CTAN members have been accused of trying to give the impression that Catholic opinions about Call To Action are mixed. This is true. Three bishops and 5000 priests and members of religious orders remained in good standing in the church while they maintained membership in Call To Action.

After addressing the charges made against Call To Action Nebraska, the signers turned their attention to Canon Law. The signers acknowledge that they are not canon lawyers. They base their observations on their reading of the Canons as well as the advice of others with more expertise in the area. The signers then applied specific Canons to their situation.

Addressing the issue of collegiality (Canon 753), the signers noted that the extra-synodal legislation was not the result of a collegial process. Bishop Bruskewitz did not confer with any other United States Catholic bishop. No other bishop followed Bishop Bruskewitz's lead or spoke publically in favor of the legislation. While applicable throughout the diocese, the legislation is not uniform in the region (Canon 1316).[78]

The signers pointed out that automatic penalties are reserved for particularly grave offenses (Canon 1318); they believe they have made the case that their membership in Call To Action or Call To Action Nebraska is not a particularly grave matter. Furthermore, the bishop did not attempt any other means of correction before he issued his extra-synodal legislation (Canon 1341).[79]

The signers claimed Bishop Bruskewitz's extra-synodal legislation denied their right to due process (Canon 1717), their right to the sacraments (Canon 843), their right to assemble and associate in groups (Canon 215), and their right to make their needs and desires known to the hierarchy (Canon 212).[80]

While the extra-synodal legislation was intended to be medicinal (i.e., intended to cure), the signers believe there is no evidence that it has achieved that goal. Membership in both Call To Action USA and Call To Action Nebraska grew after the publication of the legislation. Signers asked, "Is there evidence that the legislation is the product of mature reflection?" They answer that it seems not to be the case. First, Bishop Bruskewitz was frequently quoted in the press saying he was shocked by the media attention paid to the situation and that such a response was unintended. Second, the legislation was enacted very quickly. The extra-synodal legislation was promulgated only two days after CTAN Co-Chair Lori Darby was quoted in the *Omaha World Herald* saying that CTAN would parallel the goals of the national organization. The timing of the legislation most certainly does not affirm the assertion of mature reflection.[81]

Further evidence that the extra-synodal legislation was not having its intended medicinal result was found in the rhetoric of Bishop Bruskewitz. For example, in response to the first letter written to Bishop Bruskewitz from Call To Action Nebraska, Bishop Bruskewitz expressed his opinion that Catholic dissenters do not act with integrity. In the same letter, the bishop wrote that the CTAN Co-Chairs and the rest of the group do not "possess the competence, ability or authority to determine authentically what is essential or non-essential in Catholic doctrine, Catholic moral teaching, or Catholic Church law." The signers also mentioned a joke Bishop Bruskewitz made during his speech at the annual Churches Forum and reported in the *Southern Nebraska Register* about not being "in the excommunicating mood today." Those who are impacted by the legislation find that joke to mock them.[82]

The signers suggested that one might view the extra-synodal legislation as "a boisterous bit of rhetoric in its own right." They cite the bishop's statement that the penalties were necessary so that the prohibition would not be considered "just his opinion." This statement demonstrated that he considers "his authority to punish as a source of rhetorical power" and he chose the most extreme punishment possible.[83]

The lack of clarity of the extra-synodal legislation also called into question whether or not it functions medicinally. For example, in the United States, according to Ecclesiastical Law, no one under eighteen can be excommunicated. This important piece of information was not mentioned in the extra-synodal legislation and it was only mentioned in the secular media after the excommunication was to have taken effect. A number of the groups listed in the legislation are Masonic youth groups. Another example of lack of clarity is the use of the term "in and of the Diocese of Lincoln" to refer to those impacted by the legislation. Unsure who the term included, CTAN consulted a Canonist who advised that the legislation forbids one from receiving the sacraments in the Lincoln diocese. That is, "We are told that one of the consequences of the fact that our excommunication is legislative rather than by decree is that it does not apply outside Bishop Bruskewitz's jurisdiction." The Chancery has made no acknowledgement of this important piece of information.[84]

The signers noted an event that took place in July 1996. Jim McShane had been invited to address a local gathering of MENSA about the excommunication controversy in the Lincoln diocese. The meeting was open to the public and Msgr. Thorburn attended. He was willing to answer questions about the Chancery's position. At that meeting he reportedly said that if Bishop Bruskewitz rescinded or amended the extra-synodal legislation, then it would be the same as admitting that he could be wrong. Of course, bishops are not infallible. However, the signers note Msgr. Thorburn was most likely acknowledging that the bishop has found himself "in a difficult spot." Still, "such understanding would be difficult to extend if our sacramental life is being sacrificed to preserve Episcopal face. The request for such understanding could hardly encourage confidence in the Bishop's disinterested concern for those whom he has excommunicated."[85] The bishop appeared to show concern for those impacted by the legislation when he stated, "In obedience there is peace." Members of CTAN do not believe such peace is worth unquestioning obedience to such a biased and unjust piece of legislation. Rather, the signers cite the words of Pope Paul VI: "If you want peace, work for justice."

The signers addressed the issue of why Call To Action Nebraska continues. Among other reasons, they note that in the diocese of Lincoln, "a lack of discussion is taken to mean that everyone is satisfied with the status quo." Certainly, the harsh penalty issued by the extra-synodal legislation to those who wish to dialogue on serious issues must serve to silence others who might raise a question, too. The signers then list issues they believe require attention including the authority crisis in the church, the priest shortage, the status of women, persistence in faith among the young, subsidiarity, and divisiveness (including the lack of participation in diocesan affairs of minority people, the contempt shown for the excommunicates, the dismissive attitude toward issues, and the bishop's greater solicitude for his own freedom than for that of his flock).[86]

As the detailed response to the extra-synodal legislation drew to a close, the signers noted:

> As long as loyalty to the Church is defined as quiet acceptance of such injustice, the worse the abuses will become. Call to Action Nebraska members in the Lincoln Diocese did not seek nor did they expect to be attacked in this fashion. But we have been. And every time someone tries to show a Chancery official the injustice of what has happened to us the pressure gets worse, the accusations more inflated, the tone more bitter. It almost seems as if they are trying to provoke us into doing something that will justify what they have already done... We are determined to continue, even if the effort continues lonely and the way deserted. After all, it may be that the constraints which prevent others from speaking in this matter represent a movement of the Holy Spirit to empower the voice of the laity in the church.[87]

Reaching Out to Omaha

In early November 1997, two Call To Action Nebraska members, Cecilia Daly and Betty Peterson, wrote to Archbishop Elden Curtiss of Omaha.[88] They wrote as individuals, not CTAN representatives, to request a meeting to discuss the excommunication and seek advice for the next step in the appeal process. In their letter, Daly and Peterson explain that they reviewed a case that took place in Hawaii in which excommunication was overturned. In this case, the people affected discussed their situation with their Metropolitan, or Archbishop. They wrote, "We understand from very reliable sources that someone in the Vatican has indicated Bishop Bruskewitz has been warned not to issue any more such edicts and not to enforce the one already issued. This, however, still leaves us with the stigma; and we feel we must pursue any process available to us in regaining our respectable status in our Church." Daly and Peterson received no response to their letter. They wrote the Archbishop again in January 1998, enclosing a copy of the original letter. They received no response. They wrote again on March 12, 1998 again asking for an appointment. They concluded, "We trust that our first letters did reach you and sincerely hope that you will grant our wish to visit with you."[89]

Archbishop Curtiss responded in a letter dated March 21, 1998. He first acknowledged receipt of all three letters (November 12, 1997, January 6, 1998, and March 12, 1998). He then wrote, "A bishop has responsibility for the faith and order of his own diocese. Since I know of no reversal by the Holy See nor investigation into Bishop Bruskewitz's 1996 action by the NCCB I am in no position to undertake either action."[90] Curtiss then suggested they contact the Apostolic Pro-Nuncio and provided his address. Daly and Peterson wrote back to the Archbishop acknowledging receipt of his letter. They wrote that they were not asking for action, but rather, for advice. They concluded, "We regret that you feel unable to counsel us in this grave matter."[91]

A Bishop's Advice

Jim McShane received a letter dated December 30, 1997 from Archbishop Rembert Weakland of Milwaukee. Archbishop Weakland had been in Rome for the Synod of Bishops where he had asked other bishops for their opinion on what recourse members of Call To Action Nebraska had available to them. According to Archbishop Weakland, the consensus opinion was that CTAN should send a brief summary of the appeal to Archbishop Zenon Grocholewski, Supreme Tribunal of the Apostolic Signatura and ask for an English-speaking advocate. Weakland observed, "I did not sense any negativity on anyone's part with regard to taking up this issue."[92] The Apostolic Signatura is the Vatican equivalent of a Supreme Court.

Seventeen Lincoln diocesan members of Call To Action Nebraska followed this consensus opinion and sent a brief, registered, summary letter to Archbishop Zenon Grocholewski dated January 28, 1998.[93] The letter offered a brief explanation of the extra-synodal legislation and called that legislation "unjust, even abusive." Addressing the falsehoods spread about the members of Call To Action by the Lincoln Diocese, the signers state:

> For the record: our group does *not* [emphasis in original], as we have been accused by the Chancery, advocate or support abortion. Nor do we demand or even seek the popular election of Bishops. We do not deny, in whole or in part, any of the Creeds of the Church. We are not degenerates, we are not a sect, we are not opposed to the Catholic priesthood, we are not any of the awful things regularly attributed to us in the *Southern Nebraska Register,* the Diocesan newspaper.

The signers explained that they had hoped to deal with the issue "locally and without angry confrontation or coercion." They explained their initial appeal to Bishop Bruskewitz and its rejection and that, "At each step in our process we assured those to whom we spoke or wrote (as we now assure you) that we are not seeking coercive action that would result in the public embarrassment of our bishop." The letter stated that the signers hoped for "gentle intervention" that would lead Bishop Bruskewitz to change his mind. As that had not come to pass, the signers asked the Supreme Tribunal for the Apostolic Signatura for "some relief." Finally, they asked that should the Supreme Tribunal be unable to act on the matter, might they offer advice on a formal appeal as well as the name of an English-speaking advocate.

Archbishop Zenon Grocholewski recommended that Lincoln members of Call To Action Nebraska write to Cardinal Bernardin Gantin, the Cardinal Prefect of the Congregation of Bishops, to ask for help. They did so in a letter dated April 13, 1998.[94] The Secretary of the Congregation of Bishops, Msgr. Jorge Maria Majia, suggested CTAN members include more details about the situation in which they found themselves as well as providing context using the Code of Canon Law.

The appeal letter began with a brief description of the founding of Call To Action Nebraska and Bishop Bruskewitz's subsequently issued extra-synodal legislation. The signers pointed out that while the legislation listed reasons, these reasons were not substantiated. Further, "accusations were also unsubstantiated." The letter also explained the steps taken by affected members of Call To Action Nebraska to try to come to resolution. These steps included reaching out to Bishop Bruskewitz, Lincoln priests and lay people, other Nebraska bishops and other bishops in the United States. "When it became clear that that hope [of local resolution] would not be fulfilled, we appealed to the Signatura who has referred our letter to you. As we write, we have lived for two years under this troubling law."

Addressing the pain caused by separation from the sacraments as well as the effects of the legislation on their relationships in the community, the signers wrote:

> We and many others feel anguish that the Church in Lincoln has improperly attacked our good name and permitted us no redress. We suffer deeply because the Bishop would require us to remain without the Sacraments and other rites of the church, without community and without access to the ordinary means of grace—all reasons that would suffice for such penalties in no other diocese on earth.[95]

The signers asked first that the Congregation of Bishops act informally on this matter. Should an informal resolution not be possible, the signers asked for advice on the best way to move forward with a more formal appeal.

Five appendices that provided support documentation, including a list of Canons from the Code of Canon Law that the signers believed supported their position, accompanied the letter.[96] They provided a list of Canons along with commentary, "a series of notes indicating the more extended arguments which we are prepared to make if, in the judgment of the Congregation, it would be appropriate to do so." I provide a sample of the relevant Canons.

- Canon 14: "Laws. . . do not oblige when there is a doubt about the law."[97] The signers consider the extra-synodal legislation to be dubious.

- Canon 220: "No one is permitted to harm illegitimately the good reputation which a person possesses. . ."[98]

- Canon 375.2: "Through Episcopal consecration itself, bishops receive with the function of sanctifying also the functions of teaching and governing; by their nature, however, these can only be exercised in hierarchical communion with the head and members of the college."[99] Bishop Bruskewitz did not consult any other United States bishop before issuing the legislation.

- Canon 391: "It is for the diocesan bishop to govern the particular church entrusted to him with legislative, executive, and judicial power according to the norm of law."[100] Bishop Bruskewitz's extra-synodal legislation is outside the norm of law.

- Canon 1318: "A legislator is not to threaten *latae sententiae* penalties except possibly for certain singularly malicious delicts which either can result in graver scandal or cannot be punished effectively by *ferendae sententiae* penalties; he is not, however, to establish censures, especially excommunication, except with the greatest moderation and only for graver delicts."[101] In the note associated with this Canon, the signers wrote:

In our case there has been no showing of inveterate malice, not by the group nor by individuals. Perhaps the worst case to be made against us is that we called for church authorities to consider the ordination of married persons and women as a means of reducing the priest shortage. The former "offense," of course, describes the history of the church's first millennium. Well after the issuance of *Ordinatio Sacerdotalis* Cardinal Ratzinger publically said that the second offense, suggesting women's ordination, is not heretical and ought not to be considered grounds for excommunication."[102]

- Canon 1341: "An ordinary is to take care to initiate a judicial or administrative process to impose or declare penalties only after he has ascertained that fraternal correction or rebuke or other means of pastoral solicitude cannot sufficiently repair the scandal, restore justice, reform the offender."[103] Signers note that as Bishop Bruskewitz issued his extra-synodal legislation almost immediately after receiving a letter from CTAN informing him about the formation of the organization, "the imposition of the interdict and excommunication seem to be the Bishop's first, only and constant resort, not his last one."

Jim McShane mailed the letter to Cardinal Gantin on April 20, 1998. Attached to the United Postal Service shipping receipt located in the Call To Action Nebraska archives is a note that indicates that the letter was received on April 22, 1998 at 9:19 AM by a person named Pugliesi.

This letter remained unanswered for over eight and a half years. The first news of a response to the letter did not come from Cardinal Gantin.

Waiting For a Response

Meanwhile, on behalf of all the Lincoln diocesan CTAN members who signed the original document, Jim McShane wrote to the newly appointed Cardinal Prefect for the Congregation for Bishops, Cardinal Lucas Moreira Neves.[104] McShane wrote out of concern that nine months had passed with no response of any kind. After acknowledging the many reasons why they may not have received a response (e.g., a change in administration, an attempt to manage the situation informally, etc.), McShane noted that not only had the situation for Lincoln diocesan members of CTAN not improved, it had even gotten worse. McShane cited three examples. First, Bishop Bruskewitz had endorsed the book *Call to Action or Call to Apostasy?* by Brian Clowes. In this book Mr. Clowes accuses members of Call To Action of intending to destroy all church teachings. McShane refers to the book as an "ad hominem diatribe" and explains that Mr. Clowes "attributes not one activity to CTA which could plausibly be used to support the charges." Second, McShane referenced Joan Johnson's denial of communion (see Chapter 8) by one of her parish priests. Third, McShane addressed the fact that a number of the members of CTAN "are not young" and some "are in less than perfect health." Lincoln CTAN members are rightly worried about the ability to receive the sacrament of the anointing of the sick and a funeral Mass. McShane noted that the wider community is impacted by the lack of response as well because it appeared "there seems to be no one in authority at any level of the Church who is at once willing and able to act to correct the abuses so visibly visited upon us." He concluded, "Please give us some indication of what you are thinking and doing in response to our appeal. Please advise us as to what we can expect or what we should plan for as we look for amelioration through the process of appeal. At least, please give us some indication that you have received that appeal."

Around the third anniversary of the issuance of Bishop Bruskewitz's extra-synodal legislation, the *Southern Nebraska Register* published an editorial addressing the anniversary and calling the legislation a "grand blessing to our diocese."[105] The editorial acknowledged that the bishop had received a few hundred negative communications about the legislation but he had also received "tens of thousands of great, affirming and positive communications." The editorial claimed that the intended purpose of the legislation had been met: ambiguity about the organizations in question was dissipated. In reference to those impacted by the penalties, the editorial stated, "The opposition from those prohibited organizations and their supporters has been negligible and totally forgettable." Around this time CTAN members in Lincoln anxiously waited to receive a response to their appeal to the Congregation for Bishops. Surely these words felt like a callous denial of their pain.

After almost six more months of silence from the Vatican, Lincoln members once again considered writing to the Congregation for Bishops. The draft letter, which was never sent, written by Jim McShane, stated that Lincoln members believed the penalties afflicted by the extra-synodal legislation to be in abeyance because of a pending appeal. Because of this, most Lincoln diocesan CTAN members resumed participation in the sacraments. McShane noted that priests and lay Catholics are not aware of the appeal and that can and has caused problems. For example, one member, Joan Johnson, was denied communion by a priest by letter and one member was denied "at the altar rail." McShane once again begged for acknowledgement that the appeal was received and that it is under consideration. He explained, "We have made no public reference to our appeal so as to keep from creating pressures on anyone."

Though many Lincoln diocesan members of Call To Action Nebraska considered the penalties assigned by the extra-synodal legislation to be held in abeyance while their appeal was pending, a few conversations with Lincoln priests worried them. First, Jim McShane was asked to sponsor a person converting to Catholicism. He needed his pastor's reference. Fr. Joseph Nemec, Pastor of McShane's parish, told McShane that he considered himself to be his "former pastor" because the chancery had insisted that Jim and Carol McShanes' names be taken off the parish rolls. Second, Betty Peterson was told by her pastor that should she die as a member of Call To Action, he would be prohibited from providing the Mass of Christian Burial. Her pastor reported that this prohibition came directly from the chancery.

Jim McShane wrote to Bishop Bruskewitz sharing these two incidents along with the CTAN understanding that members were protected from penalty while the appeal was under consideration. McShane asked for specific rules regarding funeral, burial, and participation in other sacraments and rites. Indicating that the CTAN board would like to include answers to these questions in an upcoming mailing, McShane requested a timely response.

When he attempted to hand deliver the letter, Jim McShane found the Chancery locked. However, a priest saw McShane and opened the door. In an effort to keep accurate records, McShane had prepared a receipt for the hand-delivered letter and he asked this priest to sign the receipt. The priest blanched. According to McShane's email account of the event, "he did not want to engage himself in any way without permission of his bishop." Acknowledging that he understood that the priest, too, was subject to authority, McShane left the letter and the receipt and asked the priest to either send the signed receipt or a written explanation for why it was not signed. McShane's written account of this encounter was touching. The priest expressed sadness over the situation and, according to McShane, "We parted with kind words" and assurances of prayer.

Jim McShane received a response from Bishop Bruskewitz in a letter dated April 24, 2000.[106] Bishop Bruskewitz stated that the legislation was in full force. He stated that the letter "seems to imply that you do not realize the seriousness of your situation, the jeopardy in which you have placed your eternal salvation, the grave moral, canonical, and pastoral consequences in which you have situated yourself, and the scandal you continue to commit." The letter ended with an explanation of how members of CTAN can be reinstated into the Church.

Jim McShane wrote back to Bishop Bruskewitz.[107] While expressing appreciation for the prompt response, McShane noted that most of the questions asked remained unanswered. McShane asked if it is true that members of Call To Action and Call To Action Nebraska are indeed barred from Catholic funeral rites and burial in consecrated ground. Further, McShane asked if it is also true that members of CTA or CTAN cannot serve as sponsors at Baptism, Confirmation or as witnesses to Marriage.

Meanwhile, Call To Action Nebraska member, Betty Peterson, resigned from CTAN over the issue of the denial of Catholic burial. Peterson recalled her struggle in an interview:

Well, since my conscience felt free, it didn't bother me. But when I learned that he would deny Christian burial, then I began to think about what that would mean to my family and my friends and I, I really had a difficult time with that. And then I decided this is just another challenge to face. But I couldn't sleep comfortably thinking that if I drop dead tomorrow, my husband and children would have to grapple with this problem. And because I've always been a person who likes to have things settled and make sure that everything's okay, I finally decided that I had to make this decision to at least withdraw official member- ship in Call To Action. . . That's been a big challenge. It's one of the hardest decisions I ever made in my life. . . for about six weeks I really anguished and prayed about it and finally decided that I had to with- draw membership.[108]

In a newspaper story about this decision, Betty Peterson, then-77 years old, expressed concern for her children, "I felt this would be a pun- ishment, not so much for me but for my family . . . It's a burden I didn't want to impose on them."[109] National Call To Action Co-Director Dan Daley noted that Peterson "could have a Catholic burial if she were a member of any other diocese on earth but Lincoln."[110]

Bishop Bruskewitz wrote a short letter to Jim McShane dated May 9, 2000. In this letter he commented, "I am sorry that you still seem to be confused and that you have placed yourself in what you call a 'dreadful impasse'. I am also sorry that I feel compelled to doubt the sincerity of your inquiries. It would be pointless and futile, in my view, to repeat what I already wrote to you. May God's grace assist you."[111]

Members of Call To Action Nebraska did not receive satisfactory answers from Bishop Bruskewitz or an actual response from the Vatican to the appeal. Informal news trickled to Lincoln. In one unconfirmed report a priest is reported to have responded to a question about whether or not the appeal would be acted on by saying that all the people who are appealing the legislation are old and will soon be dead. Later, that same priest suggested the appeal was probably sitting in a drawer somewhere at the Vatican.

Bishop Bruskewitz, however, operated under no such ambiguity. Speaking at a *Wanderer* Forum in Milwaukee, Bishop Bruskewitz told the crowd that his extra-synodal legislation was "in full force."[112] He described those impacted by the legislation as "few in numbers. . . maybe 20 people. . . and it's very questionable as to whether some of those 20 ever were actually Catholics to begin with, or practiced the Catholic faith in any meaningful way."[113]

A response to a question in the *Southern Nebraska Register* "Ask The Register" column that asked what to do with an unwanted CTAN newsletter continued the attack on members of CTAN. The brief response read, "Call-to Action is a pathetic, tiny sect which seems to consist of a few fallen priests and some aging anti-Catholics. Ignore them. I recommend you take what they send you outdoors and burn it, and then apologize to the match."[114]

A Vatican Response?

On February 7, 2005, Call To Action Nebraska board member and former priest, John Krejci, a frequent communicant, attended daily Mass at Sacred Heart Church in Lincoln. Unbeknownst to him, Bishop Bruskewitz was scheduled to celebrate Mass at Sacred Heart that day. Krejci was the last person to approach the bishop to receive the Eucharist. According to Krejci, Bishop Bruskewitz gave him an unfriendly hand wave and walked away, denying the Eucharist to Krejci. Krejci approached the altar and communicated himself. Krejci described this moment in an article for *Voices of Nebraska Catholics,* the CTAN newsletter:

> Instead of giving me the host, [Bishop Bruskewitz] waved me off with a brief, but decidedly unfriendly gesture of his hand. He then whirled around and fled to the altar where he deposited the ciborium for Father Walsh, the pastor, to put away. I must have hesitated for a microsecond, for when I followed him to the altar, he had already left and taken his seat on the side. I saw the ciborium half full of hosts so I moved toward the center of the altar, picked up a host, communicated myself. I then

calmly returned to my place in the back row, all the while holding my
song book and feigning singing the Communion hymn, since I had by
then lost the page.[115]

This event marked the first time any member of Call To Action
Nebraska was denied communion in a public way. The members of
CTAN had not taken an official position on how to respond if denied
the Eucharist. John Krejci's action was a personal decision made at that
moment in those specific circumstances. While no CTAN member who
gathered to discuss this surprising denial of the Eucharist believed they
would have responded in a similar fashion,[116] none of us were in his shoes
that day. There was significant and strong empathy among those gathered
to hear about Krejci's experience for the pain Krejci felt when denied the
Eucharist by Bishop Bruskewitz. John Krejci wrote to Bishop Bruskewitz
later that day to remind him that according to Canon 1353, penalties
under appeal are considered suspended.[117]

Sacred Heart Pastor, Fr. Tom Walsh, denied John Krejci communion
on Sunday, February 19, 2005. During their short conversation at communion time, Fr. Walsh told Krejci that he had been instructed by the
bishop to deny Krejci communion. Krejci reminded Fr. Walsh of Canon
1353 and that CTAN had an appeal pending at the Vatican. Fr. Walsh told
Krejci "he was under the impression that the appeal was invalid!"[118] Krejci
wrote to Fr. Walsh after their conversation to ask for specific information
regarding the denial.[119] Specifically, Krejci wanted, in writing, the name
of the person who had instructed Fr. Walsh to deny him the Eucharist;
Krejci wanted to know under what authority the order came from the
chancery. Krejci wrote, "As you know I am uncomfortable putting you
in this position, but you have a responsibility to your conscience, your
priesthood, and to me as a layperson as well as to your bishop." Fr. David
Hintz at St. Patrick's Church subsequently denied Krejci communion and
also received a letter requesting information regarding who ordered the
denial.[120] Krejci again communicated himself.

The Lincoln diocese released a statement on March 3, 2005:

There is no evidence that an appeal from Mr. Krejci or his colleagues who have also abandoned the Catholic Church in order to belong to a sect entitled Call-to-Action is pending in Rome. It is the understanding of the Diocese of Lincoln that an appeal by Call-to-Action was dismissed because it erroneously tried to apply Canon 1353 to appeal a particular law rather than an administrative decree or judicial decision. The Diocese of Lincoln has been informed by the Holy See that every recourse regarding pertinent diocesan legislation has been rejected and the Holy See is supportive of the legislation. The particular law is valid and in effect.[121]

Further, the statement addressed whether or not a priest could deny communion to a person who was excommunicated *ipso facto*. The statement claimed that the priest would give "the benefit of the doubt to the person and presume they have repented" unless the person acts in such a public way as to be considered "notorious" in which case, "the presumption of repentance can no longer be held." Presumably, the bishop used this exception to justify denying John Krejci the Eucharist.[122]

On March 22, 2005, John Krejci had not received a response to any of his three letters. He wrote another letter to Bishop Bruskewitz including a copy of the letter he had sent to Bishop Bruskewitz on February 7, 2005 as well as copies of the letters he sent to Fr. Walsh and Fr. Hintz.[123] Krejci noted in his letter that he had received no response from Bishop Bruskewitz "except what I have read in the secular media." He once again asked Bishop Bruskewitz for a justification for his action in denying him Eucharist. He concluded his letter, "I am a patient but resolute person and do not intend to allow you to persecute me or any Call to Action member without exercising the judicial rights granted us in Church law."[124]

According to an article published in the *Omaha World Herald*, Lincoln diocesan spokesperson, Rev. Mark Huber, stated that the appeal was rejected "some time ago."[125] According to Huber, while people can appeal a judicial sentence or an administrative decree, CTAN could not appeal a law.[126] No member of CTAN had received any written or verbal notice that such a decision had been made. Then-CTAN board president,

Patty Hawk, said, "The Vatican, by rule, should have to contact us... We're the ones who requested (the appeal)."[127] St. Joseph Foundation Canonist, Charles Wilson, remarked that CTAN probably "appealed to the wrong people. . . Their appeal should have gone to the Pontifical Council for the Interpretation of Legislative Texts, which has the authority to rule on the constitutionality of a law."[128]

Jim McShane wrote to Fr. Huber to request a copy of the communication from the Vatican indicating that the appeal was denied.[129] McShane explained that "without seeing the ruling we can accept neither its alleged contents nor the ban's selective enforcement against John Krejci, a lifelong Catholic, a daily communicant and a noted supporter of peace and justice." He continued, "Without a copy, we cannot be expected to accept its existence." In response, Fr. Huber wrote to Jim McShane and suggested that he write to the Prefect of the Congregation of Bishops, His Eminence Giovanni Cardinal Re, for more information.[130]

On behalf of the CTAN board, Jim McShane wrote back to Fr. Huber and noted that Fr. Huber's letter was a non-response as it included no documentation to prove that the Vatican had, in fact, rejected CTAN's appeal.[131] McShane noted that the lack of response "reinforces the belief that no such authoritative documentation exists." McShane further noted that CTAN members would continue to regard the appeal as pending and requested that priests in the diocese be instructed to resume offering communion to John Krejci. Fr. Huber responded with a short letter once again suggesting that McShane write to Cardinal Re for more information.[132] Members of Call To Action Nebraska did not believe an official ruling had been made on the appeal and thought that if we wrote, we might "provoke Rome into making a decision that it clearly did not want to make."[133]

Jim McShane wrote to Jim Coriden, a Canon lawyer who had advised CTAN in the days after the extra-synodal legislation was issued. McShane posed a number of questions, including whether or not an appeal like ours is allowed by Canon law. McShane asked if it is reasonable to assume, given the signed receipt, that the appeal was received. He also asked if a hearing should have been held before a decision was made on our appeal. If a decision had been made, why wasn't CTAN notified? If Bishop Bruskewitz had a report of a decision made on our appeal, how could CTAN get a copy of it?[134] Coriden responded that he was "mystified by the recent revelation of a response from Rome."[135]

In December 2006, as President of the Board of Call To Action Nebraska, I received a letter in the mail from Bishop Bruskewitz and a copy of a letter he received from Cardinal Battista Re. Cardinal Re's letter to Bishop Bruskewitz is dated November 24, 2006. Copies were also sent to Jim McShane and John Krejci.[136] Cardinal Re wrote:

> You can explain to Mr. McShane that the Holy See considers that Your Excellency's ruling in the case of "Call to action Nebraska" was properly taken within your competence as Pastor of that diocese. The judgment of the Holy See is that the activities of "Call to Action" in the course of these years are in contrast with the Catholic Faith due to views and positions held which are unacceptable from a doctrinal and disciplinary standpoint. Thus to be a member of this Association or to support it, is irreconcilable with a coherent living of the Catholic Faith.[137]

In his accompanying letter, Bishop Bruskewitz asked the members of Call To Action Nebraska be informed of the steps necessary for absolution from the ecclesiastical censures.[138] After reading Re's letter, James Coriden, Professor of Church Law at Washington Theological Union, said that the Congregation for Bishops may have simply ruled that Bishop Bruskewitz possessed the authority to issue the extra-synodal legislation.[139] Coriden explained that "the language 'in contrast with the Catholic faith,' is a mild form of censure, and may not be a ruling on the substance of the excommunication."[140]

No member of CTAN wrote to Cardinal Re to ask for further information on our appeal. However, we learned from Cardinal Re's letter to Bishop Bruskewitz that Bishop Bruskewitz had forwarded to Cardinal Re one of Jim McShane's letters asking Bishop Bruskewitz for documentary proof that a decision had been made. Bishop Bruskewtiz claimed this letter was a further appeal.[141] We know this because Cardinal Re wrote:

> I have received your [Bishop Bruskewitz's] recent letters and the enclosed
> documentation concerning the association "Call to Action Nebraska."
> I read in particular the letter dated February 19, 2006, by which Mr.
> John [sic] McShane, on behalf of "Call to Action Nebraska", is asking
> for authoritative judgment of the Holy See about Your Excellency's sen-
> tence on the same association.[142]

The letter to Bishop Bruskewitz was a request that the Lincoln diocese provide documentary proof that a decision had been made on our
case; it was never intended to be another appeal. It is to this letter as well
as information provided by Bishop Bruskewitz about Call To Action that
Cardinal Re responded. This opened the appeal "in the Bishop's own
terms"[143] which means Bishop Bruskewitz could provide inaccurate information about Call To Action Nebraska. We know that he was operating
under such misinformation. For example, the *Southern Nebraska Register*
published that while Roman Catholics' statement of faith is the Nicene
Creed, Call To Action's statement of faith is "undefined."[144] This is not
true. Call To Action does not deny the Nicene Creed. Bishop Bruskewitz
claims members of CTA are not Catholics; CTA members make no such
claim. There is no indication that Cardinal Re ever saw or read the appeal
submitted by Call To Action Nebraska.[145]

CTAN board member, Gordon Peterson, and I, then-President
of Call To Action Nebraska, signed a letter of appeal that we sent to
Cardinal Mario F. Pompedda, Prefect, Supreme Tribunal of the Apostolic
Signatura.[146] We based this appeal on four grounds. First, Cardinal Re
exceeded his authority as "the Congregation for Bishops does not have
jurisdiction to make doctrinal and disciplinary judgments or decisions
regarding organizations of the Christian faithful."[147] Second, as a hearing
was never held and the Catholics who filed the appeal were never able to
offer evidence, CTAN members have been "deprived of due process of
law." Third, Bishop Bruskewitz's legislation slanders members of CTAN.
These members' reputations as Catholics have been damaged. Fourth,
CTAN members have taken no position contrary to Catholic doctrine.
We asked for an investigation and a hearing on these matters.

Our appeal was declined on the basis that the Supreme Tribunal of the Apostolic Signatura "has no competence in this matter"[148] because it involves a diocesan law and not an individual administrative act. As I explained to a reporter for the *Lincoln Journal Star*, "It does not seem to be a rejection of the appeal. It seems to be saying that this is not the proper avenue, so we need to find the proper avenue to state our case."[149] Canon Lawyer Thomas Doyle pointed out that this response indicates that CTAN had asked the wrong question all along.[150] Therefore, even after acting on the advice of canon lawyers and bishops, "it seems clear there never has been a proper appeal on the basic issue which is the validity of the law itself."[151]

Doyle addressed the diocesan press statement regarding this matter and the quote, "There is no evidence that an appeal from Mr. Krejci or his colleagues who have also abandoned the Catholic Faith in order to belong to a sect entitled 'Call To Action' is pending in Rome":

> This is a patently false and slanderous statement. Neither the bishop nor any official of the diocese has the authority to assert that John Krejci or any other members of Call To Action have abandoned the Catholic Church because of their membership in CTA. The statement refers to the organization as a "sect," a judgment which is also erroneous and reflective of a personal opinion but not objective fact. Call To Action has never held itself out to be a sect, denomination, cult or anything more than a group of people attempting to follow the teachings and spirit of Vatican Council II.[152]

Members of the Call To Action Nebraska board met with three staff members from Call To Action USA to discuss our options. The minutes of that meeting[153] indicate that a Canon lawyer told CTAN board member, Gordon Peterson, that Cardinal Re's letter was a personal letter and not an administrative decision, therefore the appeal filed in 1998 is still "lodged" with the Congregation of Bishops. Canon Lawyer Thomas Doyle also informed CTAN that Cardinal Re's letter was a personal opinion set down in a letter to Bishop Bruskewitz.[154] Doyle explained that if Cardinal Re expressed an official position of the Holy See, that position "would require an official document with the proper signatures and form and that is totally lacking in this letter."[155] Further, Doyle points out that the Congregation for Bishops does not have competence to judge whether an organization is doctrinally orthodox; that job belongs to the Congregation for the Doctrine of the Faith.[156]

After years of waiting for a response to the appeal and confronting the politics of the Vatican, meeting attendees considered whether Lincoln CTAN members had any chance of winning an appeal to the Vatican.[157] CTA-USA's Dan Daley expressed the belief that because there appear to be no checks and balances, a bishop can do "what he wants."[158] CTAN board members expressed the desire to gather more information before making a final decision on whether or not to continue the appeal.[159]

In an article for the CTAN newsletter, *Voices of Nebraska Catholics*, Jim McShane concluded, "It is awful to live one's spiritual life in an arena of tidy, and often impenetrable, even misrepresented technicalities. But since we seem to live in such a world, we had best learn how to master its byways lest we be run over by those who would abuse them."[160]

After thought and conversation, members of the Call To Action Nebraska board decided to request the advice of an advocate in Rome. At their meeting on March 27, 2007, the board decided to send the advocate the history of our situation along with a question of whether he would be willing to represent us. This request would be sent jointly from CTAN and CTA-USA. Gordon Peterson and James McShane sent such a request to Mr. Carlo Gullo of Rome.[161]

Mr. Gullo responded to our request for information in Italian. Jim McShane expressed his concern about our translation's accuracy on the fine points. What we could gather from the response is that we should appeal to the Congregation for the Doctrine of the Faith and not the Congregation for Legislative Texts.[162] Mr. Gullo explained that he does not hold expertise in the area of theology and, therefore, would not be an appropriate advocate for us.

Conclusion of the Appeal Process

At the May 7, 2008 board meeting of Call To Action Nebraska, CTAN board members decided to stop our formal appeal process. Gordon Peterson wrote about the long journey of the CTAN appeal and explained our rationale in *Voices,* the CTAN newsletter.[163] In the twelve years since Bishop Bruskewitz issued the extra-synodal legislation, CTAN was advised by highly competent canon lawyers and bishops to appeal to no less than four congregations: the Apostolic Signatura, the Congregation for Bishops, the Pontifical Council for the Interpretation of Legislative Texts and the Congregation for the Doctrine of the Faith. Those experts had to rely on canon law which lacks clarity for a situation like ours. Peterson explained that the process has been like "playing a deceptive 'shell game' with a pro who will never allow you to win.'" Peterson further pointed out that "no hearing was ever held, we were never consulted, no investigation or trial was scheduled, we were not even engaged in conversation with any Vatican official." Peterson explained that our decision is a reflection of our realism, though we still do not consider the excommunication to be valid. He concluded, "Justice can be a long-term process (we have been at it for 12 years now), and justice is something we will always seek. We will pursue it, and not just for ourselves, but for others frustrated by this system. Justice in the Church is something all of us deserve.[164]

On January 2, 1997,[165] Fr. Tissa Balasuriya was excommunicated for "deviating from central truths of the Roman Catholic Church."[166] Fr. Balasuriya was asked to sign a profession of faith that stated opposition to the ordination of women. Fr. Balasuriya maintained that his work was misinterpreted. Balasuriya claimed that being asked to sign a specially prepared profession of faith is "punitive and presumes my error." [167] Instead, he signed a profession of faith written by Pope Paul VI.

In response to the treatment of Fr. Tissa Balasuriya, which must have hit close to home, Jim McShane signed letters for the board of CTAN to the three Nebraska Bishops, the Congregation for the Defense of the Faith and the Oblates of Mary, Balasuriya's order. In the letter, McShane expressed anguish over the treatment of Fr. Balasuriya.

Msgr. Timothy Thorburn, Chancellor of the Lincoln Diocese, sent a letter to Msgr. Michael Jackels at the Congregation for the Doctrine of the Faith and a copy of the letter to Jim McShane.[168] Msgr. Thorburn's letter responded to the letter sent by the board of Call To Action Nebraska. In his letter, Msgr. Thorburn called members of CTAN "a small sect" who "at one time identified themselves as Catholics but who no longer believe in the teachings of the Catholic Church" and he called the group "wicked." Msgr. Thorburn expressed gratitude that Tissa Balasuriya was excommunicated and declared that "the process used to judge his heretical teachings, as well as that which imposed the appropriate penalty. . . was extremely fair and just."

One year after it was imposed and three days after the date of Msgr. Thorburn's letter to the Congregation for the Doctrine of the Faith, the Vatican lifted the excommunication of Fr. Tissa Balasuriya. The excommunication was lifted after days of negotiations between ten oblate priests[169] and the Congregation for the Doctrine of the Faith.[170] Balasuriya did not "retract his theological views" or sign the profession of faith written for him. Instead, Balasuriya "acknowledged 'perceptions of error.'"[171] Censured theologian, Charles Curran, found the reversal of the excommunication to be "very significant."[172] He continued, "To my knowledge, this is the first time they [Church officials] have backed away from anything so quickly and publically. . . The whole thing was so patently unjust and offensive they must have realized they made a mistake."[173]

An anonymous person sent CTAN a printout of a Catholic World News story[174] published on January 16, 1998 about the lifting of Fr. Balasuriya's excommunication. The short news brief glossed over a great many details of the story and, in fact, gave the impression that Fr. Balasuriya admitted to error. The title of the news brief was "Excommunicated Priest Returns to Church after Repentance." Someone underlined the word "Repentance" in the title two times in blue and handwrote under it, "It would be good if CTAN would follow Fr. Balasuriya's example."

If church structure offered CTAN the same means to negotiate with the Vatican, the fate of CTAN might have, indeed, followed Fr. Balasuriya's example.

Notes Chapter 7

1. Jim McShane, interview with the author.

2. Jim McShane, letter to Msgr. Timothy Thorburn, March 22, 1996.

3. Jim McShane, letter to Msgr. Thorburn, March 28, 1996.

4. Msgr. Timothy Thorburn, letter to Jim McShane, April 1, 1996. The Canons listed: 208, 209, 210, 212, 221, 223, 375, 381, 383, 386, 391, 392, 749, 752, 753, 754, 1313, 1314, 1315, 1316, 1317, 1318, 1319, 1320, 1369, 1373, 1374, 1375, 1399.

5. Jim McShane, "Memo to Lincoln Diocese Catholics claiming membership in Call To Action Nebraska," April 3, 1996.

6. Ibid.

7. Letter to Bishop Bruskewitz signed by 16 members of Call To Action Nebraska, April 4, 1996.

8. Jerry Filteau, "Nebraska Catholics Appeal Bishop's Order of Interdict," *Catholic Key,* April 18, 1996.

9. Canon 1734, Code of Canon Law, http://www.vatican.va/archive/ENG1104/__ P6Y.HTM.

10. Jerry Filteau, "Nebraska Catholics Appeal…"

11. Letter to Bishop Bruskewitz signed by 16 members of Call To Action Nebraska, April 4, 1996.

12. Jim McShane, letter to Archbishop Elden F. Curtiss of Omaha, Bishop Lawrence McNamara of Grand Island, Cardinal Joseph Bernardin of Chicago, Cardinal Bernard Law of Boston, Cardinal John J. O'Connor of New York, and Rev. Augostino Cacciavillan, Apostolic Nuncio to the United States, April 9, 1996.

13. Sr. Mary Brian Costello, letter to Jim McShane, April 16, 1996.

14. Bishop Anthony M. Pilla, letter to James McShane, April 16, 1996.

15. Jim McShane, written recollections of his meeting with Bishop Fabian Bruskewitz on April 11, 1996.

16. Jerry Filteau, "Nebraska Catholics Appeal…"

17. Ibid.

18. Jim McShane, letter to Bishop Fabian Bruskewitz, April 17, 1996.

19. Ibid.

20. Paul Likoudis, "An Interview with Bishop Fabian Bruskewitz," *Wanderer,* April 18, 1996, http://www.ewtn.com/library/ISSUES/BRUSKEWI.TXT.

21. Jim McShane, letter to Bishop Fabian Bruskewitz, April 17, 1996.

22. Bob Reeves, "Catholics in Forbidden Groups Vow to Keep Attending Church," *Lincoln Journal Star*, April 20, 1996.

23. Jim McShane, email to Mel Beckman, April 23, 1996.

24. Jim McShane, note to CTAN Executive Committee, April 23, 1996.

25. Bishop Fabian Bruskewitz, letter to James McShane, April 24, 1996.

26. For full text of *Veritatis Splendor* see http://www.vatican.va/holy_father/john_paul_ii/encyclicals/documents/hf_jp-ii_enc_06081993_veritatis-splendor_en.html .

27. For a full text of *Lumen Gentium* see http://www.vatican.va/archive/hist_councils/ii_vatican_council/documents/vat-ii_const_19641121_lumen-gentium_en.html.

28. Canon 1369: "A person who in a public show or speech, in published writing, or in other uses of instruments of social communication utters blasphemy, gravely injures good morals, expresses insults, or excites hatred or contempt against religion or the Church is to be punished with a just penalty." Available http://www.vatican.va/archive/ENG1104/__P52.HTM .

29. Julia McCord, "Catholics Seeking Change Start Chapter," *Omaha World Herald*, March 16, 1996.

30. Jim McShane, letter to Bishop Fabian Bruskewitz, May 8, 1996.

31. Bishop Bruskewitz, letter to Jim McShane, May 9, 1996.

32. John Krejci, letter to Bishop Bruskewitz, August 21, 1996.

33. Bishop Fabian Bruskewitz, letter to John Krejci, August 26, 1996.

34. "Bishop Bruskewitz Denies Appeal from Call To Action Nebraska," *Southern Nebraska Register*, May 3, 1996.

35. Bob Reeves, "Excommunication Date Looms for Local Roman Catholics: Call to Action Affiliates Ponder Ways to Appeal Bishop's Action," *Lincoln Journal Star*, May 13, 1996.

36. "Processes available to Call to Action Nebraska in response to the Imposition of Interdict and Excommunication," May 1996.

37. Bob Reeves, "Dissidents Ask for Review of Decision," *Lincoln Journal Star*, May 17, 1996.

38. Bob Reeves, "Excommunication date looms…"

39. Ibid.

40. Ibid.

41. Msgr. Timothy Thorburn, letter to John Krejci, May 14, 1996.

42. CTAN Statement for Media, May 15, 1996.

43. "Lincoln Bishop Expects Pope Would Back Him: Deadline Passes for Catholics to End Membership in Organizations that are 'Opposed to Catholic Faith,'" *Superior Catholic Herald*, May 23, 1996.

44. CTAN press release, May 16, 1996.

45. Ibid.

46. Ibid.

47. Ibid.

48. Ibid.

49. Ibid.

50. Bob Reeves, "Dissidents ask for review of decision," *Lincoln Journal Star*, May 17, 1996.

51. Letter from Lincoln CTAN members to Msgr. Timothy Thorburn, June 3, 1996.

52. Msgr. Timothy Thorburn, letter to Jim McShane, et. al., July 16, 1996.

53. Lincoln CTAN members, letter to Msgr. Robert Vasa, July 8, 1996.

54. Fr. Daniel J. Seiker, letter to Jim McShane, July 16, 1996.

55. Bob Reeves, "Tribunal Won't Take On Excommunication," *Lincoln Journal Star*, August 3, 1996.

56. Letter from CTAN Lincoln diocesan members to the priests of the Lincoln Diocese, October 24, 1996.

57. Letter from CTAN Lincoln diocesan members to the bishops, archbishops and cardinals of the National Conference of Catholic Bishops, October 25, 1996. CTAN sent in total around 300 letters to the United States bishops, Lincoln diocesan priests and lay leaders from the Lincoln Diocese. CTAN received seven responses. Two bishops expressed their belief that the matter should be handled either locally or in Rome. Two other bishops wrote to ensure CTAN of their prayers. One Lincoln diocesan priest asked to be removed from the CTAN mailing list and another wrote to express his belief that the Bishop was in the right. A third priest wrote a personal letter to a CTAN member.

58. Material sent from CTAN Lincoln diocesan members to the bishops, archbishops, and cardinals of the National Conference of Catholic Bishops, October 25, 1996.

59. Ibid.

60. Ibid.

61. Ibid.

62. Ibid.

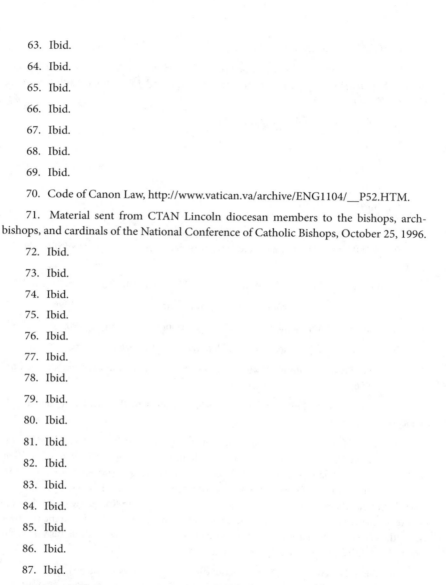

63. Ibid.

64. Ibid.

65. Ibid.

66. Ibid.

67. Ibid.

68. Ibid.

69. Ibid.

70. Code of Canon Law, http://www.vatican.va/archive/ENG1104/__P52.HTM.

71. Material sent from CTAN Lincoln diocesan members to the bishops, archbishops, and cardinals of the National Conference of Catholic Bishops, October 25, 1996.

72. Ibid.

73. Ibid.

74. Ibid.

75. Ibid.

76. Ibid.

77. Ibid.

78. Ibid.

79. Ibid.

80. Ibid.

81. Ibid.

82. Ibid.

83. Ibid.

84. Ibid.

85. Ibid.

86. Ibid.

87. Ibid.

88. Cecilia Daly and Elizabeth Peterson, letter to Archbishop Eldon Curtiss, November 7, 1997.

89. Cecilia Daly and Elizabeth Peterson, letter to Archbishop Elden Curtiss, March 12, 1998.

90. Archbishop Elden Curtiss, letter to Elizabeth Peterson and Cecilia Daly, March 21, 1998.

91. Cecilia Daly and Elizabeth Peterson, letter to Archbishop Elden Curtiss, undated.

92. Archbiship Rembert G. Weakland, letter to Jim McShane, December 30, 1997.

93. Letter from J. A. McShane and sixteen other Lincoln diocesan Catholics to Archbishop Zenon Grocholewski of the Supreme Tribunal of the Apostolic Signatura, January 28, 1998.

94. Letter from Jim McShane and seventeen other Lincoln Diocesan members of Call To Action Nebraska to Most Reverend Bernardin, Cardinal Gantin, April 13, 1998.

95. Ibid.

96. Ibid.

97. Code of Canon Law, http://www.vatican.va/archive/ENG1104/__P3.HTM.

98. Code of Canon Law, http://www.vatican.va/archive/ENG1104/__PU.HTM.

99. Code of Canon Law, http://www.vatican.va/archive/ENG1104/__P1D.HTM.

100. Code of Canon Law, http://www.vatican.va/archive/ENG1104/__P1E.HTM.

101. Code of Canon Law, http://www.vatican.va/archive/ENG1104/__P4V.HTM.

102. Jim McShane and seventeen other Lincoln Diocesan members of Call To Action Nebraska to Cardinal Gantin.

103. Code of Canon Law, http://www.vatican.va/archive/ENG1104/__P50.HTM.

104. Jim McShane, letter to Cardinal Lucas Moreira Neves, January 21, 1999.

105. "Third Anniversary," *Southern Nebraska Register*, March 19, 1999.

106. Bishop Fabian Bruskewitz, letter to Jim McShane, April 24, 2000.

107. Draft letter from Jim McShane to Bishop Bruskewitz, April 26, 2000.

108. Betty Peterson, interview with the author.

109. Bob Reeves, "Diocese Says No to Catholic Burials for Group," *Lincoln Journal Star*, April 29, 2000.

110. Ibid.

111. Bishop Fabian Bruskewitz, letter to Jim McShane, May 9, 2000.

112. Tom Heinen, "Opening Regional Milwaukee Wanderer Forum, Bishop Stresses Historical Significance of Pope," *Milwaukee Journal Sentinel*, November 6, 1999.

113. Ibid.

114. Ask The Register Column, *Southern Nebraska Register*, February 18, 2000.

115. John Krejci, "Opinion: Lincoln bishop denies Eucharist to CTAN member," *Voices of Nebraska Catholics*, March 2005.

116. Ibid.

117. John Krejci, letter to Bishop Bruskewitz, February 7, 2005.

118. Email communication from John Krejci to Patty Hawk and subsequently forwarded to members of CTAN on February 21, 2005.

119. John Krejci, letter to Fr. Tom Walsh, February 22, 2005.

120. John Krejci, letter to Fr. Hintz, March 1, 2005.

121. Faxed, "Statement of the Diocese of Lincoln," March 3, 2005.

122. "Editor's Note," *Voices of Nebraska Catholics*, March 2005.

123. John Krejci, letter to Bishop Fabian Bruskewitz, March 22, 2005.

124. Despite being denied the Eucharist, John Krejci continues to attend Mass between four and five times a week. He has been told that his picture is in at least one sacristy in the diocese, presumably so the priest and acolytes would know to refuse communion to him. John Krejci received a letter from Rocky C. Weber, a lawyer representing Bishop Bruskewitz dated December 6, 2011. Mr. Weber referred to an incident in which Krejci took the Eucharist from a ciborium held by an acolyte and informed Krejci that he is "henceforth forbidden to enter any Catholic Church, Chapel or the worship space of any other property of the Catholic Church or related entities in the Diocese of Lincoln. This includes any pubic or private function, celebration of a wedding, funeral or any other ceremony or event. If you are recognized on Catholic Church property, my Client will contract law enforcement and bring charges of trespass. If you should again take, without permission, the Most Blessed Sacrament law enforcement will be informed that a theft has occurred."

125. Angie Brunkow, "Vatican Has Turned Down Excommunication Appeal," *Omaha World Herald,* March 5, 2005.

126. "Diocese: Vatican Rejects Appeal of Blanket Excommunications," *Sioux City Journal*, March 5, 2005, http://www.votfbpt.org/Diocese_-_Vatican_rejects_appeal.pdf, accessed April 13, 2011.

127. Angie Brunkow, "Vatican Has Turned Down..."

128. Tim Drake, "Vatican Upholds Excommunications," *Catholic Exchange,* August 1, 2005, online, accessed November 3, 2005.

129. Jim McShane, letter to Rev. Mark Huber, September 19, 2005.

130. Fr. Mark Huber, letter to Jim McShane, November 9, 2005.

131. Jim McShane for the CTAN Board, letter to Rev. Mark Huber, February 19, 2006.

132. Fr. Mark Huber, letter to Jim McShane, March 13, 2006.

133. Jim McShane, "From the Lincoln Diocese: Where Does the Excommunication

Now Stand?" *Voices of Nebraska Catholics*, Spring 2007/, http://www.calltoactionnebraska. org/voices0905/frmseguevoices0905.html.

134. Notes found in CTAN archives. Dated "prior to 8 Dec 2006."

135. Text of a note from Jim Coriden to Jim McShane, undated.

136. Tom Carney, "Vatican Upholds Excommunication." *National Catholic Reporter*, December 22, 2006.

137. Cardinal Battista Re, letter to Bishop Fabian Bruskewitz, November 24, 2006.

138. Bishop Fabian Bruskewitz, letter to Rachel Pokora, December 8, 2006.

139. Tom Carney, "Vatican Upholds Excommunication."

140. Ibid.

141. Jim McShane, "From the Lincoln Diocese: Where Does the Excommunication Now Stand?" *Voices of Nebraska Catholics*, Spring 2007, http://www.calltoactionnebraska. org/voices0905/frmseguevoices0905.html. Accessed April 15, 2011.

142. Cardinal Battista Re, letter to Bishop Bruskewitz, November 24, 2006.

143. Jim McShane, "From the Lincoln Diocese: Where Does the Excommunication…"

144. S. L. Hansen, "The Differences at a Glance," *Southern Nebraska Register*, December 8, 2006.

145. Jim McShane, "From the Lincoln Diocese: Where Does the Excommunication…"

146. Rachel Pokora and Gordon Peterson, letter to Cardinal Mario Pompedda, Prefect, Supreme Tribunal of the Apostolic Signatura, December 21, 2006.

147. Ibid.

148. Velasio DePaolis, C.S., Secretary, Supremum Signaturae Apostolicae Tribunal, letter to Rachel Pokora and Gordon Peterson, January 26, 2007.

149. Bob Reeves, "Vatican Tribunal Won't Hear Excommunication Appeal," *Lincoln Journal Star*, February 21, 2007.

150. Thomas P. Doyle, "The Excommunication of the Members of Call To Action in Lincoln, Nebraska: Some Canonical Considerations," March 7, 2007.

151. Ibid.

152. Ibid.

153. Meeting minutes, February 22, 2007.

154. Thomas P. Doyle, "The Excommunication of the Members…"

155. Ibid.

156. Ibid.

157. Meeting minutes, February 22, 2007.

158. Ibid.

159. Ibid.

160. Jim McShane, "From the Lincoln Diocese: Where Does the Excommunication…"

161. Gordon Peterson and James McShane, letter and packet of information to Carlo Gullo, November 27, 2007.

162. Translation of a letter from Carlo Gullo to Gordon Peterson and James McShane, no date noted on translation.

163. Gordon Peterson, "Appeal: Shell Games," *Voices of Nebraska Catholics,* Fall, 2008 http://www.calltoactionnebraska.org/voices0909/frmseguevoices0909.html.

164. Ibid.

165. Pamela   Schaeffer,   "Vatican   Excommunicates   Balasuriya,"   *National Catholic   Reporter,*   January,   17,   1997,   http://natcath.org/NCR_Online/ archives2/1997a/011797/011797c.htm.

166. Pamela Schaeffer, "Balasuriya, Supporters Appeal to Tribunal," *National Catholic Reporter,* http://natcath.org/NCR_Online/archives2/1997a/021497/021497f.htm.

167. Pamela Schaeffer, "Balasuriya, Supporters Appeal to Tribunal."

168. Msgr. Timothy Thorburn, letter to Rev. Msgr. Michael O. Jackels, January 12, 1998.

169. "Slam Dunk Brings Balasuriya in from the Cold," *National Catholic Reporter,* February 20, 1998, http://natcath.org/NCR_Online/archives2/1998a/022098/022098g. htm.

170. Tom Roberts, "From the Editor's Desk: A Conclave Evening with Tissa," *National   Catholic   Reporter,*   April   29,   2005,   http://natcath.org/NCR_Online/ archives2/2005b/042905/042905b.htm.

171. Pamela Schaeffer, "Condemned Priest is Restored to Church," *National Catholic Reporter,* January 30, 1998. http://natcath.org/NCR_Online/archives2/1998a/013098/ bala1.htm.

172. Pamela Schaeffer, "Condemned Priest is Restored…"

173. Pamela Schaeffer, "Condemned Priest is Restored…"

174. "Excommunicated Priest Returns to Church After Repentance," *CatholicCulture. org,* January 16, 1998, http://www.catholicculture.org/news/features/index.cfm?recnum= 6721&repos=4&subrepos=1&searchid=730716.

CHAPTER 8

The Exercise of Power

But Jesus called them to him and said, "You know that the rulers of the
Gentiles lord it over them, and their great ones are tyrants over them.
It will not be so among you; but whoever wishes to be great among you
must be your servant." —Matthew 20:25–26 (NRSV)

IN THE SPRING OF 2008, I learned that a radio program to which I listened regularly, *Speaking of Faith*, was seeking the faith stories of Roman
Catholics. I went to their website and typed a short essay. Not long after,
I was contacted by a producer for the show and interviewed via phone.
Speaking of Faith aired the program called "The Beauty and Challenge
of Being Catholic: Hearing the Faithful" on May 1, 2008. [1] The program
featured a variety of Catholic voices, including mine. On the program I
said, "So I guess when I approach the communion altar here in Lincoln,
I'm almost always afraid that this is the week that they're going to turn me
away, and that's a very strange place to be in when you are about to receive
the Eucharist."

That week did come, but the refusal did not happen in the communion line. I received a handwritten letter from Fr. Lyle Johnson, the pastor
of the church I had been a member of for over ten years. The letter was
dated October 13, 2009. The text read: "Rachel, I write to inform you that
due to your involvement with Call to Action, I've removed your name
from our parish list. I would appreciate a chance to visit with you and

hear you on this. I'd ask your prayerful consideration of calling me some time—as I'm prayerful about it, too."[2] I cannot say I was blindsided by this news. I had been quoted heavily in the media and I also had recently had my picture taken for the parish directory.

I called Fr. Johnson and we met in his office. At that meeting I learned that not only was I removed from membership, Fr. Johnson had been instructed to deny me communion. I was not surprised to hear this information, though I could not have guessed how terrible it would be to hear those words spoken.

During this difficult time, I turned to my CTAN friends. Members of Call To Action Nebraska provide a community for each other. Through the difficulties, we have established a sense of identity and purpose. This has been particularly important, and perhaps easier, in Lincoln where CTAN members were unable to find fellowship in their parishes.

Business as usual for CTAN generally involves some sort of spring gathering and a picnic each fall. The group often meets weekly during Advent and Lent for prayer and discussion. CTAN members have also met to discuss a common book or to pray together in someone's home. Many of the small group gatherings happen in Lincoln, probably because the need for community is greater. The group publishes a newsletter, *Voices of Nebraska Catholics*. A handful of Lincoln Call To Action members regularly travel to the Omaha diocese on Saturday evenings for Mass and dinner together.

Amidst the business as usual, Call To Action Nebraska often finds itself speaking out on an important topic, supporting one another through a difficulty or, unfortunately, reacting to an abuse of power or misinformation spread about the group or those associated with CTAN in some way. In this chapter I detail some of these topics and events.

Nurturing Fear About Call To Action

Human Life International published a full-page advertisement in the *Southern Nebraska Register* for the booklet *Call to Action or Call to Apostasy* by Brian Clowes.[3] The advertisement prominently displayed a favorable review of the booklet written by Bishop Fabian Bruskewitz. The text of the advertisement, which appears like a newspaper story, suggests that Call To Action is responsible for the fact that so many United States Catholics have "lost their faith." The ad uses fear to promote the book by claiming that United States dioceses will disappear: "That's why opposing and defeating the dissenters is so urgent." In fact, "the Catholic Church in America has become almost completely unraveled." In the ad, Call To Action members are portrayed as "dummies" with Satan pulling their strings.

Jim McShane wrote a response to "Call to Action or Call to Apostasy" for the CTAN newsletter. In his response, McShane noted that "Clowes would have his readers simply accept that CTA and all its members in all their acts are liars, agents of the devil, who are striving to desolate the church, to shred its teachings, to shatter its structures, to undermine the sacrifice of the Mass, to replace the sacraments with mere symbolic ritual, etc."[4] According to McShane, Clowes understands dialogue to be "an effort to legitimize sin and lies."[5]

Jim McShane noted that in his book Brian Clowes does not quote one person who spoke for Call To Action. Instead, he quotes people who have spoken at CTA conferences. "He then attributes to them the worst possible interpretations he can force onto their words, and then asserts that the worst sense is the intent of all members of CTA, all dissenters, all liberals."[6] McShane notes that Clowes' book is propaganda.

Attacks on Women Speakers

Over the years, CTAN has invited a variety of speakers to address us. The Lincoln diocese, using its diocesan paper, issued vicious attacks on many of them.

Patty Crowley

Patty Crowley was scheduled to speak at the CTAN conference in May 1997 but had to cancel her appearance due to a family funeral. Instead, she met with CTAN members in October of that year and talked with them about her experience on the Papal Birth Control Commission.

Patty and her husband, Pat Crowley, founded the Christian Family Movement. They had four birth children, an adopted child and a number of foster children. Even in her 80s, Patty Crowley remained an active and engaged Catholic. She served as a lector and Eucharistic Minister at her parish. She and her daughter traveled to the local federal corrections center every week to visit incarcerated women. She helped found a women's shelter called Deborah's Place where she continued to volunteer. She was also involved in works that helped the elderly. Crowley developed a program for volunteers who cleaned elderly people's apartments and she served on the board of HOME, Housing Opportunities and Maintenance for the Elderly.[7]

The Vatican invited Patty and Pat Crowley to serve as two of thirty-four lay representatives on the Papal Birth Control Commission that began meeting in 1963 and grew in numbers through 1965 when it reached fifty-eight members.[8] The commission, created by Pope John XXIII, met for a total of four years. The result of the commission's work was a "majority report" that recommended the church no longer forbid contraception.[9] However, a few Vatican conservatives urged Pope Paul VI not to change the church's policy on birth control. In 1968, Pope Paul VI issued his encyclical *Humanae Vitae* which forbade all birth control except the rhythm method. Crowley and her husband were "devastated." She continued, "My husband said he couldn't believe it."[10]

In an unsigned "Ask the Register" column of the *Southern Nebraska Register*, a Lincoln diocesan priest referred to Patty Crowley as a "very old degenerate who roams about promoting sexual immorality."[11] The writer continued, "Nobody pays much attention to what she says, except perhaps some depraved members of the Call-to-Action sect. Her views deserve no consideration whatsoever." According to coverage in the *National Catholic Reporter*, Ms. Crowley's attorney, Algis Augustine, contacted the *Southern Nebraska Register* demanding an apology and the name of the author. Augustine claimed that the *SNR* had engaged in defamation against Ms. Crowley. Rocky C. Weber, an attorney who represented the

Southern Nebraska Register, explained that what was written was "clearly an opinion regarding the positions of a public figure."[12]

The *National Catholic Reporter* contacted the editor of the *Southern Nebraska Register*, Fr. Ken Boroviak. Fr. Boroviak refused to release the name of the person who wrote the column and he would not indicate whether or not he approved or disapproved of the comments regarding Ms. Crowley.[13] The *NCR* asked Fr. Borowiak if a "superior" read the column before it went to press. He replied, "No comment."[14]

In response to this attack on Ms. Crowley, Jim McShane wrote the following to the *Southern Nebraska Register* editor, Fr. Borowiak:

> Have you any evidence whatsoever to adduce to support this accusation? Of course not. Mrs. Crowley is a person of good standing, whose Christian Family Movement was the source of many graces to many families, parishes and communities. Her support for single parents and in particular for unwed mothers and their children would win her the title "degenerate" in no loving community in the world. Her reputation for propriety and goodness won her a place on a papal commission where in conscience she was bound to provide the best advice her intelligence and her conscience could muster. If the question she was asked were not open to the sort of answer she offered, it would have been mere hypocrisy on the part of Paul VI to ask her for it. Because the Pope eventually rejected her advice and that of the overwhelming majority of others on that commission does not make her or her peers degenerate for having offered it. Neither does she become degenerate for describing the process whereby the decision was made. Truth telling is rarely degenerate and it is unbecoming of men of the cloth to say otherwise. . . Such an attack on an elderly woman, hospitalized at the time with pneumonia, is so unkind as to be despicable. I understand that you may not have known her physical condition, but that is surely another example of the recklessness of the *Register's* remarks.[15]

After the personal attack against her was published in the *Southern Nebraska Register*, Patty Crowley received many letters of support. At one point she began to save them in a scrapbook.[16] Crowley began the scrapbook with a definition of "degenerate." Included in the scrapbook were letters from friends and strangers, lay people and priests and three letters from bishops, one was a copy of a letter a bishop sent to Bishop Bruskewitz that "chid[ed] him for his insensitivity."[17] One writer included a sarcastic response he received from someone in the Lincoln Chancery who wrote, "Your letter will get all the attention it deserves."[18] Another writer asked Bishop Bruskewitz to admit that he wrote the response in question.

Patty Crowley died in 2005 at the age of 92.

Sr. Joan Chittister

The Benedictine Mission House/Christ the King Priory and retreat center in Schuyler, Nebraska drew sharp criticism from the Lincoln diocese in spring 1999. Benedictine sister, Joan Chittister, was scheduled to give two presentations at the center. Sr. Chittister had served as President of the Leadership Conference of Women Religious and as the prioress of her religious order in Erie, Pennsylvania[19] and she is a vocal member of Call To Action. Though Schuyler is located in the Omaha diocese, Msgr. Thorburn told a reporter from the *National Catholic Reporter* that, "It was very disturbing that [Chittister] was speaking in an area very close to the diocese of Lincoln."[20] Msgr. Thorburn wrote to the monks: "I shall be obliged in conscience to do all that I can to discourage anyone from considering a religious vocation in your community, from frequenting the St. Benedict Center, to repent for my past speaking favorably about it and to do what I can to prevent the advertising of your facility in the diocese of Lincoln."[21] Msgr. Thorburn wasn't the only Lincoln priest to take umbrage with Sr. Chittister's talk in the Omaha diocese. Lincoln diocesan vocation director, Fr. Robert Mataya, disinvited a representative from the Schuyler monastery from participating in Vocation Education Day.[22]

Omaha Archbishop Curtiss requested that Sr. Chittister avoid both discussing the issue of women's ordination and making "aggressive arguments against the church."[23] Sr. Chittister said she planned to stick to a message that follows the "spirit of Jesus in the gospels. . . I see nothing in either lecture that violates that position, however. So, no, nothing [in my talk] has been changed."[24]

The international Benedictine community supported Sr. Chittister and the Schuyler community that invited her. Archabbott Wolf Notker, head of the congregation, told a reporter for the *National Catholic Reporter*, "I personally appreciate Sr. Joan Chittister. . . Of course, she may not have statements that please everybody in the church, but I think we should be open enough to listen to other opinions."[25] The spokesperson for the monks in Schuyler, Brother Tobias Dammert, said, "Sister Joan is Catholic as Catholic can be. But she is not afraid to say what needs to be said. Sometimes she is misunderstood."[26]

The diocese took another opportunity to attack Sr. Joan Chittister when it learned that she was to speak in Lincoln at a CTAN conference. This notice was published in the *Southern Nebraska Register* under the headline "Warning To All Catholics":

> The Call-to-Action sect is advertising an anti-Catholic rally in Lincoln in the coming week. It is said to feature a collection of fallen-away priests, who are bitter enemies of the Church, and a Pope-hating feminist. Some members of that sect masquerade as Catholics and, under that disguise, try to lure unsuspecting people away from the Catholic Faith. Catholics should beware of this and avoid that gathering.[27]

Those who would accept this warning are generally not people who would attend Call To Action events. Others did attend, however. Over 400 people, representing twenty-two states, attended the April 5-6, 2002 meeting.[28] Sr. Joan Chittister acted as a major draw for the conference. In a news conference after her speech, she responded to a question about her reaction to Bishop Bruskewitz calling her a "Pope-hating feminist." Chittister acknowledged Bishop Bruskewitz's right to his opinion but noted that the Gospel calls us to "love your neighbors and even your enemies."[29]

Rosemary Radford Ruether

In response to news that Garrett-Evangelical Theological Seminary Theology Professor, Rosemary Radford Ruether, was scheduled to speak at Nebraska Wesleyan University, the *Southern Nebraska Register* printed an unsigned opinion piece with the title, "She's Phony."[30] The *SNR* article claimed that Ruether is "no Catholic" and that "it approaches the absurd to call her squalid teachings 'theology.' Relying on the Ignatius Press book *Ungodly Rage* by Donna Steichen, the article claims that Ruether "seems very excited about feminine witchcraft." Ironically, the editorial ends by suggesting that Catholics should not turn to the secular media for accurate religious information though it printed the untruth that Nebraska Wesleyan had "condom distributing machines." According to the NWU student newspaper, there were rumors of protests at the lecture but the protests did not come to pass.[31] Administrators from the Lincoln Catholic high school, Pius X, wrote a letter to the NWU president expressing concern over what they perceived to be hostility to Catholicism with Reuther's lecture being one example.[32] Then-NWU President Jeanie Watson, did not reveal the other concerns listed in the letter. It is perhaps significant that at that time two NWU professors and one NWU adjunct instructor were active members of Call To Action Nebraska.

Another opinion article in the *Southern Nebraska Register* stated that Call To Action Nebraska "seems to have been involved in the appearance of Rosemary Radford Ruether at a local Protestant college, where she is reported to have attacked traditional family life."[33] Call To Action Nebraska had nothing to do with the invitation to Reuther to speak at Nebraska Wesleyan University. However, after Reuther agreed to speak in Lincoln, she did accept an invitation by CTAN to attend a meal and prayer service that evening in the home of two members of CTAN. The *SNR* article claims that the service was a Mass celebrated by a "priestess." In fact, the service was not a Mass and there was no priestess, rather a female CTAN member acted as prayer leader.[34] Further, Reuther did not attack "traditional family life." In her presentation, she pointed out that family life in Biblical times does not mirror the oft-cited "family values" of today.

Sr. Jeannine Gramick

Call To Action Nebraska's fourth annual spring conference featured Sr. Jeannine Gramick and James Biechler. Sr. Gramick is a co-founder of New Ways Ministry, an organization that ministers to lesbian, gay, bisexual and transgendered (LGBT) Catholics, which is based in Maryland. Sr. Gramick worked with the LGBT community from 1971 – 1999. In 1999, the Congregation for the Doctrine of the Faith forbade her from continuing this work. Bishop Bruskewitz wrote a letter to Sr. Gramick before her presentation stating that he had the authority to forbid her to speak in the Lincoln diocese and that he was using that authority to do so.[35] Sr. Gramick checked with canon lawyers who told her that Bishop Bruskewitz could not stop her from speaking. Sr. Gramick's censure involved "pastoral work involving homosexual persons."[36] Her presentation at the CTAN conference, entitled, "Conscience and Development of Doctrine: Whose Responsibility?" did not involve such pastoral work. Gramick noted that "I may still speak and write, even about homosexuality. It would be unfair to make the prohibition more stringent than it is (Canon 18)."[37] Gramick wrote back to Bishop Bruskewitz and asked to meet with him but Msgr. Thorburn said a meeting "would not be likely."[38]

After Sr. Jeannine Gramick's presentation at the Call To Action conference, the *Southern Nebraska Register* published an unsigned opinion piece that began: "In a failed attempt to infect decent people with their ideological pathologies, the anti-Catholic sect Call-to-Action has recently reached into a theological sewer and brought to Nebraska Sister Jeannine Gramick SSND, an apostle of perversion."[39] This opinion piece misleads the reader by claiming that Sr. Gramick has been "Condemned by the Holy See for her false and immoral doctrines." Sr. Gramick had been asked by the Congregation for the Doctrine of the Faith to stop her ministry because she would not reveal her personal beliefs about homosexual acts. The Vatican wanted Sr. Gramick and her co-minister Fr. Nugent to publically state that they supported the Church's position on homosexual acts.[40]

The *Southern Nebraska Register* opinion piece ended by calling into question the "mental processes" of Call To Action members and reflected, "Fortunately, no one of significance pays any attention to their raving, except perhaps their friends and supporters in the secular media."[41]

Of course, Call To Action Nebraska members had no recourse to correct the mistakes and misperceptions fostered by the *Southern Nebraska Register* article. Still, members of CTAN tried to respond. CTAN Board Chair, Patty Hawk, and CTAN Board member, Pat Sullivan, sent a letter to Omaha Archbishop Curtiss specifically addressing the April 14, 2000 opinion piece published in the *Southern Nebraska Register*.[42] Hawk and Sullivan took issue with the *SNR*'s characterization of CTAN as a sect. They also explained that having been present at the CTAN conference at which Sr. Gramick spoke they felt that to call her "'an apostle of sexual perversion' is unspeakably virulent and so far from the example of Christ that I cannot imagine such being stated in his name." Hawk and Sullivan note that the viciousness evident in the latest *Southern Nebraska Register* column caused them and other CTAN members to wonder why no one in the hierarchy had spoken out against it. They asked Archbishop Curtiss to correct "this false and unchristian teaching" so that "we may be seen, even in Lincoln, as a Church of justice and mutual love, not one of attempted character assassination by name-calling and false statements."

A subsequent *National Catholic Reporter* editorial describes Bishop Bruskewitz's response to the fact that Call To Action Nebraska did not disband after he issued his extra-synodal legislation as "an impotent rage and rampage nothing short of scandal."[43] Citing that the bishop is the publisher of *The Southern Nebraska Register*, the editorial states, "In the Catholic world the bishop is usually the publisher, and what appears is neither more nor less than what the publisher wishes." Quoting directly from editorials in the *Southern Nebraska Register* about Patty Crowley, Rosemary Radford Ruether and Sr. Jeannine Gramick, the *National Catholic Reporter* editorial noted "the sheer lack of civility and decency, not to mention charity, in the vitriol coming from the Lincoln chancery."[44]

CTAN Members Singled Out

Joan Johnson Denied Communion by Parish Priest

True to the promise made just after Bishop Bruskewitz promulgated his extra-synodal legislation, no CTAN members were denied communion for a time. This changed in September 1998. Call To Action Nebraska board member and daily communicant, Joan Johnson, received a letter from Rev. Jeremy Hazuka, a second-year priest at St. Joseph Church, Johnson's parish. Fr. Hazuka wrote that he saw Johnson in the picture of the board in the CTAN Newsletter. He told her, "Out of conscience I must inform you that you should not be receiving the Eucharist unless you leave Call to Action and have the excommunication lifted. I am the person distributing Holy Communion, and feel that I cannot, in good conscience, give Communion to a person who has left the fold of Christ."[45] Joan Johnson responded to Fr. Hazuka in a letter excerpted below:

> Thank you for your letter of concern. I am sorry that you have been drawn into this in only the second year of your priesthood. I do realize that you have made a pledge of obedience to the Bishop. I have not. You indicate that your decision to deny the Eucharist to me is based on conscience. Since you have never spoken to me personally, you probably don't realize that my decision to remain a member of CTA is also a matter of conscience. . . My faith goes to the very core of my being. It defines who I am, and at this point in my life, my faith is safeguarded by being a member of CTA. . . With CTA membership that includes bishops, priests, religious and many lay people who have devoted their lives to working for the Church, it seems to me there is an indication that there are things that need to be openly discussed. As a member of CTA, it is not expected that I subscribe with the same enthusiasm to every issue on the table. I am impressed with the way CTA treats everyone with respect and acts as a sounding board in a non-divisive way for issues facing the Church. There is a slogan that has recently

been promoted in this diocese. WWJD. I sincerely doubt that Jesus would deny the Eucharist to anyone who remains firmly convinced after months of prayer and reflection that they were following their conscience. I have made the decision to attend daily Mass as often as possible. Out of respect for your decision to follow your conscience, I will not approach the Eucharistic table when you are the celebrant. God will know that with a clear conscience and a heavy heart I desire to receive Him and will judge us both accordingly.[46]

One other incident occurred that gave Joan Johnson pause. A priest from the Milwaukee diocese who asked to be moved to the Lincoln diocese was temporarily assigned to Johnson's parish. Once during daily Mass with that priest, Joan Johnson was the last in line for communion. When she reached the front of the line, the priest told her he had run out of hosts. Johnson said, "That doesn't happen. A priest either breaks a host in two or goes to the tabernacle and gets more. He knew there was one more communicant. I don't think it was a coincidence he ran out of hosts. After that, I made sure I was not the last one in line."[47]

Mel Beckman and John Krejci Forced to Choose

In December 2001, Ralph Hueser called Call To Action Nebraska board member and newsletter editor Mel Beckman to a meeting. Pastoral Minister Hueser had been instructed by Omaha Archbishop Curtiss to inform Beckman that he had to choose between editing the CTAN newsletter and editing the *Nebraska Criminal Justice Review*, a Holy Family parish publication. Mel decided to give priority to editing the *Nebraska Criminal Justice Review*.[48] CTAN board member and Sociology professor, John Krejci, served on the board of the *Nebraska Criminal Justice Review* at that time; he resigned from the board of *NCJR*. The *NCJR* board was unhappy that their colleagues were faced with this decision.[49] They explained that the *NCJR* addresses social justice issues, not theological issues. In addition, *NCJR* board members were not required to hold any particular religious belief; in fact, most of the *NCJR* board members were not even Catholic.

Lincoln Diocesan Noncompliance
in Sex Abuse Audits

In the early part of the 2000s, cases of sexual abuse of children by United States Catholic priests made headlines around the country. Catholics and non-Catholics questioned how bishops could move known child sex abusers from one parish or ministry to another with no warning to the priest's new community.

The United States Conference of Catholic Bishops (USCCB) met in June 2002 to address the issue of sex abuse and minors. Writing about that meeting in the *Southern Nebraska Register*, Bishop Bruskewitz noted the presence of protesters, "Except for hearing some screaming folks upon my arrival, the various protesting groups did not bother me. My inside room kept me from being annoyed by them."[50]

Bishop Bruskewitz shared that, at that meeting, the bishops approved a "Charter for the Protection of Children and Young People." Bishop Bruskewitz explained that national bishops' conferences "are not empowered to enact any binding Church laws... except in a few matters." Though then-USCCB President, Bishop Wilton Gregory, called the Charter "mandatory," Bishop Bruskewitz pointed out, "There seems to be some type of shame-control intended."

A Catholic News Service article reported that Bishop Bruskwitz believed that the Charter approved at the Dallas meeting "was a hasty reaction to media pressure that will not address the core problem— dissent from church teaching on sexual morality."[51] The report indicated that Bishop Bruskewitz's "unscientific conclusion" is that because most of the sexual abuse of minors in question took place against adolescent boys, it is "rooted in societal acceptance of homosexuality."[52] Bishop Bruskewitz believed that homosexuals should not be ordained to the priesthood, "I don't think drug addicts should be pharmacists, I don't think alcoholics should be bartenders. I don't think kleptomaniacs should be bank tellers and I don't think homosexuals should be priests."[53]

Perhaps unsurprisingly, Bishop Bruskewitz did not comply with all of the guidelines laid out in the Dallas Charter. A *Lincoln Journal Star* article reported that the Lincoln diocese did not participate in a nation-wide study designed to "determine the extent of sexual abuse of minors by priests" because Bishop Bruskewitz believed that there were "inherent flaws" in the study design.[54] While the diocese conducted background checks on all new employees, individual priests were allowed to decide if they would conduct background checks on current employees and volunteers. Lincoln Chancellor, Fr. Huber, reportedly told a reporter for the *Lincoln Journal Star* that Bishop Bruskewitz would implement the recommendations "he thinks are truly helpful."[55] At the time, the Lincoln diocese was the only diocese that refused to participate in the John Jay study.[56] Regarding the background checks, Fr. Huber told the *Omaha World Herald*, "If someone has worked with you all your life and you've known them . . . it doesn't seem appropriate [to conduct a background check]."[57]

Jim McShane commented on this matter. He told a reporter, "The American bishops are trying very hard to alleviate any concerns people have about the safety of their children and this bishop has decided 'nobody can make me do it.'"[58] The national director of the Survivors Network of Those Abused by Priests (SNAP), David Clohessy, expressed concern that Bishop Bruskewitz's refusal to fully comply "lacks compassion for abuse victims."[59] According to a report in the Call to Action News, Bishop Bruskewitz did participate in the audit in 2003 but refused to participate again in 2004.[60]

Chairwoman of the USCCB's National Review Board, Dr. Patricia Ewers, called for "strong fraternal correction" of Bishop Bruskewitz because he declined to participate.[61] In an interview published in the *Wanderer*,[62] Bishop Bruskewitz expressed indignation that Dr. Ewers would call for his fraternal correction saying, "Sometimes you have to react. If I'm attacked, they are going to get a mouthful of porcupine quills."[63] He continued, "I was speechless with indignation, and I refuse to be bossed around by these people."[64]

CTAN Members Threatened with Arrest

Over 1,000 Catholics from across the country signed a petition to Bishop Bruskewitz that was also copied to CTA-USA and Bishop Skylstad, president of the United States Conference of Catholic Bishops. The petition protested Bishop Bruskewitz's lack of justice in his handling of the Call To Action Nebraska appeal, exclusion of females from ministries open to them and refusal to participate in the USCCB adopted audit regarding sex abuse in the church. Members of Call To Action Nebraska scheduled a prayer service for the afternoon of Friday, June 1, 2007. CTA-USA co-director, Dan Daley, planned to join the group for this service which was to take place outside the Lincoln cathedral. The service was to culminate in the delivery of the petition to the chancery. In a news article published before the scheduled prayer service, I was quoted as President of CTAN that Bishop Bruskewitz is not required to participate in the audit; however, by not doing so he promotes "a sense of suspicion. . . . We have to be vigilant."[65]

Because CTAN members planned to gather in a public place, we filed for a Permit to Gather. That permit was granted. The chancery was also notified of the CTAN prayer service and a group of Bishop Bruskewitz's supporters planned a counter-protest for the same time. CTAN learned of this counter protest when I received a phone call from Captain Kim Koluch of the Lincoln Police Department alerting me that the chancery had instructed them to arrest any member of Call To Action Nebraska who stepped foot on church property. Koluch told me, "They do not want those petitions."

Members of CTAN called an emergency meeting to discuss our options. We decided to cancel the prayer service and instead hold a small press conference in the morning. The counter-protesters learned of this change and around 100 people, many of them children, gathered during our press conference. When I began to address the gathered media, the protesters began to sing loudly the hymn "Immaculate Mary." It seemed the intention was to drown out my words. I distinctly remember the moment and thinking, "That is our hymn, too" and I, and the rest of our number, jointed the counter-protesters in the hymn.

In my prepared words I noted that members of Call To Action Nebraska believed that the presence of counter-protesters would negatively affect our ability to pray. I concluded, "Though we have changed our original plan, we stand by our message. We must speak for those who cannot. Children are among the most vulnerable in society and every effort, mandated or not, must be taken to ensure their safety."[66] After we spoke to the media, we walked toward the chancery to deliver our petitions to Bishop Bruskewitz. We were stopped at the edge of church property by police officers.

Around 100 people gathered that afternoon at the chancery to express their support for Bishop Bruskewitz. They presented their own petition to Bishop Bruskewitz who attended the gathering, blessed the crowd and accepted their petitions.[67] The local media covered our CTAN press conference as well as the counter-protests.[68]

Msgr. Timothy Thorburn wrote a letter to the editor of the *Lincoln Journal Star* in which he explained the necessity of the presence of police officers during the Call To Action Nebraska prayer service. Msgr. Thorburn claimed that CTAN had "past inclinations toward violent disruptions." Msgr. Thorburn further commented, "it would have been imprudent not to have the police present."[69]

CTAN has never engaged in any violent disruptions nor have we been inclined in that direction. We have made every effort throughout our existence to seek peaceful resolution to our disagreements. Perhaps Msgr. Thorburn referred to John Krejci communicating himself at Mass after the bishop waved him away while he was in the communion line. If one would consider John Krejci's response to be an act of violence, one should also consider that Krejci might have experienced the denial of the Eucharist as an act of spiritual violence. In any case, Krejci's actions were not planned actions of the Call To Action Nebraska organization; they were his own immediate response to a personally devastating situation.

Msgr. Thorburn concluded by saying that members of CTAN did not protest because of the audit. Rather, "its members are mad that the Vatican twice upheld the Lincoln Diocese in its excommunication of Call to Action members, ruling that they are an anti-Catholic sect. Complaints about the audit are simply the closest stick, as the saying goes, with which to beat the dog." As demonstrated in Chapter 7, no evidence has ever been given to members of CTAN indicating that the Vatican had responded to our appeal. In addition, members of CTAN are neither anti-Catholic nor a sect. Continually repeating those points does not make them true. As Jim McShane noted in a CTAN newsletter article, "CTA is neither a 'sect' cut off from the Church nor a 'religion' separate from it. . . Repeated assertions or accusations that we are or do something else cannot change fundamental realities; by themselves they can not make us guilty of what they accuse us of."[70]

CTAN members were not alone in their frustration that Bishop Bruskewitz would not participate in the USCCB-approved sex abuse audits. Later that month, David Clohessy, Executive Director of Survivors Network of those Abused by Priests (SNAP), stood outside the Lincoln Cathedral. He told a reporter for the *Lincoln Journal Star* that he was requesting the United States Conference of Catholic Bishops to persuade Bishop Bruskewitz to participate in the sex abuse audits or publically censure him for his noncompliance.[71] Almost a year later another member of SNAP held a press conference outside the Lincoln Cathedral. SNAP member Bob Schwiderski again drew attention to Bishop Bruskewitz's refusal to participate in the sex abuse audits.[72] Schwiderski called for Bishop Bruskewitz to be banned from all events during the upcoming United States visit of Pope Benedict XVI.

As we were unable to deliver our petitions to Bishop Bruskewitz in Lincoln, Nicole Sotelo, CTA-USA staff member, and I attempted to deliver the petitions to the United States bishops at the United States Conference of Catholic Bishops Fall Assembly in Baltimore. After a joint press conference with Call To Action USA and the Survivors Network of Those Abused by Priests, we attempted to enter the hotel where the bishops were gathered to deliver the petitions. We were blocked from doing so by hotel security.[73] A security officer told us he would send a representative from the USCCB to come to us to collect the petitions. No one came.[74] Msgr. Thorburn called this attempt a "publicity stunt."[75]

Bishop Bruskewitz was asked about the Call To Action petitions in an interview with the *Catholic World Report*. He told the reporter:

> The antics of Call to Action in these last few months have simply been publicity stunts in which they are trying to call attention to themselves. The group in Lincoln is incredibly small. They are mostly dissidents from the 1960s era who have abandoned the Catholic faith. They don't have any children in our Catholic institutions that I know of. They have made themselves into an anti-Catholic sect, and so it is absurd for them to pretend to be concerned about children's safety in the Church. They have some slight nuisance value for themselves, but they really don't annoy me by and large, and except in the eyes of a few journalists in the secular media they really don't count for anything in this part of the world.[76]

When discussing the authority of the United States Conference of Catholic Bishops to publicly censure him, Bishop Bruskewitz noted that the USCCB had no reason to reprimand him, "But it would make no difference to me if they did, because they have no authority."

Continuing to Speak Out on Sex Abuse Audits

Members of Call To Action Nebraska gathered on the sidewalk in front of the Chancery Office near the Cathedral of the Risen Christ on Wednesday, April 28, 2010 for a vigil and prayer service. Participants gathered peacefully to speak, sing, pray, and express concern that the Lincoln diocese continues to refuse to participate in the sex abuse audits of the United States Conference of Catholic Bishops. In a press release, I am quoted as having said:

> When Lincoln Bishop, Fabian Bruskewitz, refused to participate in audits designed to give minimum assurance that steps are being taken to protect children of this diocese, he said, "No one has authority over me." He is, sadly, correct. In the Lincoln diocese, Catholics are told they should trust the bishop. Members of the Lincoln diocese may trust their

bishop, but the bishop must also be accountable to the children of his diocese. . . [77]

Once again, as CTAN members gathered, spoke, sang, and prayed, a group of twenty-eight protesters gathered nearby and prayed and sang as well. According to a *Lincoln Journal Star* article, "Some Bruskewitz supporters said they had no idea why Call to Action members had gathered on Wednesday but, regardless, they want people to know they do not consider Call to Action members Catholic."[78] Once again, CTAN members were threatened with arrest if they stepped onto church property and police officers were present to monitor the activity. This made for an interesting exchange when Bishop Bruskewitz supporter Mary Quintero, standing on the church grounds, called out to CTAN members to invite them to join their group of bishop supporters. She encouraged us, "It's a short walk to home." Patty Hawk responded to Quintero, "We were told we weren't welcome," referring to the threat of arrest if any member of the group stepped foot on church property.[79]

Call To Action Nebraska Celebrates Ten Year Anniversary

Call To Action Nebraska celebrated its tenth anniversary at a conference entitled, "Called by the Spirit: Moved to Action" on June 2 & 3, 2006. Sr. Simone Campbell, National Coordinator of NETWORK, a Catholic social justice lobbying organization, spoke to the group on June 2 on the topic of "The Theology of Insecurity." On Saturday, those gathered participated in a workshop conducted by staff from *Pace e Bene,* an organization that promotes nonviolence. The conference concluded with an outdoor prayer service that took place near St. Mary's Church, the old cathedral, in downtown Lincoln, Nebraska. During the prayer service CTAN members echoed Pope John XXIII's call to open the windows of the Church and let in the Holy Spirit.

In response to the conference, Bishop Bruskewitz once again referred to Call To Action as "an anti-Catholic sect composed mainly of aging fallen-away Catholics, including ex-priests and ex-nuns."[80] I would agree with this one point: the members of Call To Action, just like the members of the Catholic Church and every breathing person in the world, are aging.

Bishop Bruskewitz Celebrates 50 years of Priesthood

On July 16, 2010, Bishop Bruskewitz celebrated the fiftieth anniversary of his ordination to the priesthood. An article in the *Lincoln Journal Star* marking this anniversary noted that both the bishop's supporters and detractors would describe him as devout and stubborn "with unyielding orthodoxy and ultra-conservative views."[81] In the article, Bishop Bruskewitz was also described as a leader, a teacher, principled, kind, charitable, charismatic, decisive, and resolute. Bishop Bruskewitz was quoted as having said, "I am not a dictator. But I do think that bishops have, by Catholic doctrine, the three-fold duty to teach, to sanctify and to govern the Catholic people ... in spiritual matters."[82] He noted that he would have to answer to God for how he used that responsibility.

Bishop Bruskewitz explained that "matters of truth have only two options: true or false. I don't think that it's being arrogant. It think it is being kind and charitable to speak the truth and that is an important part of what a bishop has to do."[83]

Though Bishop Bruskewitz believed that he was being kind and charitable by speaking truth as he sees it, members of Call To Action do not necessarily experience his words or manner in that way. I am sure examples of Bishop Bruskewitz's kindness and charity are legion. However, when he spoke to or about members of Call to Action, he used harsh, demeaning, and misleading language. CTAN member, Rod Diercks', description of the members of CTAN stands in contrast to the caricature of Call To Action members presented by Bishop Bruskewitz:

> They bring thoughtfulness, they bring love, they bring a concern for
> their families and the world in a way that's just very touching. These
> people really reach out and you can see it, you can see it in not only

what they do, but you can see it in their actions. You can hear it in their voice, in what they say. They're just very welcoming people who really see more potential in the church. They see more potential in everybody, in all kinds of people. And they try to help people reach their potential.[84]

When I conducted my interviews for this book, I asked members of Call To Action Nebraska what they wished non-members knew about CTAN. Many people wished non-members knew that members of CTAN are not threatening—we aren't wild-eyed radicals. For example, Jerry Johnson said:

> Our bishop doesn't always tell the truth about people. . . He calls us terrible names in the *Southern Nebraska Register*. One of the things that, in a way, strikes me as funny: we are about the straightest group of people I know in so many ways that it is sort of funny. We get accused of all this stuff, you know, and we are almost disgustingly well behaved.[85]

Bishop Bruskewitz's Resignation

When a bishop turns 75 years old, the Code of Canon Law requires him to submit a letter of resignation, though the pope could wait years to replace a bishop after he submits his resignation. Bishop Bruskewitz celebrated his 75th birthday on September 6, 2010. He announced his plans to continue living in Lincoln, Nebraska and make himself available to the new bishop, should the new bishop choose.[86]

On September 14, 2012, Pope Benedict XVI appointed Bishop James D. Conley the next Bishop of the Lincoln Diocese.[87] Bishop Conley told a *Lincoln Journal Star* reporter that he does not plan to change the conservative philosophies or practices of the diocese,[88] including overturning the excommunications. He said excommunication "can have a medicinal purpose" to persuade people to return to the Church.[89] He told the reporter, "Bishop Bruskewitz has been a true champion of the Catholic faith and personal hero of mine for many years."[90] Bishop Conley was installed Bishop of Lincoln on November 20, 2012.

Conclusion

I spent the 2010-2011 academic year on sabbatical in Galway, Ireland. On Holy Saturday, 2011, I wrote the words that opened this chapter. Being struck from the rolls of my parish was not an easy thing to happen and it wasn't an easy thing to write about. Later that evening, I attended my favorite liturgy of the year, the Easter Vigil, with these memories heavy on my mind and heart. On Easter day, I wrote the following reflection:[91]

> I arrived early and was pleased to see that my favorite spot was unoccupied. Just as I started to sit down, Fr. Dick said from across the church, "Oh, Rachel. Come here." He asked a young woman, Ella, and me to participate in the liturgy by carrying lanterns during the part of the liturgy called the Service of Light. We processed, carrying lit lanterns, to the altar from opposite sides of the church where two other people dressed the altar. We then processed outside where Fr. Dick lit the Easter fire, blessed it, and lit the Easter candle.
>
> After spending the day thinking about getting, quite literally, expelled from the church in Lincoln, this small event held great significance to me. It felt wonderful to be counted on to help out when a need arose. Fr. Dick knows about my situation and that didn't stop him from including me.
>
> The Service of the Light, it seems, did me a service as well. On Easter day I went for a stroll in the sunshine with the words of the Easter Exsultet resonant in my spirit.
>
> Accept this Easter candle,
> a flame divided but undimmed,
> a pillar of fire that glows to the honor of God.
>
> Let it mingle with the lights of heaven
> and continue bravely burning
> to dispel the darkness of this night!

Notes Chapter 8

1.   The radio program is now called "On Being," the program referenced is available online at: http://being.publicradio.org/programs/being_catholic/.

2.   Fr. Lyle Johnson, letter to Rachel Pokora, October 13, 2009.

3.   Published in the June 18, 1999 edition of *Southern Nebraska Register*, page 24.

4.   Jim McShane, "*Southern Nebrska Register* Describes Call To Action as an 'Evil Working' Sect," *Voices of Nebraska Catholics*, Winter 1998.

5.   Ibid.

6.   Ibid.

7.   Tom Roberts, "Bruskewitz's Paper calls Crowley 'Degenerate,'" *National Catholic Reporter*, January 30, 1998.

8.   Ibid.

9.   Bob Reeves, "Catholic Activist Predicts New Contraception Policy," *Lincoln Journal Star*, October 7, 1997.

10. Ibid.

11. "Ask the Register," *Southern Nebraska Register*, November 7, 1997.

12. Tom Roberts, "Bruskewitz's Paper calls Crowley 'Degenerate.'"

13. Ibid.

14. Ibid.

15. Jim McShane, letter to Fr. Kenneth Borowiak, November 10, 1997.

16. Tim Unsworth, "Chill that Surrounded the Crowleys Finally Melting in Patty's Scrapbook," *National Catholic Reporter*, August 14, 1998.

17. Ibid.

18. Ibid.

19. "Feminist Nun's Visit Criticized by Top Lincoln Diocese Official," *Lincoln Journal Star*, June 20, 1999.

20. Teresa Malcolm, "Chittister Visit Irks Neighboring Chancellor," *National Catholic Reporter*, June 4, 1999.

21. Ibid.

22. Ibid.

23. Ibid.

24. Ibid.

25. Ibid.

26. "Feminist nun's visit criticized…"

27. "Warning To All Catholics," *Southern Nebraska Register*, March 29, 2002.

28. Bob Reeves, "Local Call to Action Gets National Support," *Lincoln Journal Star*, April 7, 2002.

29. Ibid.

30. "She's Phony," *Southern Nebraska Register*, February 25, 2000.

31. Crystal Chesshire, "Worry Over Speaker Comes to Naught," *Cornerstone*, March 3, 2000.

32. Jessica Johnson, (March 3, 2000). "Pius X High School Administrators Write Letter of Concern to Watson," *Cornerstone*, March 3, 2000.

33. "Tragic Figure," *Southern Nebraska Register*, April 14, 2000.

34. I was that prayer leader.

35. Bob Reeves, "Nun Urges Catholics to Follow Consciences," *Lincoln Journal Star*, April 9, 2000.

36. Tom Roberts, "Gramick on Conscience in Lincoln," *National Catholic Reporter*, May 5, 2000.

37. Ibid.

38. Bob Reeves, "Nun Urges Catholics to Follow Consciences."

39. "Tragic Figure," *Southern Nebraska Register*.

40. Gramick and Nugent's story did not end here. They were summoned to Rome to meet with the respective heads of their congregations. Fr. Nugent complied with demands and remained a Salvatorian priest. Gramick expressed that keeping silent would be a violation of her conscience. She was dismissed from her order, the School Sisters of Notre Dame. See Pamela Schaeffer, "Gramick Says No to Vatican Silencing, Expects Dismissal," *National Catholic Reporter*, June 16, 2000. Call To Action Nebraska sponsored a prayer service in support of Sr. Gramick.

41. "Tragic figure," *Southern Nebraska Register*, April 14, 2000.

42. Patty Hawk and Patricia Sullivan, letter to Archbishop Elden Curtiss, May 10, 2000.

43. "Catholics of Lincoln Deserve Better than This," *National Catholic Reporter*, May 5, 2000.

44. Ibid.

45. Rev. Jeremy Hazuka, letter to Joan Johnson, September 21, 1998.

46. Joan Johnson, letter to Rev Jeremyu Hazuka, October 4, 1998.

47. Joan Johnson, interview with the author.

48. Mel Beckman, email to Patty Hawk, December 21, 2000.

49. Ralph Hueser, letter to Archbishop Curtiss, March 1, 2001.

50. Bishop Fabian Bruskewitz, "An Ordinary Viewpoint: The Dallas Meeting-I," *Southern Nebraska Register*, June 28, 2002.

51. "Bp. Bruskewitz: Dissent, Homosexuality are Core Problems of Abuse Scandals," *Southern Nebraska Register*, July 26, 2002.

52. Ibid.

53. Ibid.

54. Bob Reeves, "Lincoln Diocese Doesn't Comply with Sex-Abuse Policy," *Lincoln Journal Star*, January 7, 2004.

55. Ibid.

56. Bob Reeves, "Lincoln Diocese Opposes Study," *Lincoln Journal Star*, January 10, 2004.

57. Angie Brunkow, "Lincoln Diocese Says it is Dealing with Sexual Misconduct," *Omaha World Herald*, January 11, 2004.

58. Joe Ruff, "Nebraska Bishop Says No to Some Anti-Abuse Measures," *East Valley Scottsdale Tribune*, January 31, 2004.

59. Ibid.

60. "Bishops' Second Annual Sex Abuse Report: In CTA's View, the Crisis is Far From Over," *Call to Action News*, April-May 2005.

61. "Church Reports Decline in Sex Abuse Allegations," *Tablet*, April 8, 2006, http://217.8.242.153/article/245.

62. "The Wanderer Interviews… Bishop Bruskewitz on Defying the NRB," *Wanderer*, April 23, 2006.

63. Ibid.

64. Ibid.

65. Bob Reeves, "Call to Action Members to Present Petition to Bishop," *Lincoln Journal Star*, May 30, 2007.

66. Official statement of Call To Action Nebraska on our June 1, 2007 action.

67. Bob Reeves, "Bishop's Supporters Upstage his Critics," *Lincoln Journal Star,* June 2, 2007.

68. In a small, related article published in *Lincoln Journal Star*, Bob Reeves reported

that I had misused my work email address by using it for Call To Action correspondence. Several Nebraska Catholics sent emails to me and my employer suggesting that my use of my work email indicated my employer's support of Call To Action. One person indicated he would contact the *Lincoln Journal Star*. I was taken by surprise. First, I admit with chagrin that I had never even considered that using my email in this way would indicate that my employer supported these efforts. Second, as I had already been researching Call To Action, I considered my involvement in the organization as part of my scholarly pursuits as well as personal. Nonetheless, it was bad judgment and I immediately signed up for a private email account and asked that my email address be changed on the Call To Action Nebraska and Call To Action USA websites to that new private account.

69. Msgr. Timothy Thorburn, "Audit is not the point," Letter to the editor, *Lincoln Journal Star*, June 13, 2007.

70. Jim McShane, "Setting the Record Straight: Response to the 'Ask the *Register*' Article of May 21, 1999," *Voices of Nebraska Catholics*, Summer 1999.

71. Bob Reeves, "Victims' Advocacy Leader Asks Bishops to Censure Bruskewitz," *Lincoln Journal Star*, June 15, 2007.

72. Deena Winter, "Man Urges Lincoln Bishop to Take Part in Abuse Audit," *Lincoln Journal Star*, April 5, 2008.

73. See Lynn Anderson, "Child Abuse in Church Found to Mirror Society." *Baltimore Sun*, November 13, 2007.

74. Rachel Pokora, "From the chair: Reflections on Baltimore Experience," *Voices of Nebraska Catholics*, Winter 2007.

75. Chris Burbach, "Lincoln Bishop Again Faces National Criticism," *Omaha World Herald*, November 13, 2007.

76. George Neumayr, "Shadows and Light: Bishop Bruskewitz on Call to Action's Petition Against Him and Other Controversies in the Church," *Catholic World Report*, April 2008.

77. CTAN press release, April 28, 2010. Available, CTAN archives.

78. Erin Andersen, "Catholic Groups at Odds over Handling of Sex Abuse Audits: Call to Action Nebraska, Bishop's Supporters Gather in Lincoln," *Lincoln Journal Star*, April 29, 2010.

79. Ibid.

80. Bob Reeves, "Catholic Group Calls for More Openness," *Lincoln Journal Star*, June 4, 2006.

81. Erin Andersen, "Bishop Bruskewitz Reflects on 50 Years of Ordained Life," *Lincoln Journal Star*, July 17, 2010.

82. Ibid.

83. Ibid.

84. Rod Diercks, interview with the author.

85. Jerry Johnson, interview with the author.

86. Erin Andersen, "Bishop Bruskewitz Reflects. . ."

87. "Bishop of Lincoln, Neb., retires; Denver auxiliary named his successor," *National Catholic Reporter*, September 14, 2012, http://ncronline.org/news/people/bishop-lincoln-neb-retires-denver-auxiliary-named-his-successor.

88. Erin Andersen, "New bishop 'not going to mess around with' philosophies of Lincoln diocese," *Lincoln Journal Star*, September 14, 2012, http://journalstar.com/life-styles/faith-and-values/new-bishop-not-going-to-mess-around-with-philosophies-of/article_d4889fb0-fe5c-11e1-b16f-0019bb2963f4.html.

89. Joe Duggan, "A new take on tradition for incoming Lincoln bishop," *World-Herald Bureau*, November 9, 2012 http://www.omaha.com/article/20121109/NEWS/711099908/1685.

90. Erin Andersen, "New bishop 'not going to mess around...'"

91. This reflection is excerpted from a longer version printed in *Voices of Nebraska Catholics*, Vol 14 (2), Spring 2011.

CHAPTER 9

Power and Authority in Church Structure

Opposition is not a fundamental contradiction of solidarity. … There are countless examples of people quarreling . . . precisely because they have in their hearts a concern for the common good.[1]—Karol Wojtyla, before he became Pope John Paul II

WHEN I WAS IN EIGHTH GRADE, my classmates at St. Jude School in Grand Rapids, Michigan and I decided we would like to have a Valentine's Day dance. Our principal said we could not for some unremembered reason, so we turned our attention to alternatives. Using the pay phone outside the gym, I called my mom during our lunch break and asked her if we could hold a dance at our house. She said, "No." That evening, I asked my mom if we could talk about the request. I said something like, "If you tell me what you are worried about, maybe we can work something out." So my mom and dad and I talked about it. By the end of the discussion, I had their permission to hold a dance in our living room. I don't remember all their rules, but I have great memories of that party.

A year or so later I was telling this story to a high school friend of mine and her mother overheard me. She later told my friend that she thought I was a bad influence because I showed great disrespect to my parents when I didn't take "no" for an answer. I was surprised to hear this interpretation of what had happened because I thought the interaction I had with my parents showed the utmost respect and that respect had flowed in both directions.

By no one's understanding were my parents permissive. They were extremely involved in the lives of their children and there were many things they did not allow their children to do. My sister and I always understood why, though. Perhaps the activity wasn't safe or it was "too mature" for us. Whatever their reason, I never remember my parents saying, "because I told you so." My parents believed it was their responsibility to help us grow to be fully functioning adults which meant, among other things, helping us to develop the ability to reason, make good choices and take responsibility for ourselves. As we grew and tried new things, my parents engaged us in conversations about our experiences that taught us how to think reasonably, responsibly, and morally.

My parents were always interested in my reactions and views. They wanted to hear what I felt. I was given the opportunity for age-appropriate input into family decisions. I accepted my parents' authority and felt comfortable with the way they exercised it. I never went through a rebellious phase. My mom and dad think it is because I never had anything against which to rebel. I agree. My parents were reasonable people with rules that I knew were for my own good and they cared about how the rules affected me. My parents never had to insist they were in charge because I always knew it.

The Family Metaphor and Church Authority

Roman Catholics frequently use a family metaphor when they discuss the Catholic Church. This metaphor makes sense in that, like a family, many people join the Catholic Church as infants at baptism. Like a family, we have strong ties to the institution and consider it a vital part of our identity. For example, Omaha Chancellor Fr. Gutgsell has said, "You can disagree in family. You can have hard feelings. You can even stop talking to each other. You never stop being family."[2] Tom Fox, editor of the *National Catholic Reporter*, spoke at the second Call To Action Nebraska meeting. Fox said the church is "a raucous family getting together around a meal."[3] Omaha Archbishop Elden Curtis likened Catholics who stay away from Mass and hold dissident beliefs to children who rebel against their parents.[4]

I expect my church, like my family, to treat me like a fully functioning and mature adult. The family metaphor sheds some light on why the church does not treat me in this way. One way to understand the conflict in the Lincoln diocese between members of CALL and Call To Action Nebraska and the bishops is to consider differing views of effective family functioning. In one approach, children are taught to think and reason and given more and more responsibility until they reach adulthood at which point they are treated as adults.

Another approach to family places the head of the household as the final word at all times. This head expects to be treated with respect and respect is shown through obedience. A person who doesn't show the proper respect could be considered outside the family. Lincoln Catholic Pam Tabor illustrated this approach when she told a reporter that the church could be compared to a family in which the children follow the orders of the head. She said, "You may ask questions, but once the parent says, 'This is not allowed,' you're not truly a member of that family unless you accept that."[5] In this view of the church, lay people, regardless of age, are treated as children who must bow to the authority of their priest, the bishop and the pope.

Fr. Michael Crosby, a priest from Wisconsin, addressed this approach when he explained his belief that the average Catholic still operates like a child. He said, "You're dealing with adults who are children when it gets to their faith life. They are not well-informed, just believing something because the bishop says it."[6] CTAN member Joan Johnson believes the hierarchy "preach to us like we are in second grade. I think that means that many Catholics do not have a deep understanding of their faith and I honestly think it is not their fault."[7] Former Lincoln resident and CTAN member, John Burke, noted that adults in the Lincoln diocese are treated like adolescents. He believes that this treatment stems from a mistrust of how adults would respond if given the chance to discuss their ideas and experiences.[8] Omaha CTAN member, Pat Sullivan, noted that Archbishop Curtiss entitled his column in the archdiocesan paper "Your Shepherd and Teacher." Sullivan explained her reaction, "Whoa! I'm not a sheep and I'm not a child! I can learn, yet. Yes, I've got lots to learn yet. But it still makes me feel demeaned when I see that. And I think in the tone that he takes in these things that he's doing an injustice to the vast majority of Catholics here. I think the church in general is doing that; I think they're underestimating people a great deal."[9]

One might understand Bishop Bruskewitz's governance in Lincoln by looking at how he used the family metaphor, as well. In a *Southern Nebraska Register* article about the excommunication of Call To Action, he is quoted as having said, "Parents have to tell children that they can't test everything in the medicine cabinet or drink everything under the sink. The Church is our mother and gives us these instructions as protection against dangers we might not perceive. . . It is liberating, not enslaving."[10] Bishop Bruskewitz practiced what he preached. A newspaper article pointed out that before he became bishop of the Lincoln diocese, Bruskewitz and his more liberal bishop in Milwaukee, Archbishop Rembert Weakland, had differences. However, he "never disobeyed Weakland."[11] Bishop Bruskewitz frequently reported that he would obey the pope if the pope told him to repeal the extra-synodal legislation that led to the excommunication of CTAN members or participate in the USCCB sex abuse audits.

Priests in the Lincoln diocese are taught where they fit in the line of family authority. Charles R. Morris, a journalist writing for *Commonweal* magazine, interviewed Rev. Joseph Nemec, the thirty-nine-year-old pastor of Lincoln's St. Teresa's Parish. Morris asked Fr. Nemec, in light of his youthful appearance, about his relationship with the parishioners of St. Teresa's. He responded: "I'm their *father*. . . That's what a pastor is. . . We're very participative here, but, as in any good Catholic family, parents love their children and still control them. They need to be told what's right and wrong with the love and care of a father [emphasis in orginal]."[12] Fr. Nemec understands himself to be the head of the parish family. The lay people of the parish are the children who may not know what is right and wrong. Morris observed that the obedience demonstrated by this statement flows "in a clear, straight line. Children honor and obey their parents. Parents honor and obey their pastor. Pastors honor and obey their bishop. And bishops honor and obey the pope, who speaks for Jesus Christ."[13] Morris explained how this view of "strict orthodoxy" and obedience is paired with "a very exalted view of the priesthood."[14] The Lincoln diocese attracts young men to the priesthood from other parts of the country.[15] This might be one reason why. Morris wrote that if a priest "is submissive and obedient to his superiors, he expects the same from this flock . . . because he is a local spokesman of a vast salvific enterprise—of the one true church, the chosen vessel for an eternal deposit of faith bequeathed directly from the hand of Christ."[16]

According to the metaphor of family as enacted in the diocese of Lincoln, lay people are to submit to their father, the priest. Lay people and priests are to submit to their bishop. For example, Rev. Damian Zuerlein, a priest in the archdiocese of Omaha, signed his name to the 1990 Call To Action *New York Times* advertisement. According to an article in the *Omaha World Herald*, Zuerlein now "declines to address that issue" saying, "I have to teach what the church teaches, whether I wish for change or not."[17] Zuerlein submitted to the will of his superiors. Lori Darby noted in an interview, "There are a lot of people who, for whatever reason, are forced to be silent. And that silence gives an illusion that the Roman Catholic Church is all on one page."[18] CTAN member Charles Kelliher reinforced this point. Kelliher had been a priest in the Lincoln diocese. He left the active ministry in the early 1970s and moved to Kearney, Nebraska. After the move, Kelliher said he "could speak out, because my job wasn't threatened. I could be, I would say, more true to my conscience, more true, more honest with what I really felt."[19]

Certainly, there are multiple ways that authority is exercised in families and this is true in the church as well. Msgr. Thorburn told a journalist that people might be confused when they hear different messages coming from different bishops. He said, "It's very much like families. The father and mother praise and teach differently in all families."[20] While bishops might exercise their authority in different ways, the fact is, how they do so is their choice.

Bishops Flavin and Bruskewitz dealt with Catholics who sought change differently. Bishop Flavin chose not to answer repeated questions and requests for meetings. His non-response was a response in itself. From reports of interviews with the bishop, we understand that Bishop Bruskewitz understood his insistence on obedience to be a demonstration of love. When asked about the harshness of his letter to John Krejci and Lori Darby in which he writes that as dissidents they lack integrity, Bishop Bruskewitz explained, "I think that saying things in a clear and precise way, establishing boundaries, serves the purpose of love. Love is deceitful if it is not truthful, and truth must be, in my view, an important component of love."[21]

One might turn to communication theory to understand Bishop Bruskewitz's "clear and precise" approach, specifically to the idea of person-centered messages as described in Jesse Delia's theory, Constructivism.[22] A sender creates a person-centered message with a goal or multiple goals in mind. The message is designed to be most effective for a particular receiver in a particular context. To send a person-centered message, the sender must have an understanding of the receiver and an ability to use that understanding in a practical way. The meaning of the message doesn't change, but the message is constructed in such a way that the person is most open to hearing and considering it. Bishop Bruskewitz's letter to John Krejci and Lori Darby in which he accuses the two of lacking integrity was not person-centered. If Bishop Bruskewitz intended members of Call To Action Nebraska to prayerfully consider his concerns, he might have avoided opening his letter to John Krejci and Lori Darby with a personal insult.

Of course, it can be difficult to know how other people might hear a message and this may be particularly so for people who hold a great deal of power. Sandra Harding and Julia Wood's Standpoint Theory teaches us that a person who holds little or no power understands the powerful better than the powerful understand the powerless.[23] This is out of necessity for survival—survival in a job, a family, or even a church. Bishop Bruskewitz demonstrated a lack of understanding of members of Call To Action Nebraska, though I believe he thought he understood us. He read

Brian Clowes book and Mary Jo Anderson's article about Call To Action. Both of these sources make outrageous claims about CTA members. Bishop Bruskewitz has claimed that many CTAN members in his diocese were never very involved Catholics. This is, again, an outrageous claim. A cursory knowledge of the members of CTAN will find them to have been involved in almost every possible ministry, from music to lectoring, from RCIA sponsor to catechist. Some CTAN members are daily communicants. What standard was Bishop Bruskewitz using when he claims CTAN members were uninvolved Catholics?

With words that highlight his knowledge of his own authority in his own diocese, Bishop Bruskewitz dismissed concerns that his extra-synodal legislation might suggest church division because there are some bishops who are members of Call To Action. He remarked, "As far as I know, there are no Catholics in the Diocese of Lincoln who are bishops who are members of Call to Action. Therefore, it doesn't really affect me directly."[24] The only people affected by Bishop Bruskewitz's legislation are people over whom he exercises control and those people include no Roman Catholic bishops. I assume Bishop Bruskewitz did not mean to imply that if something does not impact him directly, he has no concern for it. He did, however, dismiss the concern that some Catholics were confused by his legislation because it differed so greatly from what was enacted in other dioceses.

Bishop of New Ulm, Minnesota, Raymond Lucker, used the family metaphor in his discussion of power and authority. Lucker referred to the arbitrary use of power as one of the church's most pervasive problems.[25] Lucker is quoted as having said, "Where problems can't be discussed. . . the family is dysfunctional."[26] Yet this seems to be the type of family advocated by the "father knows best" ideology of church family. At the time he issued the extra-synodal legislation, Bishop Bruskewitz was described by Notre Dame Professor of History, Jay Dolan, as "an extreme example of a new breed of bishop."[27] This new breed wants "to stifle any discussion or debate, rule by fiat, by their authority."[28]

Bishop Bruskewitz's focus on obedience was well documented. He told members of Call To Action Nebraska that peace comes from

obedience. He wrote that Vatican II taught, "With ready Christian obedience, lay people as well as disciples of Christ should accept whatever their
sacred pastors, as representatives of Christ decree in their role as teachers and rulers in the Church."[29] In this same column, Bishop Bruskewitz
noted that those in authority will have to answer to God for how they
have cared for those placed under them.[30] Put simply, Bishop Bruskewitz
said, "Bishops speak in the name of Christ, and the faithful are to give
them appropriate obedience."[31]

A mature person has a grasp of what he or she knows and doesn't
know. S/he also knows when to turn to others for answers to important
questions or information that will help in reasoning through a difficult matter. Within a family, one person may know a lot about invest-
ing money and another might be the expert on first aid. Similarly, asking
to be treated like an adult member of the church does not mean that
one believes s/he has all knowledge and control. Rather, it is asking to
be treated with respect and acknowledged for the gifts one brings to the
table. Joan Johnson expressed this idea in an interview,

> I hoped that our leaders would recognize that we are all on our faith
> journeys together, that top-down, all encompassing authoritarian rule,
> based on the whims of those making the rules did not recognize where
> each individual was at on the journey at any given moment. God in His
> infinite wisdom has given each one of us differing gifts that he expects
> us to use for his greater honor and glory.[32]

Acknowledging each individual's gifts is a way to honor the work of
the Holy Spirit. Bishop Bruskewitz touched upon this idea when he wrote
". . . the Second Vatican Council talks about a right which is linked with an
obligation on the part of lay people to give their opinion and advice when
they have special skills and knowledge or particular competence in some
matters pertaining to the good of the Church." [33] However, as he continues, he is careful to assert the authority of the bishops over the opinion
and advice of lay people: "Once again, this does not necessarily mean
that 'those whom the Holy Spirit has raised up to shepherd the Church'

necessarily must heed the advice or accept the opinions expressed."[34]

This concern with the authentic authority of a bishop explains, in part, why Bishop Bruskewitz perceived danger in dialogue. In a speech he presented in Mundelein, Illinois, Bishop Bruskewitz addressed what he saw to be the limits of dialogue. One of these limits involves a skewing of the relationship between teacher and student. Bishop Bruskewitz stated, "If the Church, for example, as such, enters into dialogue, it must be clearly seen that the Church is already in possession of a certain measure of truth, and the purpose of dialogue is to make sure that the terminology in which this truth is phrased is acceptable and can be accommodated by the one who is the partner in the dialogue."[35] Bishop Bruskewitz does not appear to believe that the teacher has much of anything to learn from the student besides the best way to phrase a fact.

Organizational Structure

Several years ago I realized that had I accepted a job in a more mainstream diocese, I would likely have joined a parish in which I felt comfortable. Surely, I would have been nurtured and challenged to grow, but I would not have faced the urgent faith questions that I confronted when I moved to the Lincoln diocese. I have reflected on occasion that if Bishop Flavin and Bishop Bruskewitz had given even an inch, I might not have taken so much responsibility for my faith journey. Their refusal to acknowledge or compromise on even the most modest requests, such as female readers or Eucharistic ministers, prompted me as well as members of CALL and Call To Action to seriously question the very structure of the Catholic Church.

Jim McShane expressed a similar idea in an interview. He explained how the years of involvement in CALL and CTAN have impacted him:

> I think I'm further left than I probably would have been without the bishop. Hell, we were trying to get to a place where lay people, men and women, could read together. And this was a job for lay people. It didn't have to be men or women, I'm not talking about the sacred priesthood, I'm talking about an essentially minor service role in the church which

was forbidden to my wife and daughter for no good reason. I hadn't thought much about women's ordination. And as with most things that you don't think much about, you don't you know, you don't get too far down the line towards adopting them, on the one hand. On the other hand, it was very clear that there was no way that a group isolated to the Lincoln Diocese was going to have any effect on any of these matters whatsoever. That was clear. That as long as we were identifiable as belonging within this border, we were subject to authority, our existence was a matter of bemusement to our co-parishioners, but they were certainly too fearful, most of them, to find out what we were about much less to join us.[36]

Bishops Flavin and Bruskewitz denied seemingly reasonable requests, such as women readers and dialogue about controversial issues and they demonized the faithful, practicing Catholics who made the requests. After years of observing such behavior by the bishops, Jim McShane indicated he reached a new understanding about the powerlessness of the laity.

The idea that those whose small requests are denied become more progressive might reach back to the first Call To Action gathering sponsored by the Untited States bishops in 1976. Sociologist Fr. Andrew Greeley, criticized the bishops' Call To Action gathering and Cardinal Berardin. Bradford E. Hinze noted that Greeley portrayed the participants in the 1976 Call To Action conference as "radical and marginal to the everyday life of the vast majority of American Catholics."[37] Hinze continued, "Those many participants who wanted honest discussion about the need for genuine church reform were portrayed as radical opponents of the bishops and as in some way radically unfaithful to the church. But in fact, the vast majority of those involved in Call To Action were and remained faithful Catholics responding generously and in good faith to the U.S. bishops' invitation."[38] Hinze suggests that these portrayals might, to some extent, have "contributed to the unnecessary radicalization of those who had invested in the process initiated by their own bishops...."[39]

Perhaps at that time the viewed radicalization could be deemed unnecessary. However, as the effects of denying the laity a voice in church matters become more and more evident in the United States, a thorough examination of the structures of the church becomes necessary if the church is going to minister fully and with integrity.

Examples abound of power run amuck in the Catholic Church. Perhaps most shocking have been the continual revelations of cover-ups of child sexual abuse. While the sexual abuse of children occurs in a myriad of institutions, what makes the abuse that happened in the Catholic Church even more tragic than abuse in other arenas was the way it was allowed to happen again and again by the bishops, the men who held the authority to do something about it. The same structural problems that led to the transferring of abusive priests from one parish to another are at work in the problems experienced by members of CALL and Call To Action Nebraska: Bishops protect the institution of the Church. Lay people are not to question the authority of the priest. Lay people are not to question the authority of the bishop. The message is clear: the job of the lay person is to obey.

Power in the Organizational Structure

Power is often understood as an overt phenomenon—the ability to get someone to do something. However, power is more complex than that; it operates on many levels. Critical theorists teach us that when we look at power, we need to not only look at what happens, we must also look at what does not happen. Who speaks and who keeps quiet? Whose voices do we acknowledge and whose voices are not acknowledged? Whose ideas are considered and whose ideas are ignored? Clearly, power in the Catholic Church manifests itself through privileging some voices and silencing other voices. Further, because this power is exercised in the church, the silencing of some voices happens in the name of God.

In the church in Lincoln, voices have been silenced in multiple ways. Some silencing occurs through blocking alternative points of view. John Burke, CTAN member before he and his family moved out of Nebraska, commented on the way Lincoln youth were only exposed to certain voices. Burke was a counselor at Pius X High School in Lincoln. He remarked on

what he heard about what was happening at the Newman Center at the
University of Nebraska at Lincoln.

> I heard, for example, that students that weren't going to daily Mass there
> would get calls. . . why aren't you at Mass? Why aren't you doing this?
> And there'd even be some coercion to break up with boyfriends or girl-
> friends. And I heard this from former students. . . I'm reading [in] the
> *Register* [the list of]. . . the candidates for the priesthood and it amazed
> me how many of them had been through the Newman Center. And
> that, that raised a huge red flag for me. I saw myself coming from a
> small Midwestern town being sucked into Opus Dei. I saw the whole
> thing. And I felt like I knew just what those young men were going
> through. And I just wanted to talk to them and say, before you make
> these commitments, and before you get too entrenched in this mind-
> set, you really ought to look at some other things. But you don't get
> that chance. And here it's difficult. . . I remember at Pius my first year,
> they had some new priests teaching and they found out I went to Notre
> Dame. And I could tell they were kind of scoffing at the whole thing.
> And I asked them if they'd read. . . Richard McBrien. . . some of the
> other works and they said, "well, no, we wouldn't even read that." You
> know. . . "that would lead us astray, that'd be a temptation just to even
> read it." And I'm thinking, well, that's really not a balanced or holistic
> approach to Theology. . . And I think that's what disturbed me the most,
> is seeing the young people sucked in, and making some big, in some
> cases lifelong commitments, decisions, based on the limited experience
> they had at the Newman Center or in this Diocese.[40]

When Bishop Flavin did not acknowledge or respond to the pleas of
the faithful, he silenced their voices. When Bishop Bruskewitz defined
members of Call To Action Nebraska as anti-Catholic, he silenced
their voices. When Bishop Bruskewitz wrote that he would meet with
John Krejci only after he "regularized" his situation with the Church, he
silenced a voice. Members of CALL and Call To Action Nebraska tried
to have their voices heard in their diocesan newspaper but they were

denied that opportunity. Certainly, the entire appeal process was silencing as well. Though Bishop Bruskewitz often initiated media coverage, he appears to fault CTAN members who spoke to the media. However, this was the only avenue open to them to defend themselves against wild accusations. Joan Johnson noted that Bishop Bruskewitz "really stretches the truth about some of our members, and yet we have no mechanism to respond. . ."[41] Silenced voices.

A bishop is in charge of his own diocese. Recall CALL and CTAN member, Kay Haley's, comment on how Bishops Flavin and Bruskewitz used this power:

> I think it's wonderful for a bishop to be in charge of his diocese, but it's also like it's his very own little kingdom and he's like a little king and that's the way he wants to treat it. He alone has authority and the Archbishop of Omaha can't do anything. He's answering only to the pope. So it can be a real problem if you have a man like Bishop Flavin who wanted to build a fence around the diocese. Or Bishop Bruskewitz. . . [42]

The experiences documented in this book demonstrate the need for lay people to have an official means to have their voices heard in the church—one that does not depend on the granting of that right by their bishops. Further, priests and bishops must change the church culture of protecting the institution over protecting the rights of individual parishioners. Though it was clear through private communication that bishops and priests from around the country disagreed with both Bishop Flavin and Bishop Bruskewitz, they felt powerless to have any influence. In effect, the organizational structure of the church led them to silence themselves. If a priest is viewed as disobedient, a bishop could strip him of his faculties. This is a heavy threat to hold over a person, especially a person in mid-to-late life who has built his whole life in the institution.

As noted, Bishops generally refrain from criticizing each other in public. Regarding Bishop Bruskewitz and his extra-synodal legislation, Fr. Thomas Reese stated, "One of the problems that occurs when a bishop goes rogue like this is that episcopal courtesy requires that bishops do not get in fights in public, so even those bishops who disagree with him, won't say anything."[43] Reese believed the bishops would "burn up the telephone wires talking to each other about how they are going to handle Bruskewitz."[44] Reese explained that silence does not equal agreement when it comes to the bishops. The bishops, he said, "do not wash their laundry in public."[45]

One might suppose that this policy is comforting if one is a bishop. If, however, like members of CALL and CTAN, you find yourself in the crosshairs of a "rogue" bishop, you have absolutely no recourse for justice. In that case this policy looks and feels different; it feels demeaning and abusive. As it was reported shortly after the extra-synodal legislation was promulgated:

> The response from the official church? Officially, a silence. "It's not likely that we would get involved," a spokeswoman for the National Conference of Catholic Bishops said the other day. "The bishop is in charge of his diocese, and that is the principle upon which we operate. He is the chief teacher." A spokesman at the Vatican Embassy in Washington declined comment. The press office at the Holy See in Rome referred the matter back to the National Conference. However, the *NCR* has reported that, in the back channels of the church, bishops all over the country are buzzing, consternating, working the phones as to what it all means.[46]

Certainly, the bishops cared about what Bishop Bruskewitz's legislation meant for them. What is unclear is if they cared about what the action meant for those at whom it was directed. When we hear reports of our appeal filed in a drawer somewhere with the hope that the problem will die with us, what are we to think? Are we to imagine that the bishops care about us or that they care about not upsetting the status quo? The official response is... silence. Rosalind Carr noted in an interview that this was a lesson she learned early through her experience with Catholics for Active Liturgical Life. She explained, "We would write to the bishops and say, 'women can't read, we don't have any Eucharistic ministers' and the bishops would say, 'Oh dear' and pat our hands and say, 'your bishop can do whatever he wants. We don't intrude on him.' And so we already knew we were isolated and alone. So we knew those other people were out there, but they didn't really care about us."[47] As Lori Darby observed, "When [you] are silent about injustice, you are participating in perpetuating that injustice."[48] Indeed, silence gives assent to the re-creation of the same unjust structure.

Jesuit moral theologian, Richard McCormick, pointed out in an essay in *America* magazine that though a bishop has authority in the church, he might "not exercise true leadership."[49] McCormick explained that the use of power does not necessarily lead to influence. McCormick defines authority as "the right to speak and to decide for a particular group, and to bind its members to the goals and methods of the group. It is the right to command and order."[50] In contrast, McCormick defines leadership as "the capacity of influencing the behavior of others in a given situation toward some goal or objective."[51]

We can treat formal authority as if it has an independent value and when we do, individuals or groups are controlled. McCormick's description of a controlled group sounds an awful lot like what members of CALL and Call To Action experienced and continue to experience in the Lincoln diocese: "Discussion is closed and draws upon very limited competence. The controlled are told what they may and may not do, not what they can achieve. They are reminded of the importance of a structure, not of their own importance. They are constrained, not challenged; they are prohibited, not promoted."[52] In contrast, leadership leads to the liberation of individuals so that they can reach their full potential[53]

Changing the Organizational Structure

Do I mean to suggest that the entire organizational structure of the Catholic Church is corrupt? No, I do not. Do I mean to call all teaching authority of the bishops into question? No, I do not. What I do suggest is that the institution conduct a thorough review of its structure and this review must include the voices of the laity. We must be honest about the social construction of this structure. Organizational structure is created and sustained as people act in patterned ways over time. The Catholic Church offers a unique case as some church members treat each aspect of church structure as if it was handed straight from God. Any familiarity of church history will show, however, that the church has made mistakes in the past and the church has changed and grown as human knowledge has grown.

When I visit some Catholic websites, I often read blog entries that express the opinion that Catholic dissenters are egotists who want total control of the church. These responses seem an extreme reaction to a desire to discuss issues and problems. CTAN member John Burke noted:

> I don't see that as certainly one of the main motivations is to gain con-
> trol as much as to alleviate control over people that are being oppressed
> in one form or another. And we're not, we're not always talking about
> major forms of oppression, or overt, major overt oppression, but the
> subtle oppression that occurs within systems that we, you know, even
> now in a lot of ways I'm unaware of.[54]

Members of Call To Action are asking that the church take a careful and honest look at these structures and make necessary adjustments. Burke discussed a presentation he heard in which the speaker said the Hebrew meaning of sin is being "off the target." Burke appreciated this understanding and used it to express his belief that members of Call To Action aren't "necessarily trying to be the archer all the time." Rather they are "just trying to realign the target a bit. . . put things back in balance. . . look at how we've gotten offline in some subtle ways, as well as maybe some more overt ones."[55]

Disagreement in the church goes back to its very origins, before much structure was even in place. St. Peter and St. Paul differed in their belief on whether or not the Gentiles needed to first convert to Judaism and follow Jewish law in addition to following Christ. Peter believed they should. Paul did not. St. Paul addressed this matter (1 Cor 4: 3-5, RSV):

But with me it is a very small thing that I should be judged by you or by any human court. I do not even judge myself. I am not aware of anything against myself, but I am not thereby acquitted. It is the Lord who judges me. Therefore do not pronounce judgment before the time, before the Lord comes, who will bring to light the things now hidden in darkness and will disclose the purposes of the heart. Then every man will receive his commendation from God.

Though Peter is considered the first pope, in the end, Paul's view prevailed.

Do bishops hold teaching authority? Yes, they do. But does that authority mean that everything a bishop or priest does is divinely inspired? No, it does not.

What is the Solution?

If we truly believe that the Holy Spirit is at work in all the people of God, we must devise a way for all the people of God to have their voices heard. Anything less than that is an affront to the Holy Spirit. The structure of the church must change so that there are official outlets for the many and varied voices of the church. Would such a change be complicated and messy? Yes, it would. But complicated and messy is a condition of this life. As Avery Dulles observed, "the Catholic Church stands to gain from a prudent introduction of certain American democratic values and practices as urged by the liberals."[56]

Some might argue that pastoral councils invite lay voices into church discussions. This involvement is possible only if those with authority allow it. Pastoral councils are consultative bodies. Further, they are not even required to exist. Reflecting on the Archdiocese of Omaha's pastoral council, Mel Beckman remarked, "The Archdiocese has a pastoral council but it's very much the Archbishop's council and he controls it and it's not really a consultative thing. The decisions are made behind the scenes, most people don't know who makes them."[57]

Even if a bishop listens to the people on a pastoral council, an effort must be made to bring diverse voices to the table. Joan Johnson recalled the Lincoln diocesan Synod that took place in 1996. Johnson said, "It was clear that Bishop Bruskewitz had an agenda from day one when he came to Lincoln. But he needed to legitimize that agenda and he did it through this Syndod. It was a total sham. Only those who totally agreed with this agenda were allowed to participate as representatives."[58] The bishops must invite alternate voices to the table, listen to them, and seriously and prayerfully consider alternative perspectives.

Certainly, the bishops could benefit from talking to lay people and really listening to them. When asked about what she finds most difficult in the church, CALL member Mary Jo Bousek answered, "the lack of the hierarchy listening to the people in this diocese. I've been here long enough that I'm out of touch with how it works in other places but I know the Catholic Church is not a democracy. It's not a democracy! I hear that so many times. No, it's not a democracy but don't you want the hierarchy to listen to the people?"[59] For real change to occur, the organizational structure must be scrutinized. As Patty Hawk observed, "It's not about making certain changes. . . it's about creating and evolving and nurturing a healthy church environment. That's not going to happen with one change. It's not even going to happen with 150 changes. It's going to happen with constant dialogue and reflection and a sense of community and celebration."[60] Carol McShane expressed a similar idea, "I would love to see CTA succeed, of course, in women in the ministry. But if they came and handed that to us today, it would be a hollow victory because there's so much other reform that has to take place. We have to reform our way of thinking about church, about community. We have to reform our way of thinking about the hierarchy."[61]

Change doesn't happen quickly in the Catholic Church, but it does happen. Lay people can impact the direction of the church. As one Omahan CTAN member stated, "If you look back historically, any major changes, most major changes that have come. . . they're connected [to] somebody in the trenches little by little putting pieces together. . . But they don't occur just because of what's happened right here, it's all the stuff back here that was sort of laying the groundwork."[62] Many members of CTAN see their work as laying the groundwork for the changes they hope to see in the church. I know I may not live to see the changes I hope for, but I also know that without this groundwork, future generations may not either.

Second, we must treat our fellow Catholics with love and respect. I call on the words of Fr. Avery Dulles as he discussed different approaches to the relationship between Catholicism and United States culture:

> Each group should respect the intentions of the others and humbly recognize its own limitations. The internecine struggles between opposed factions are a scandal and a waste of energies that could more profitably be devoted to the common mission of the church as a whole to minister to the salvation of the world. By generously recognizing the diverse gifts of the Holy Spirit, all can help build up the body of Christ in unity and strength."[63]

In reading some online Catholic discussions, one notes a sense of glee as one Catholic cheerfully pushes another out the door. Shouldn't we, as Dulles suggests, offer the benefit of the doubt to the other—to assume that all persons mean well, even when we disagree with them?

In an interview, CTAN member John Burke explained how throughout his life he has had experience with a wide variety of Catholics, from Opus Dei to very liberal. He explained that these experiences were very good for helping him understand the diversity within the Church. He said, "It helped me understand how to discern people that are searching from people who are being intolerant of each other." He explained that when he moved to Lincoln, "I had no problem with people having more conservative viewpoints, more conservative theology than me, it's when they're chastising those that don't as somehow being less holy, less Catholic, less in touch with God, that is really bothersome."[64]

A Lincoln CTAN member who has moved out of state addressed her experience of CTAN as a group of people who approached things positively and did not try to insult others. Explaining what she was afraid she might find when she attended a CTAN gathering, she said:

I was concerned at first that is would just be this opportunity to just lash out at the people who were lashing out at them. You know just kind of a forum for retaliation, but it wasn't at all. I thought Call To Action was so loving towards people. I mean you could feel comfortable in expressing your frustration. But I think the focus always came back to a positive light. You know, I never felt like "Oh well, that was just a session to let it all out and air your complaints." I never felt like that was the purpose of Call To Action. . . So it was like, you don't stoop to that level of name calling and condemning other people because then you become like that. It was like it was above that, which was always refreshing to me.[65]

Another Lincoln CTAN member shared, "The most important thing that people need to know about Call To Action is that people who belong to it love the church. The true basis is not anger but it is love of something better and love for the opportunity that there be something better."[66]

Why is it important?

Members of Call To Action are frequently asked, "Why do you stay in the Catholic Church?" Sometimes the question is not asked very nicely. Each person's answer might be different, but most people seemed to agree that "This is my church" and "I am the church." When I was interviewed for the radio program, Speaking of Faith, I explained:

I have a friend who is gay and he tells me this story about sitting in church as a child and knowing that he was gay and hearing the priest talk about how that's wrong and how he would just beg God to change him. And I think, if I stay quiet, how many more kids are going to hear these things? It's a responsibility to listen to the Spirit moving in you. And so, if I leave, I feel like I'm not following my calling.[67]

Other interviewees cited the words of St. Peter, "Lord, to whom shall we go?"[68]

Each interview I conducted for this book was unique in some way. One Lincoln CTAN member who asked to remain anonymous told me about her relationship with the Catholic Church. I had known this woman for quite awhile but I was surprised by what she shared. Her story touches the theme I mentioned above:

> Being a Catholic has always been very painful for me. Since I was eight
> years old and that was the first time I remember. . . I had to go to con-
> fession and they told me all about hell and I took it all literally. I was
> scared to go to communion. . . I could not go to communion without
> immediately going to confession first. . . I would get so scared about
> being clean. . . they told us you had these dark spots on your soul. . . I
> would get physically sick. . .[69]

She reflected on her hope for Call To Action, "I was hurt and I don't want them to hurt anymore. Whatever little I can do to stop some of this stuff."

While no other bishop has followed in Bishop Bruskewitz's footsteps and excommunicated members of Call To Action, other characteristics of Catholic life in Lincoln are spreading to other dioceses. As an editorial in the *National Catholic Reporter* stated:

> If Bruskewitz is, as one person put it recently, 'a loose cannon on
> the barque of Peter,' his behavior might not come as a total surprise.
> Episcopal appointments in recent years have had to pass through a nar-
> row corridor of strict orthodoxy as defined by a small clique of prelates
> in Rome, with virtually no regard to pastoral considerations or input
> from the local clergy or laity. The result has been not that the world's
> Episcopal ranks are now characterized by a healthy balance of conser-
> vative, moderate and progressive voices, but rather that narrow-minded
> ideologues dominate. In such a climate, extremism flourishes, strict
> adherence to church law is viewed as the highest of virtues and recourse
> to censure is increasingly the means of governance.[70]

Though Bishop Bruskewitz was not named to another, higher, position in the church, three priests from the Lincoln diocese have been made bishops. Two of these bishops have demonstrated some tendency to emphasize their own authority and silence voices of dissent.

Thomas Olmsted was ordained bishop in 1999. His first assignment was Coadjutor Bishop of the Diocese of Wichita, Kansas. He became Bishop of Wichita in 2001. In 2003, Bishop Olmsted was named Bishop of Phoenix, Arizona.[71] Bishop Olmsted made national news when he removed the Catholic designation of St. Joseph's Hospital and Medical Center when the administrators there would not acknowledge his authority over the hospital's ethics committee.

The case above question involved a heartbreaking situation.[72] A pregnant woman, already a mother of four young children,[73] developed pulmonary hypertension. With no treatment, both mother and baby had almost no chance of survival. Doctors recommended termination of the pregnancy to save the life of the mother. Sr. Margaret Mary McBride, a member of the ethics committee at St. Joseph approved the surgery. St. Joseph's holds that the procedure was an indirect abortion while Bishop Olmsted insists the procedure was an abortion. Bishop Olmsted publicized that Sr. McBride and any other Catholic who participated in the operation had excommunicated themselves. Bishop Olmsted reportedly wrote a letter in which he referred "numerous times to his authority as bishop."[74] He wrote, "There cannot be a tie in this debate. Until this point in time, you have not acknowledged my authority to settle this question. . . Your actions communicate to me that you do not respect my authority to authentically teach and interpret moral law in this diocese."[75]

Robert Vasa became bishop of the Baker, Oregon diocese in 2000. In 2011 Bishop Vasa was named coadjutor to the Santa Rosa, California diocese and bishop June 30, 2011.[76] Bishop Vasa is known for requiring all Eucharistic Ministers, lectors, cantors and catechists in the Baker diocese to sign or verbally profess an "Affirmation of Personal Faith" called by some a "loyalty oath." Bishop Vasa explained that the statements in the affirmation "represent the authentic and authoritative teaching of the Catholic Church and acceptance of these tenets is expected of every Catholic."[77] In discussing the affirmation, Bishop Vasa explained that those serving the church are representatives of the church and care must be taken that they not lead "the little ones" astray.[78] After affirming, "I believe and profess all that the Holy Catholic Church teaches, believes and proclaims to be revealed by God," the following areas are singled out for affirmation:

> the inviolability of human life, the sinfulness of contraception, the evil of extra-marital sexual relationships, the unacceptability of homosexual relationships, the wrongness of cohabitation before marriage, the significance of the Real Presence of Christ in the Eucharist, the legitimacy of Marian devotions, the existence of hell and purgatory, the uniqueness of the Catholic Church, the legitimacy of the Holy Father's claim to infallibility and the moral teaching authority of the Catholic Church.[79]

The fact that Bishop Vasa chose to emphasize these teachings and not mention love of God or neighbor, peace, or justice is instructive.

When Bishop Vasa left the Baker diocese, he left behind a polarized diocese. An article in the *National Catholic Reporter* quotes members of the Baker diocese with conflicting views of Vasa.[80] Some describe him as having "hard-line policies, rigid theological interpretations and… markedly top-down leadership style short on compassion." Another person is quoted as describing him as "warm, friendly and down to earth" as well as "the best thing to happen to this diocese." Certainly, some were pleased with Bishop Vasa and his Affirmation of Personal Faith, but Richard Groves is quoted as having said that the affirmation hurt many people: "I know people in their 70s and 80s for whom the church was the center of their lives—and they are heartbroken. They have been made to feel like outsiders. It is like if you do not toe the line, if you do not accept a very rigid, narrow approach to Catholicism, you do not have a place here."[81]

Bishop Vasa brought a version of his loyalty oath with him to the Santa Rosa diocese.[82] Catholic and non-Catholic teachers and administrators in the Santa Rosa diocese Catholic schools are being required to sign a contract addendum called "Bearing Witness." Bishop Vasa wrote the addendum. When signed, the addendum indicates that the employees agree that they are "a ministerial agent of the bishop" and that they reject, among other things, contraception, abortion, and same-sex marriage.[83] (This requirement was temporarily withdrawn as this book went to press.)

For thirty years faithful, committed Catholics have been working together to give voice to the voiceless in the diocese of Lincoln, Nebraska. Through all the adversity, they built a strong community that welcomes newcomers. Mary Hawk described her impression of the Call To Action members:

> Well, in terms of the way they treat each other, I would say respect would be probably the first thing. All of these people are educated. All of them are articulate. Some of them are extremely educated. And they're conscious of how they are communicating with one another. . . This group, again, who have personally taken it upon themselves to understand the theology of the church and the theology of Christ, take the time, even though they are so far and away ahead of me in my understanding, they take the time to ensure that everybody understands what they're trying to communicate. . . this community of Catholics, Nebraska Call To Action, knows that they are planting seeds they may never see bloom, but they know they will bloom. They just may never, it may not happen in their lifetime. But they are undaunted. They know that generations before them have planted seeds from which they've benefited, and they're doing the same for generations to come. They laugh a lot. Again, I think that they are, they are a community. . . These people need one another and they are there for one another. I think they are the essence of what the church is supposed to be—a microcosm of what Christ wanted.[84]

Mary Hawk's description matches my own.

I leave the reader of this book with a question: What kind of family do Roman Catholics want to create together? Do we want a family with an authoritarian father who demands blind obedience? Or do we want to create a family in which each member is treated with respect and dignity and each person's gifts are celebrated and utilized? I want the latter. God gave me a brain and the ability to reason. I received the gifts of the Spirit at Baptism and Confirmation. Surely these gifts should not be allowed to stagnate.

For over thirty years the leadership of the Roman Catholic Church in the diocese of Lincoln has attempted to silence alternate voices. They have been unsuccessful. Though we have suffered for it, CALL and CTAN members have raised our voices time and again. The suffering is not the only story, however. By being true to our call and the voice of the Spirit, we find great peace.

Notes Chapter 9

1.   Stephen Buttry, "Catholic Dissenters Look to Centuries of Precedent," *Omaha World Herald*, April 28, 1996.

2.   Stephen Buttry, "Dissenters Can't Imagine Leaving Church Family," *Omaha World Herald*, May 12, 1996.

3.   Ibid.

4.   Ibid.

5.   Bob Reeves, "Many Rally Behind Bishop Who Issued Ban on 12 Organizations," *Lincoln Journal Star*, April 20, 1996.

6.   Bob Reeves, "Call To Action was Praised by Cardinal: Group Now Forbidden by Bishop," *Lincoln Journal Star*, April 21, 1996.

7.   Joan Johnson, interview with the author.

8.   John Burke, interview with the author.

9.   Pat Sullivan, interview with the author.

10.   S. L. Hansen, "Holy See Upholds Excommunication Penalty for Call To Action: Bishop Calls for Reconciliation, Hopes for an End to Opposition," *Southern Nebraska Register*, December 8, 2006.

11.   Kristi Wright, "An Orthodox Life: Bishop Thrust into Spotlight Prefers to Tend Flock," *Omaha World Herald*, April 21, 1996.

12.   Charles R. Morris, "A Tale of Two Dioceses: From Lincoln to Saginaw," *Commonweal*, June 6, 1997.

13.   Ibid.

14.   Ibid.

15. Bob Reeves, "Priest Shortage Hasn't Hit Local Diocese—Yet," *Lincoln Journal Star*, April 22, 1996.

16. Charles R. Morris, "A Tale of Two Dioceses…."

17. Stephen Buttry, "Catholic Dissenters Look to Centuries…."

18. Lori Darby, interview with the author.

19. Charles Kelliher, interview with the author.

20. Jeff Zeleny, "Nebraska Catholics Face Being Excommunicated," *Sunday Eagle Tribune*, April 14, 1996.

21. Paul Hendrickson, "Questions of Faith: They Say They're Good Catholics. But Their Bishop is Threatening Excommunication," *Washington Post*, April 12, 1996.

22. For an introduction to Constructivism and person-centered messages, see Chapter 8 of Em Griffin, *A First Look at Communication Theory*, 8th ed, New York: McGraw Hill, 2012.

23. For an introduction to Standpoint Theory, see Chapter 35 of Em Griffin, *A First Look at Communication Theory*, 8th ed, New York: McGraw Hill, 2012.

24. Leslie Wirpsa, "Bruskewitz Elaborates on Recent Decree," *National Catholic Reporter*, April 12, 1996.

25. "Bishop Lucker: Which Church Teachings are Really Essential?" *Call To Action News*, Spring 1996.

26. Ibid.

27. Leslie Wirpsa, "Excommunication Decree Sows Confusion: Three Bishops Belong to Condemned Group," *National Catholic Reporter*, April 5, 1996.

28. Ibid.

29. Bishop Fabian Bruskewitz, "An Ordinary Viewpoint: The Lay Vocation I," *Southern Nebraska Register*, May 10, 1996.

30. Ibid.

31. Stephen Buttry, "Shepherds Guide Restive Flock," *Omaha World Herald*, May 14, 1996.

32. Joan Johnson, interview with the author.

33. Bishop Fabian Bruskewitz, "An Ordinary Viewpoint: The Lay Vocation II," *Southern Nebraska Register*, August 2, 1996.

34. Ibid.

35. This speech was given on April 10, 1999. A text of the speech can be found at: http://www.dioceseoflincoln.org/Archives/about_talks_limits-dialogue.aspx.

36. Jim McShane, interview with the author.

37. Bradford E. Hinze, *Practices of Dialogue in the Roman Catholic Church: Aims and Obstacles, Lessons and Laments*, New York: Continuum, 2006, 82.

38. Bradford E. Hinze, *Practices of Dialogue...* 89.

39. Bradford E. Hinze, *Practices of Dialogue...* 82.

40. John Burke, interview with the author.

41. Joan Johnson, interview with the author.

42. Kay Haley, interview with the author.

43. Leslie Wirpsa, "Excommunication Decree Sows Confusion...."

44. Ibid.

45. Ibid.

46. Paul Hendrickson, "Questions of Faith...."

47. Rosalind Carr, interview with the author.

48. Lori Darby. Interview with the author.

49. Richard A. McCormick, "Authority and Leadership: The Moral Challenge," *America*, July 20/July 27, 1996.

50. Ibid.

51. Ibid.

52. Ibid.

53. Ibid.

54. John Burke, interview with the author.

55. Ibid.

56. Avery Dulles, "Catholicism and American Culture: The Uneasy Dialogue," *America*, January 27, 1990.

57. Mel Beckman, interview with the author.

58. Joan Johnson, interview with the author.

59. Mary Jo Bousek, interview with the author.

60. Patty Hawk, interview with the author.

61. Carol McShane, interview with the author.

62. Interview with the author, name withheld at interviewee's request.

63. Avery Dulles, "Catholicism and American Culture."

64. John Burke, interview with the author.

65. Interview with the author, name withheld at interviewee's request.

66. Interview with the author, name withheld at interviewee's request.

67. "The Beauty and Challenge of Being Catholic: Hearing the Faithful," *Speaking of Faith*, May 1, 2008, http://being.publicradio.org/programs/being_catholic/transcript.shtml.

68. John 6:68.

69. Interview with the author, name withheld at interviewee's request.

70. "Bruskewitz Attack Adds a Chill to Chilly Church," *National Catholic Reporter*, April 12, 1996.

71. Diocese of Phoenix, Arizona, http://www.diocesephoenix.org/bishop/olmstedIndex.htm.

72. See Michael Clancy, "Phoenix Bishop Gives Ultimatum to Hospital," *National Catholic Reporter*, December 16, 2010, http://ncronline.org/news/faith-parish/phoenix-bishop-gives-ultimatum-hospital.

73. Jerry Filteau, "Catholic Health Association Backs Phoenix Hospital," *National Catholic Reporter*, December 22, 2010, http://ncronline.org/news/catholic-health-association-backs-phoenix-hospital.

74. See Michael Clancy, "Phoenix Bishop Gives Ultimatum. . ."

75. Ibid.

76. Diocese of Santa Rosa website, http://santarosacatholic.org/thebishop.html.

77. Bishop Robert Vasa, Letter to Lay Ministers, Diocese of Baker Pastoral Guidelines, Appendix 29, April 2004, http://www.diocesephoenix.org/bishop/olmstedIndex.htm.

78. Bishop Robert Vasa, "Giving Testimony to the Truth," Diocese of Baker Pastoral Guidelines, Appendix 29, April 23, 2004, http://www.diocesephoenix.org/bishop/olmstedIndex.htm.

79. Ibid.

80. Dan Morris-Young, "'I Suspect Jesus was Not all that Popular': Bishop Vasa Reflects on his Time in Baker, Ore., Diocese," *National Catholic Reporter*, March 21, 2011, http://ncronline.org/news/accountability/i-suspect-jesus-was-not-all-popular.

81. Ibid.

82. John A. Coleman, "Church Loyalty Oaths Revisited," *America*, June 29, 2012, http://americamagazine.org/content/all-things/church-loyalty-oaths-revisited.

83. Dan Morris-Young, "California bishop adds belief requirements to teacher contracts," *National Catholic Reporter*, March 11, 2013, http://ncronline.org/node/47291.

84. Mary Hawk, interview with the author.

Selected Bibliography

George Cheney, Lars Thoger Christensen, Theodore E. Zorn and Shiv Ganesh, *Organizational Communication in an Age of Globalization: Issues, Reflections, Practices,* 2nd ed. Long Grove, IL: Waveland Press, 2011.

John A. Coleman, "Church Loyalty Oaths Revisited," *America,* June 29, 2012, http://americamagazine.org/content/all-things/church-loyalty-oaths-revisited.

Bernard J. Cooke, "Call To Action: Engine of Lay Ministry," in *What's Left?: Liberal American Catholics,* ed Mary Jo Weaver (Bloomington, IN: Indiana Unviersity Press, 1999).

James A. Coriden, "Even in Lincoln, Doubtful Laws Don't Apply, " *Commonweal,* April 19, 1996. http://findarticles.com/p/articles/mi_m1252/is_n8_v123/ai_18221780/.

James D. Davidson, Andrea S. Williams, Richard A. Lamanna, Jan Stenftenagel, Kathleen Maas Weigert, William J. Whalen, and Patricia Wittberg. *The Search for Common Ground: What Unites and Divides Catholic Americans* (Huntington, IN: Our Sunday Visitor Publishing Division, Our Sunday Visitor, Inc. 1997)

Stanley A. Deetz, *Democracy in an Age of Corporate Colonization: Developments in Communication and the Politics of Everyday Life.* Albany, NY: State University of New York Press, 1992.

Avery Dulles, "Catholicism and American Culture: The Uneasy Dialogue," *America, 162,* no 3 (1990).

Eric M. Eisenberg and H. L. Goodall, Jr. *Organizational Communication: Balancing Creativity and Constraint,* 4th ed. (Boston: Bedford/St. Martin's, 2004).

Anthony Giddens, *The Constitution of Society.* University of California Press, 1984.

Bradford E. Hinze, *Practices of Dialogue in the Roman Catholic Church: Aims and Obstacles, Lessons and Laments.* New York: Continuum, 2006.

Paul Likoudis, "An Interview with Bishop Fabian Bruskewitz." *The Wanderer,* April 18, 1996, http://www.ewtn.com/library/ISSUES/BRUSKEWI.TXT.

Richard A. McCormick, "Authority and Leadership: The Moral Challenge," *America,* July 20/July 27, 1996.

Charles R. Morris, "A Tale of Two Dioceses: From Lincoln to Saginaw," *Commonweal, 124*, no. 11 (June 6, 1997).

Dennis K. Mumby, *Communication and Power in Organizations: Discourse, Ideology and Domination.* Norwood, NJ: Ablex Publishing Corporation, 1988.

Mary Jo Weaver and R. Scott Appleby, *Being Right: Conservative Catholics in America.* Indianapolis: Indiana University Press, 1995.

Index

A

Abortion,
CTA non-position, 168; CTAN non-position, 206645

Adkins, Barb, 122

Adult education, 67
CALL concern, 71; priest, presence (requirement), 72

Allen, Jenny, 37

Anderson, Mary Jo, 136
CTA accusations, outrageousness, 271; *Southern Nebraska Register* article, 131–132

Andreatta, Tullio, 55

Apostolic Delegate to the United States, CALL documentation, 66

Apostolic Pro-Nuncio
Catholics Speak Out letter writing, 152; McShane communication, 186

Apostolic Signatura, 211

appeal, 227
competence, absence (*See* Supreme Tribunal of the Apostolic Signatura)

Appleby, R. Scott, 20
Being Right, 3–4

Archbishops, McShane communication, 186

Artificial contraception, public approval/Catholic Church disapproval, 129

Augustine, Algis, 240–241

Authority, questions, 43–44

Automatic penalties, 200

B

Balasuriya, Tissa
excommunication, 227; Thorburn opinion, 228; Vatican lifting, 228; treatment,
McShane opinion, 227

Banks, Adelle M., 136, 175, 176

"Bearing Witness" (Vasa), 287–288

Beckman, Mary Ann, 121

Beckman, Mel, 136
Archbishop perspective, 281; editing choice, 248; excommunication knowledge/response, 139; Gutsgell contact, 121–122; interviews, 134, 174, 177; public dissent comment, 161; Weavings perspective, 118

Being Right (Weaver/Appleby), 3–4

Benedictine Mission House/Christ the King Priory, Lincoln diocese criticism, 242

Benedict XVI, Pope, 1
smaller but purer (phrase), 5

Bentley, Rosalind, 176

Bernardin, Joseph, 174
CTA comments, 142–143; Greeley criticism, 274; Vatican World Communications award; (1987), delivery, 115

Berrigan, Daniel, 6

Beutler, Patty, 89

Biechler, James, 245

Bishops
authority: editorial assertion, 128; Flavin perspective, 63; CALL communication, 76; Carr perspective, 278–279; CTA gathering, Greeley criticism, 274; kingdom, Haley perception, 277; leadership, exercise, 279; legitimate authority, acceptance, 194–195; obedience, dogmatic matter (Cannon), 43; position, power, 6; power: editorial assertion, 128; knowledge, 94; problems, Reese perspective, 277–278; retirement age, 94; role, 4–5; spiritual vitality, concerns, 64; strict orthodoxy, 269

Block, Stephanie, 179

Boland, Raymond (extra-synodal legislation comment), 143

Boroviak, Ken, 241

Bousek, Mary Jo, 53, 54, 112
CALL member, 32; excommunication perspective, 151; hierarchy, listening (absence), 282; interview, 134, 177; Lincoln Catholic Church, relationship, 109; reader, role, 37

Bowles, Richard J., 25

Breaking Open the Word sessions, 15–16

Bruskewitz, Fabian, 136, 174, 177
agenda, legitimization, 282; ambition, Hawk perspective, 149–150; automatic penalties, 200; behavior, *National Catholic Reporter* perspective, 285–286; bishop, assignment, 94; book reading suggestions, CALL member reactions, 101–103; CALL interaction, 96–103; *CallSpirit* newsletters, delivery, 98; CALL Steering Committee, meeting: request, 98; restrictions, 100–101; Catholic treatment, 270; commendation (Donohue), 153; consecration, 95; correspondence, 11; CTA appeal, 183, 185–189; CTAN Steering Committee letter, 124; Bruskewitz response, 125; CTAN student report, 120; *Dateline NBC* appearance, 197; defining power, 131–133; description, 96; dialogue, perception, 273; diocesan priest letter, McCown response, 107; discussion/debate, stifling, 271; distrust, McShane perception, 188; docile obedience, expectation, 205–206; embarrassment, Buckley, Jr. perspective, 150; excommunication efforts, 137–138; extra-synodal legislation: abeyance, ruling, 216–217; appeal, response, 190–194; application, Vatican opinion, 150; Associated Press article, 158; Bernardin comments, 142–143; Canons, usage/explanation, 184–185; concerns, dismissal, 271; Gutsgell response, pressure, 161; issuance, 1–2, 16–17, 126–130; legal authority, 148; McBrien response, 146; rescinding,

Priests' Senate (impact), 199; support, 153; validity, perspective, 183–184, 200–201; Wilson comments, 145; extremism, propagation, 154; face-to-face meeting, 187–190; first appeal, 185–186; response, 190–194; formal canonical warning, 126–127; fraternal correction, 250; group excommunication, 18; Human Life International support, 153; impact, effectiveness, 19; Institute of Religious Life support, 153; justice, absence, 251–254; Krejci meeting, opportunity, 194; letters, 110, 111; harshness, 99–100; life/death issues, linkage (McBrien comments), 161–162; local/national communication, 199–209; McCown meeting, 96–97; McCown perceptions, 102–103; McShane meeting, 187–190; media, attention, 96–97; noncompliance (Dallas Charter), 249–254; notoriety, Seiker perspective, 154; Pastoral Bulletin, 96; pastoral love, exercise/responsibility, 189; perception of CALL, letter, 99; priesthood, fiftieth anniversary, 256–257; requests, denial, 274; resignation, 257; Roman Catholic definition, 132–133; subsidiarity, preference, 194–197; support, 252; targeting, 1–2; Wanderer Forum speech, 219; Weakland, differences, 268

Buckley, Jr., William F., 177
Bruskewitz perspective, 150

Burger, John, 181

Burke, John, 267–268
excommunication comment, 163; extra-synodal legislation comment, 150–151; parish life comments, 154–155

Burke, John (interview), 177–179

Busswell, Charles A., 127

Buttry, Stephen, 178, 179

Buttry, Steve, 54

C

CALL. *See* Catholics for Active Liturgical Life

CallSpirit, 53, 56–57

archives, exploration, 24; Carr remarks, 108–109; Catholic news, coverage (absence), 30; Catholic Social Services Bureau report, 85–86; final publication, 108–109; McCown comment, 88; newsletters, delivery, 98

Call To Action (CTA)
abortion, stance (avoidance), 168; authentic teachers (role), U.S. bishops (emphasis), 115; behavior, perception, 284; Bruskewitz information, 131; "Call for Reform in the Catholic Church" (pastoral letter), 116; CALL member interest, 113; Catholic Church affiliation, continuation (reasons), 284–289; Catholic option, mixture, 206; Cody, impact, 115; conference, Krejci/Darby appearance, 164; convention (1976), 115; CALL attendance, 117–118; CTAN involvement, 119; fear, nurturing, 238–239; funeral rite ban, 217; legislation response, 138–139; Lucker support, 143–144; McCown disagreement, 119; members, Hawk perception, 288; membership, numbers, 126–127; musical dramas, development, 115; *New York Times* advertisement, 116–117; organization, education, 131;petitions, *Catholic World Report* coverage, 254;press releases, 138–139; Reese perspective, 129; Ruetz comments, 169–170; Vatican discussion, 139; Vatican World Communications award, Bernardin delivery, 115

Call To Action Nebraska (CTAN), 117–119
actions, 160–173; advice, 211–214; appeal, 183, 185–186: brokered solution option, 195; development, 197–199; justice, absence, 251–254; options, 194–197; process, cessation, 227–228; response, 190–194; winning, chances, 226; Bruskewitz attack, 1–2, 125–126; Canon Law support, 213–214; charges, addressing, 201–202; communication, 210; conference ("It's a Matter of Conscience"), 165; Daley, speech/attendance, 166; Krejci welcome letter, 166; Darby, exit,

171–172; defense, rubrics/laws (usage), 203; defiance, Bruskewitz claim, 205–206; Diercks description, 256–257; direct Vatican appeal, 196; enforcement, 130–131; excommunication threat, 139; extra-synodal legislation appeal, 185–186; formation: announcement, 121–126; bishops, responses, 125; founding, 113; funeral rite ban, 217; Gantin appeal letter, 212–213; Gutsgell attendance, 162; identity/purpose, establishment, 238; information inaccuracy, Bruskewitz supply, 224; interdict, response, 155–159; involvement, 19–20; Krejci/Darby, co-chairs (designation), 124; legislation: member decision, 155–159; reaction, 138–139; *Lincoln Journal Star* article, 126; liturgy, Bruskewitz concern, 187–188; Majia suggestion, 212; mass, illegality (Bruskewitz claim), 203–204; McShane service, impact, 273–274; media: attention, 139–141; interaction, Bruskewitz comments, 191–193; meeting: Bruskewitz/Curtiss awareness, 122; Daley attendance, 152; members: attack, 247–248; Bruskewitz perception, 167–168; interview, 11; numbers, doubling, 158; withdrawal/reinstatement, 155–159; non-appeal options, 194–195; non-Catholic creed, usage (Bruskewitz claim), 202–203; *Omaha World Herald* article, 126; open meetings, policy development, 122–123; Permit to Gather, acceptance, 251; Peterson resignation, 217–218; prayer service, police officers (presence), 252; press release, 138, 173, 180; protests/polemics, organization (Bruskewitz claim), 204; responses, considerations, 170–173; retreat, 18–19; state meeting, initiation, 119–121; Steering Committee: Darby, comments, 170–171; student observers, exit, 121; Steichen opinion, 167; support, 152–155; Synod of Bishops opinion, 211; tenth anniversary celebration, 255–256; Vatican appeal, avoidance, 199–200; Vatican contact, requirement, 222

Call to Action or Call to Apostasy? (Clowes)

advertisement, 238–239; Bruskewitz endorsement, 215; McShane response, 239

Call To Action USA (CTA-USA), 114–117
Bruskewitz targeting, 1–2; conferences, advertisement, 18; Daley (co-director), 152; Detroit Call to Action conference (1976), recommendations (usage), 116–117; press release, 178; Profiles in Courage and Faith, document, 152

Call to Holiness, national conference (1996), 164
purpose, 166; *Southern Nebraska Register* opinion piece, 168–169; speakers, 164, 166

Cannon, Cecil M., 55; accusations, 43
bishop obedience, 43; dogma, term (usage), 43

Canon Law
ambiguity, 130; bishop retirement age, 94; Canon 14, 213; Canon 212, 207; Canon 215, 207; Canon 220, 213; Canon 391, 221; Canon 753, 200; Canon 843, 207; Canon 1316, 200: impact, 149; Canon 1317, 200; Canon 1318, 200, 206–207, 213–214: stipulation, 149: viewpoint, 186; Canon 1341, 207, 214; Canon 1353, 220: application attempt, 221; Canon 1369, violation, 204; Canon 1717, 207; CTAN usage, 213–214

Cardona, Dolores (Sheehan meeting), 65

Carlson, John, 136, 181

Carr, Rosalind K., 54
bishop perspective, 278–279; *CallSpirit* remarks, 108–109; CTAN inactivity, 155; Eucharist, receiving (concern), 74; excommunication comments, 155–156; interview, 178; letters, 90, 111, 112; survey explanation, 37

Casey, James V.
Denver archbishop, 24–25; interview, 25

Casler, Leight (Vasa conversation), 129–130

Cathedral of the Risen Christ, 24–25

Catholic Church
affiliation, reasons, 284–289; Americanism, impact, 6; authority, 10–11; change, slowness, 282–283; child sexual abuse, cover-ups, 275; church hierarchy, equivalence attempt (Bruskewitz), 128–129; communication, 7–8; CTAN relationship, 284–289; data collection, 11–12; gender discrimination, 41; hierarchy, listening (absence), 282; love/respect, absence, 74; loyalty, definition, 209; opposition: Curtiss perspective, 160–161; Vasa perspective, 149; organizational structure, 9–10, 273–275: change, 279–281; power, understanding, 275–279; reification, 9; scrutiny, 282; penalties, types, 200; power, 10–11: examples, 275; reform: context, 24–30; efforts, 23–24; sabotage, Cannon accusation, 43; structure, 59: impact, 9; typology, 5–6

Catholic community, bishop role, 4

Catholic faith, doctrine (opposition), 106

Catholic Hispanic community, response (improvement), 108

Catholicism, United States culture (relationship), 283

Catholic news, coverage (absence), 30

Catholic News Service, Vatican officials interview, 150

Catholics
childlike behavior, 267–268; isolation, Flavin (impact), 78; legislation response, 145–151; opinions, differences, 42; types, 5–6

Catholic schools, Flavin dedication, 30

Catholics for Active Liturgical Life (CALL)
Bruskewitz: bishop assignment, 94–95; interactions, 96–103; perception, letter, 99; *CallSpirit* (final publication), 108–109; church structure, 59; conciliation: failure, 82–84; filing, delay, 80; formal request, 80–81; Haley comment, 84; CTA awareness, 117;

disbanding, 24, 93; dissidents, perspective, 60–61; documentation, 66–67; education: discussion, 72; improvement/impact, 93–94; encouragement/support, 86–87; Flavin, response (absence), 48–49; formation, 42: reason, 24–25, 45; founding, 23–24, 33–35; hope, 87–88; initial meetings, 45–51; leadership, change, 78–79; legitimacy claim, Bruskewitz avoidance, 104; McCown, chairperson, 78–79; McShane: meeting chair, 45–46; president, service, 51; service, impact, 273–274; meetings: courage, 60, Haley reflection, 50; members: interview, 11; question/protest, ability, 43; negative assessment (Bruskewitz), 105; negotiations, 59–60; organization, Catholic identity, 60; Patron Saint, selection, 50–51; personal spiritual growth (Vatican II years), 30–31; Peterson (founder), 26; petition, response time, 81–82; plans, 64; Position Paper, 54: McShane, involvement, 47–48; statement, 63; priests, relationships, 27–28; resistance, 60–62; Roman Catholic churches, impact, 60–61; teaching duties, loss, 88

Catholics for Active Liturgical Life (CALL) Steering Committee Bruskewitz book suggestions, problems, 101–102; Bruskewitz meeting restrictions, 100–101; Bruskewitz prejudgment, 99–100; canon lawyer, contact, 62; disbanding, 108–110; meeting request (Bruskewitz), 98; Catholics for a Free Choice, 127

Catholic Social Services Bureau, *CallSpirit* report, 85–86

Catholics Speak Out, letter writing, 152

Catholic World Report (Call To Action petitions coverage), 254

Catlin, Roger, 54, 55

CCD. *See* Confraternity of Catholic Doctrine

Celibate-only priesthood, Curtiss support, 160

Chancery, McShane lockout, 217

Charron, Joseph, 168

"Charter for the Protection of Children and Young People" (bishop approval), 249

Cheney, George, 21

Chicago archdiocese, autocratic style, 115

Chicago Call To Action, travels, 115–116

Child safety, bishops (impact), 250

Chittisler, Joan Lincoln diocese attack, 242–243; support, 243; women's ordination, issue (discussion), 242–243

Christ, body/blood, 13 focus, 15

Christensen, Lars Thoger, 21

Christifidelis, 140

Christus Dominus (Vatican II document), 66

Church authority, family metaphor (relationship), 266–273; changes, U.S. Catholics response, 3; commitment, 4; congregation, women (impact), 42; environment, health, 282; hierarchy, Johnson perspective, 267–268; loyalty, definition, 209; penalties, types, 200; sabotage, Cannon accusation, 43; strict orthodoxy, 269; teachings, laity (differences/disagreements), 129

Clohessy, David, 253

Clossey, Pat, 180

Clowes, Brian, 180 *Call to Action or Call to Apostasy?,* 215; CTA accusations, outrageousness, 271; Human Life International report, 164–165

Code of Canon Law, 176 revisions, 148–149

Cody, John, 115

Communication
definition, 8; perspective, 7–8

Communion, Johnson denial, 215

Conciliation
failure, 83–84; formal request, 80–81; Haley comment, 84; process, Flavin nonparticipation, 82

Confraternity of Catholic Doctrine (CCD), 63
CALL focus, 67; CALL members, teaching duties (loss), 88; education quality, location (McShane difficulty), 70; Flavin/Seiker interaction, 69–70; outreach, renewal, 108; programs: funding, Vitzhum explanation, 68–69; usage, 64; signup, opportunity, 14

Congregation for Bishops
appeal, 227; CTAN communication, member consideration, 216

Congregation for Legislative Texts, appeal, 226

Congregation for the Doctrine of the Faith, appeal, 226, 227

Conley, James D., 257

Conscience, primacy (McInerny comment), 146

"Conscience and Development of Doctrine: Whose Responsibility?" (Gramick presentation), 245

Cooke, Bernard J., 133

Catholic permissions, perspective, 139

Cordaro, Frank (Thorburn communication), 168

Coriden, James, latae senteniae penalties usage (comment), 148–149

Coriden, James A., 176, 185
McShane letter, 222–223

Costello, Mary Brian, 186

Creativity, constraint (balance), 8

Crosby, Michael (Catholic analysis, 267–268

Crowley, Pat, 240

Southern Nebraska Register attack, 240–241

Crowley, Patty
CTAN conference speaker, 165: appearance, cancellation, 239–240; Lincoln diocese attack, 239–242; Southern Nebraska Register attack, 240–241: McShane response, 241

Culture Wars (Catholic magazine), 167

Culver, Virginia, 175

Curran, Charles, 228

Curtiss, Elden
celibate-only priesthood affirmation, 160; CTAN Steering Committee letter, 124: Curtiss response, 125; Daly/Peterson communication, 210; Hawk/Sullivan letter, 246; letters, 135, 179; A Pastoral Letter on Catholic Doctrine and Practice, 160–162; Thorburn letter, 121

Curtiss, Elden F.
legislation response, 160–162; pastoral letter, 178

D

Daley, Dan, 119, 251
CTA-USA co-director, 152

Daley, Sheila (justice perspective), 139

Dallas Charter guidelines, 249
Bruskewitz noncompliance, 249–254

Daly, Cecilia (excommunication letter), 210
Curtiss response, 210

Dammert, Tobias, 243

Darby, Lori
CTAN co-chair designation, 124; CTAN exit, 171–172; CTAN experience, 172–173; CTAN meeting perspective, 119–120; death threat, 171; founding co-chair, 18; integrity, absence (Bruskewitz accusation), 270; interviews, 134, 135; letters, 173, 181, 182; pain/strength, 159

Dateline NBC (Bruskewitz appearance), 197

Davidson, James D., 20, 135

Davis, Julie/Alton (Bruskewitz perspective), 154

Day, Dorothy, 6

Deborah's Place, 240

Deetz, Stanley A., 21

Delias, Jesse, 270

DeMolay, 127

Detroit Call to Action conference (1976), recommendations (usage), 116–117

Dialogue, danger (Bruskewitz perception), 273

Diercks, Rod, 256–257

Diocesan Council of Catholic Women, Vatican II study, 31

Diocesan Development Program (DDP), 54
usage, 37

Diocesan priests
Bruskewitz letter, McCown response, 107; communication, 64–65

Diocesan Tribunal
appeal, Thorburn perception, 198; Vasa chair, 195

Diocese of Lincoln
communication, improvement, 63; Kelliher, priest role, 27; non-instituted readers, Bruskewitz allowance, 103–104

Discursive closure, evidence, 10–11

Dissenting opinions, Vasa perspective, 129–130

Dissipating Ambiguities
Bruskewitz claim, 147; McShane comment, 147; Reese comment, 147; *Southern Nebraska Register* publication, 127–128

Dolan, Timothy, 271
USCCB president election, 4

Donohue, William (Bruskewitz perspective), 153

Doyle, Thomas, 225–226

Duffey, Virginia, 55

Dufford, Bob, 51

Dulles, Avery, 21
Catholic Church perspective, 281; Catholicism, United States culture (relationship), 283; Catholics, typology, 5–6

E

Eastern Star, 127

Ecumenical activities, Flavin participation (absence), 81

Ecumenism, 78

Eisenberg, Eric M., 21

EMEs. *See* Extraordinary Ministers of the Eucharist

Encyclical On the Development of Peoples (1967), 114

Eucharistic Ministers
role, 13, 15; Thorburn/Bruskewitz perspective, 130–131; usage, absence, 17

Evangelization, impediment, 201

Ewers, Patricia, 250

Excommunication
Balasuriya incident, 227–228; Bousek comments, 151; Burke comment, 163; Carr comments, 155–156; Daly/Peterson letter, 210: Curtiss response, 210: Hawk comments, 157; Hill comments, 145; impact, 162–163; justice, Daley perspective, 139; Kelliher interpretation, 158; knowledge, 138–139; Krejci media statement, 196–197; Matthews comments, 147–148; McCauley comments, 148; McManus perspective, 148; MENSA gathering, Thorburn comments, 208–209; psychological effect, 162–163; reversal (Balasuriya), 228; support, 153; Thorburn comments, 208–209; validity, 163

Extraordinary Ministers of the Eucharist (EMEs)
absence, impact, 64; usage: absence, 73; refusal, 81

Extraordinary Ministers of the Holy
　Communion usage, ban, 73
Extra-synodal legislation
　abeyance, 216–217: Bruskewitz consider-
　ation, 217–218; adjudication, Bruskewitz
　(impact), 199; appeal, 183: brokered solu-
　tion option, 195; CTAN development, 197–199;
　Krejci names, absence, 196–197; options, 194–197;
　Thorburn perspective, 196; Vatican response,
　218–219; Bernardin comments, 142–143;
　bishops, response, 142–144; Bruskewitz
　issuance, 1–2, 16–17; Burke com-
　ments, 150–151; Catholic response,
　145–151; clarity, absence, 201, 208;
　copy, Chancery fax, 205; CTA/CTAN
　response, 138–139; CTAN appeal,
　185–186: process, cessation, 227–228; Vatican
　response, absence, 222; CTAN members,
　decisions/responses, 155–159; CTAN
　non-appeal options, 194–195; Curtiss
　response, 160–162; dueling conferences,
　164–170; excommunication, effects,
　162–163; first appeal, 185–186; Green
　comment, 145; impact/worries, 161;
　issuance, 126–130; Kelliher comment,
　144; letters to the editors, discussion,
　141; local diocesan tribunal, involve-
　ment, 195; local/national communica-
　tion, 199–209; Maguire comment, 146;
　McBrien response, 146; media coverage,
　140: Chancery, blame, 204–205; medicinal
　approach, evidence (absence), 207;
　medicinal result, absence, 207–208;
　National Conference of Catholic
　Bishops, noninvolvement, 278; non-
　media response, 152–155; penalties,
　abeyance, 216; promulgation, 278; reac-
　tion, 137; rescinding, Priests' Senate
　(impact), 199; Southern Nebraska
　Register: blessing, 215–216; publication, 127,
　184; subsidiarity, preference, 194–197;
　Untener comment, 144; U.S. bishop
　response, 142–144; validity, perspective,
　183–184, 200–201

F
Faith
　example, 12–20; seriousness, 16; treat-
　ment, 13
Family
　household head, impact, 267; meta-
　phor: church authority, relationship, 266–273;
　Lucker usage, 271–272; Roman Catholic
　creation, 288–289
Ferguson, Tom
　Danko meeting, 71; TEC program ini-
　tiation, 70–71
Fessio, Joseph, 164, 166
Fidelity (Catholic magazine), 167
Filteau, Jerry, 135, 176
First Vatican Council. See Vatican I
Flavin, Glennon P., 52
　autocratic directives, explanation, 50;
　autocratic leadership style, 30; bishop
　authority perspective, 63; Bishop of
　Lincoln appointment, 30–31; CALL
　communication, failure, 63; CALL posi-
　tion paper, 47–48; Catholic isolation,
　78; Catholic treatment, 270; commu-
　nication, 45–51: problem, 62–63; refusal, 75;
　conciliation: attempt, 80–84; process, nonpar-
　ticipation, 82; control, 76–77: characteriza-
　tion, 27; ecumenical activities, absence,
　81; episcopacy, characteristic, 25–26;
　Hansen support, 44–45; intransigence,
　67; laity voices, silencing, 276–277;
　lector expansion, 33–34; lector policy:
　opinion pieces, 40; perspectives, 40; reactions,
　39–40; letter, 90, 91; letters of acknowl-
　edgment/support, 86–87; McCown:
　communication, 79; meeting, 79–80; McShane
　communications/updates, 47–49; media
　interaction, refusal, 76; meeting, 78–86:
　absence, 61–62; Peterson, letter/meeting,
　84–86; power, 60–62: abuse, 84; priest:
　control, 76–77; laity, separation, 28–29; priori-
　ties, 30; requests, denial, 274; succes-
　sion, 24–25
Formal authority, value, 279
Fox, Thomas C., 52, 53, 56, 89

CTAN speech, 266–267; *National Catholic Reporter* commentary, 50

Freemasons, 106, 127
Catholic membership, ban (Curtiss affirmation), 160; Church position, 131; marriage, 158; members, cessation, 162

Funeral rites, CTA/CTAN member ban, 217

Fussell, Anita, 52, 55, 110
Lincoln Journal Religion Editor, 26

G

Gabig, Joseph, 60

Gagnon, Cardinal (interview), 165

Ganesh, Shiv, 21

Gantin, Bernardin (CTAN appeal letter), 212–213

Gately, Sr., Edwina (CTAN conference speaker), 165

Gaudium et Spes, 165–166, 180

Gay/lesbian legal marriage, Catholic opinion, 129

Gedris, Agatha, 3

Gehringer, Joel, 177

Gender discrimination, 41

George, Francis (bishop role discussion), 4

Gergen, Genevieve, 55

Germany, Catholicism, 32–33

Giddens, Anthony, 21
structure, duality, 8

God
human rights source, 6; nation sovereignty, 6

Goodall, Jr., H.L., 21

Goodstein, Laurie, 20, 136, 176

Gramick, Jeannine
Lincoln diocese attack, 245–246; *Southern Nebraska Register* attack, 245–246

Grand Island Independent (extra-synodal legislation coverage), 140

Greeley, Andrew, 274

Green, Thomas (extra-synodal legislation comment), 145

Gregory, Wilton, 249

Grocholewski, Zenon, 211
CTAN letter, 211–212; recommendation, 212

Gullo, Carlo (Peterson/McShane request), 226

Gumbleton, Thomas, 65, 127

Gurrieri, John A.
encouragement, 86; letter, 92

Gutgsell, Michael, 122
extra-synodal legislation response, pressure, 161; family perspective, 266; public dissent examples, 160–161

H

Haley, Kay, 53, 56, 92
bishop perspective, 277; CALL meetings, 50; conciliation comment, 84; priests, exodus, 29–30; Vatican Council examination, 32

Hanifen, Richard (extra-synodal legislation comment), 143

Hanigan, Joe, 30

Hansen, Eulalia, 55
lector policy support, 44–45; McShane response, 44; support, 44

Hardes, Dales, 52–53
Oblate of Mary Immaculate, diocesan guidelines, 34

Harding, Sandra, 270–271

Hastings Tribune (extra-synodal legislation coverage), 140

Hauke, Manfred, 101

Hawk, Mary, 19–20
excommunication comments, 157; interview, 178

Hawk, Patty, 19–20

Bruskewitz perspective, 149–150; church environment, health, 282; excommunication perspective, 140; interview, 174, 176; Vatican contact, requirement, 222

Hawk, Teresa, 134

Hazuka, Jeremy, 247
Johnson Eucharist denial/response, 247–248

Heinen, Tom, 136

Hemlock Society, 127

Hendrickson, Paul, 173, 176
diocese perspective, 137

Hennessey, Patricia (CCD experience), 67–68
letter, 68

Hill, Richard (excommunication comments), 145

Hinze, Bradford E., 133

Hitchcock, Helen Hull, 100–101

Holomon announcement, 61

Holy Eucharist, usage (expansion), 108

Holy Spirit
belief, 281; Christ, promise, 77; impact, 5; movement, CALL following, 60; opening, 15; work, opportunity, 197–198

Homebound, Holy Eucharist (usage), 108

Homosexual practices, CTAN approval (Bruskewitz claim), 206

Hooper, John, 20

Housing Opportunities and Maintenance for the Elderly (HOME), 240

Huber, Mark, 21, 250
appeal rejection statement, 221–222; correspondence, 11

Hueser, Ralph, 248

Hughers, Jane Wolford, 114

Humanae Vitae (Paul VI issuance), 240

Human Life International

Bruskewitz petition drive, 153; report publication, 164–165; *Southern Nebraska Register* (advertisement), 238–239

Human rights. source, 6

Huspenl, Dennis, 174

I

Ignatius Press, Call to Holiness, 164

Imesch, Joseph L. (support), 87

Imposed penalties, 200

Inestimabile Donum, 39–40

Instituted lectors
characteristics, 36; policy, Bruskewitz perception, 106–107; Institute of Religious Life, Bruskewitz support, 153

Interdict, lifting (report/falsity), 190–191

It's a Matter of Conscience (CTAN conference theme), 165

J

Jackels, Michael (Thorburn letter), 228

Job's Daughters, 127

Johnson, Dirk, 175
Kellihers, communication, 118

Johnson, Jerry
commentary, 257; CTAN membership retention, 156; outrage, 23; Sheehan meeting, 65; UNL faculty worship prohibition, 75

Johnson, Joan, 53, 90
children, education (decision), 70; communion denial, 215, 247–248; CTA annual conference advertisement, impact, 117; CTAN membership retention, 156; excommunication, 138; faith journey, recognition, 272; interviews, 110, 134, 173, 178; letter, 133; nursing home survey, 74; Vatican II comment, 93

Johnson, Lyle, 237

John XXIII (Pope), enthusiasm, 25

Jones, E. Michael, 167
Justice, Daley perspective, 139

K

Kalin, Leonard, 77
Kealy, Thomas, McShane communication, 47
Kearney Hub (extra-synodal legislation coverage), 140
Keating, Karl, 52
 Flavin encounter, 27
Keeler, Bob, 136, 175
Keleher, James (extra-synodal legislation comment), 143
Kelliher, Charles, 52, 53
 active ministry exit, 269; excommunication interpretation, 158; extra-synodal legislation comment, 144; interview, 175, 178; Johnsons, communication, 118; priest, 25: role, 27
Kent, Stephen M., 179
King, Jr., Martin Luther, 190
Koluch, Kim, 251
Komonchak, Joseph A., 20, 21, 110
Konrady, Daniel J., 141
Kozeny, Tom, 52–53
Krejci, Jean, 181
 extra-synodal legislation reaction, 141; restrictions/repercussions, 162
Krejci, John, 181
 Bruskewitz: gesture, unfriendliness, 219–220; meeting opportunity, 194; communion, Walsh denial, 220; CTA convention delegate, 117; CTAN co-chair designation, 124; Eucharist denial, explanation request, 221–222; founding co-chair, 18; integrity, absence (Bruskewitz accusation), 270; interview, 178; letters, 135, 173, 174; *NCJR* resignation, 248; pain, Bruskewitz (impact), 220; self-communion, 219–220, 252; sin, awareness, 157

Krisman, Ronald K.
 comment, 86; letter, 92

L

Laghi, Pio, Mahoney discussion, 83
Laity, 73–75
 advice/opinion, 272; bishop attention, 281–282; church teaching, differences/disagreements, 129; concerns, expression, 63; conversation, bishops (involvement), 282; participation, Flavin limitations, 81; priests, separation (Flavin encouragement), 28–29; voices: denial, impact, 274–275; silencing, 276–277
Lamanna, Richard A., 20, 135
Latae sententiae penalties, usage (Coriden comments), 148–149
LDCCW. *See* Lincoln Diocesan Council of Catholic Women
Lector guidelines, 33–35
Lector policy. *See* Lincoln lector policy
Lector program, Flavin expansion, 33–34
Lector training, completion, 155
Letters of acknowledgment/support, 86–87
Liberalism (Catholics type), 5–6
Life/death issues, Bruskewitz linkage (McBrien comments), 161–162
Likoudis, Paul, 176
 Gagnon interview, 165; interview, 177
Lincoln Catholic Church, discrimination/autocracy (Bousek perception), 109
Lincoln Diocesan Call To Action, excommunication threat, 139
Lincoln Diocesan Council of Catholic Women (LDCCW), 44
 contact, 55–56; Hansen, lector policy support, 44
Lincoln diocese
 access, 2; adult education, CALL

concern, 71; bishops, discussions, 65; Bruskewitz consecration, 95; Chancery, McShane lockout, 217; changes, NCR story, 33–34; guidelines, changes, 34; joining, requirement, 17–18; Kealy (Vicar General), 65; lector policy, opinions, 41–42; lector program, Flavin expansion, 33–34; liturgical guidelines, 33–34; local/national media attention, 139–140; McShane/Vasa conversation, 46; media attention, 139–141; outlier status, 4; priests: discussions, 65; exodus, 29–30; physical appearance (Flavin concern), 28; relationship, 29; religious education, 67–73; sacramental needs, Flavin ability (problem), 81; Scripture readings, women (prohibition), 87; sex abuse audit noncompliance, 249–255: continuation, 254–255; virtue/loyalty, discussion, 49–50; voices, silencing, 275–276; women, role (limitation), 37

Lincoln Journal Star, 26
CTAN story, 126; extra-synodal legislation: copy, fax, 205; coverage, 140; interdict, lifting (report), 190–191; lector policy announcement, 107

Lincoln lector policy
announcement language, 36–37; CALL, formation, 45; Catholic reaction, 35–45; change, 34–35: Bruskewitz concerns, 105; Lincoln Journal Star announcement, 107; regulations, 105–106; Southern Nebraska Register announcement, 107; change, Bruskewitz, impact, 103–108; Flavin implementation, 38; gender-based concerns (Bruskewitz), 104; implementation, reason, 41; initiation, 39; logical extension, 42; mass, Scripture reading (restrictions), 73; meeting, 35; negative side, Bruskewitz perception, 104–105; non-installed lectors, female service, 105; opinion pieces, 40–41; reader opinions, 41–42; regulations (Bruskewitz), 105–106; *Lincoln Star* editorial, 42

Liturgical renewal, CALL Steering Committee request, 108

Liturgical review, commitment, 23

Liturgical wholeness, CALL concern, 48

Local diocesan tribunal, involvement, 195

Loudon, Betty Lou, 55

Lucker, Raymond, 127
CTA support, 143–144; extra-synodal legislation comment, 143–144; family metaphor, usage, 271–272

Lumen Gentium, 191

M

Maguire, Daniel (extra-synodal legislation comment), 146

Mahoney, Roger (letter), 91, 92

Mahoney State Park
liturgy, affirmation (Bruskewitz concern), 187–188; location, 119; mass: Bruskewitz perception, 192; permissions, 121; meetings, Bruskewitz students (exit), 201–202; organizational meeting, 190

Majia, Jorge Maria, 212

Malcolm, Teresa, 175

Martin, Regis (Bruskewitz perspective), 153

Mass, Scripture reading
Bruskewitz allowance, 95–96; Flavin restrictions, 73

Matthews, Sandy, 176
excommunication comments, 147–148; interview, 179

McBride, Margaret Mary, 286

McBrien, Richard
extra-synodal legislation comment, 146; life/death issue linkage comments, 161–162

McCaslin, Jack, 119
ministry prohibition/excommunication, Bruskewitz order, 121; Thorburn letter, impact, 120–121

McCauley, Dave (excommunication comments), 148

McClory, Bob (CTAN conference speaker), 165

Bruskewitz perception/comments, 167–168

McCord, Julia, 134, 136, 175, 180

McCormick, Richard, 279

McCormick, Tom, 117–118

McCown, Diana, 52, 53, 89
  Bruskewitz diocesan letter response, 107; Bruskewitz meeting, 96–97; CALL chairperson, 78–79; Casey interview, 25; Flavin: communication/response, 79; meeting, 79–80; interviews, 109–110, 112, 134; Letter From Our President, 109; letters, 91, 92, 111

McGovern, Ray (CTAN conference speaker), 165

McInerny, William (primacy of conscience comment), 146

McManus, Frederick R. (excommunication perspective), 148

McNamara, Lawrence, 21
  CTAN Steering Committee letter, 124

McShane, Carol, 53, 54, 56, 89, 90
  Bruskewitz book reading reaction, 102; CALL: position paper, 47–48; presidency, 51; CTA success, 282; excommunication, psychological effect, 162–163; Flavin meeting, absence, 61–62; interviews, 110, 111, 173, 174, 176; Kealy communication, 47; lector policy meeting, 35; Lincoln Journal Star: article, 34–35; interview, 194–195; memo, 133; priest appearance comment, 28; response (women's touch), 44; Vasa meeting, 46

McShane, Jim
  Bruskewitz meeting, 187–190; CALL/CTAN involvement, impact, 273–274; Canon list, receipt, 184–185; Coriden letter, 222–223; CTAN observers, discussion, 122; dissipating ambiguity comment, 147; extra-synodal legislation response, 138; extra-synodal letter, bishop responses, 186; letter to Thorburn, 123: Thorburn response, 123–124; Neves communication, 214–215; Newman Center problems, perspective, 75

Media coverage, Chancery (blame), 204–205

Media interaction, Flavin refusal, 75–76

Medicinal penalty, Canon Law (impact), 130

Michigan State University (MSU), student parish involvement, 15

Moen, Peggy, 180
  interview, 167

More, Thomas, 193

Morgenroth, Anton (presentations), 71–72

Morris, Charles R., 21
  Commonweal interview, 268–269; conservative vision, risk, 5

Morris-Young, Dan, 136

Morton, Gene (Sheehan meeting), 65

Mother Angelica
  Call to Holiness appearance, 164; network, 154

Mother's Day Massacre, 61

Mullen, Richard L., 55

Mumby, Dennis K., 21

N

Nation, sovereignty, 6

National Abortion Rights Action League (NARAL), 206

National Catholic Reporter (NCR), 30
  Bruskewitz behavior, 285–286; Catholics, characteristics, 59; extra-synodal legislation coverage, 140; Fox commentary, 50; Lincoln story, 33–34; reading, 18

National Conference of Catholic Bishops, McShane communication, 186
  CALL conciliation: failure, 83–84; process, Flavin nonparticipation, 82; public knowledge, vote, 83; request, 80–81; formal conciliation attempt, 80

National Council of Catholic Women (NCCW), position paper, 55–56

Nebraska Criminal Justice Review (NCJR), Krejci resignation, 248

Nebraska Wesleyan University (NWU), problems, 16–17

Nemec, Joseph, 268

Neo-conservatism (Catholics type), 5–6

Neuhaus, Richard, 177

Neves, Lucas Moreira (McShane letter), 214–215

Newman Center
adult education, 67; Burke perspective, 275–276; classes, attendance, 31–32; misgivings, 89–90; students, worship, 72

Newport, Frank, 135

New Ways Ministry, 245

New York Times (Call to Action advertisement), 116–117

Nicene Creed
CTAN acceptance, 224; CTAN displacement, Bruskewitz claim, 190; usage, CTAN refusal (Bruskewitz claim), 203

Noel, Thomas J., 52

Non-Catholic creed, CTAN usage (Bruskewitz claim), 202–203

Non-installed lectors
dress code, 106; female service, 105; publicity, reduction (Bruskewitz explanation), 106–107

Nursing homes
Holy Eucharist, usage (return), 108

Nursing homes, communion (distribution request/refusal), 74

O

Obedience, requirement, 5

O'Brien, Nancy Frazier, 21

Olmsted, Thomas, 286

Omaha Catholics, Weavings (creation), 118

Omaha World Herald
CTAN article, 126; extra-synodal

legislation coverage, 140; Jones, comments, 167

Opus Dei, 283

Order of St. Peter's Seminary, establishment, 154

Ordinatio Sacerdotalis, 189–190, 214

Organizational structure, 9–10, 273–275
change, 279–281; power, understanding, 275–279; reification, 9; scrutiny, 282

Orgren, James, 177

Orsy, Ladislas
comment, 87; letter, 92; support, 85

Orthodoxy, litmus test, 10

Orwig, Jim
extra-synodal legislation comment, 146; interview, 175

P

Papal Birth Control Commission (Crowley experience), 240

Parish councils, establishment, 108

Parish life, difficulty (Burke), 154–155

Pastoral Constitution on the Church in the Modern World, 165–166

Pastoral council, bishop attentions, 281–282

Pastoral Letter on Catholic Doctrine and Practice, A (Curtiss), 160–162

Pastors
acceptance, Vatican II opinion, 272; control, 10

Paul VI, Pope, 133
encyclical letter (5/114/71), 114; faith profession, Balasuriya signing, 227

Peterson, Betty, 52, 53, 89
CALL founder, 26; CTAN resignation, 217–218; excommunication letter, 210; Curtiss response, 210; lector policy meeting, 35; Sheehan meeting, 65

Peterson, Elizabeth A., 55

Peterson, Gordon, 91, 92

appeal letter, 224–225; CALL Vice President, 80; conciliation procedures, Mahony discussion, 81; letter, Flavin meeting, 84–86

Peterson, Mary Jo, 51

Pettinger, Alfred N., 52

Pew Forum on Religion and Public Life, 135

Pieczynski, Linda (CTA President comment), 164

Pilla, Anthony, 186

Pius X High School, 37

Planned Parenthood, 127

Plattsmouth Journal (extra-synodal legislation coverage), 140

Pokora, Dan/Marie
Catholic identification, 12–13; permissiveness, 266

Pokora, Rachel
appeal letter, 224–225; communion, denial, 238; parish membership removal, 237–238; sabbatical, 258

Politics of Prayer: Feminist Language and the Worship of God (Hitchcock), 100

Pompedda, Mario F. (Peterson/Pokora appeal letter), 224–225

Pontifical Council for the Interpretation of Legislative Texts, appeal, 227

Power
understanding, 275–279

Power, exercise, 237

Prayers of the Faithful, 40

Press, communication, 75–76

Priesthood vocation, Flavin dedication, 30

Priests
appearance, McShane comment, 28; communication, 76–77; exodus, 29–30; Flavin control, 76–77; laity, separation (Flavin encouragement), 28–29; physical appearance, Flavin concern, 28; relationships, 29

Profiles in Courage and Faith (CTA-USA document), 152

Prophetic radicalism (Catholics type), 5–6

Public dissent
Beckman comment, 161; Gutsgell examples, 160–161

Q

Quinlan, Margaret, 55

Quinn, John R., 21

Quintero, Mary, 255

R

Radday, Harold (letter), 133

Radicalization, necessity (absence), 274–275

Rainbow Girls, 127, 158

Ratzinger, Joseph
Christianity perspective, 5; conscience, 1; female ordained priests, perspective, 166–167

Re, Battistia, 222–223
documentation request, 224; letter/administrative decision, contrast, 225–226

Reedy, John, 56
bishop perspective, 277–278; editorial response, 49–50

Reese, Thomas, 129
ambiguity dissipation perspective, 147

Reeves, Bob, 133, 135, 136, 173, 175, 177–181
McShane contact, 190

Religion
education, 67–73 concerns, documentation, 67–68; school location, 70; media ignorance, Bruskewitz opinion, 151; seriousness, 16

ReligiousSisters, Sisters' Council (usage), 74

Religious sisters (Eucharistic Ministers),

Flavin prohibitions, 77

Reuther, Rosemary Radford, 101

Ribadeneira, Diego, 135, 175

Rite of Christian Initiation of Adults (RCIA) program, involvement, 15–16

Rite of Institution of Readers, usage, 36

Roman Catholic, Bruskewitz definition, 132–133

Roman Catholic Church
CALL, relationship, 60–61; dedication, 51; experience, change, 2–3; hierarchy, power, 7; interest, CTA promotion, 132; marriage preparation program, examination, 16; ordained ministry, women (involvement), 42; structure, complexity, 9; Rotelle, John E.; encouragement, 87; letter, 92

Ruether, Rosemary Radford, 111, 179
Lincoln diocese attack, 244; Nebraska Wesleyan University speech, 244; *Southern Nebraska Register* attack, 244

Ruetz, Robert (CTA comments), 169–170

Ruff, Joe, 179, 181

S

Saint Michael the Archangel Chapel, 127

Sanchez, Mary, 174, 175

Schaeffer, Pamela, 134, 180, 181

Schevtdhuk, Liz, 54, 55

Scripture readings, women
Bruskewitz allowance, 95–96; Flavin prohibition, 87

Second Vatican Council. *See* Vatican II

Seiker, Daniel (Vasa communication), 199

Seiker, Francis (CTAN membership renewal), 155

Seiker, Marilyn, 52, 54, 92
CALL member, 26; CTAN membership

renewal, 155; Flavin meeting, 69–70; freedom, hope, 88; interview, 177, 178; Vatican II examination, 33

Seminary training, UNL problems, 77

Service of Light, 258

Sex abuse audits
attention, 254–255

Sex abuse audits, Lincoln diocese non-compliance, 249–255

Sharn, Lori, 135

Sheehan, Daniel, 89
assistance, McCown gratitude, 83; communication, 65–66; letter, 92; Peterson communication, 65

Sisters' Council
formation, 77; usage, 74

Smaller but purer (Benedict XVI phrase), 5

Smith, Darci, 133

Society of Saint Pius X (Lefebvre Group), 127

Soleto, Nicole, 253

Southern Nebraska Register (SNR), 33–34
Anderson article, 131–132; Crowley attack, McShane response, 241; defamation claim, 240–241; Dissipating Ambiguities, publication, 127–128; editorial, Reedy response, 49–50; excommunication information, 138–139; extra-synodal legislation, publication, 127, 184; Human Life International advertisement, 238–239; Kealy, editor, 47; lector policy change, announcement, 107; Overheard at the Call to Holiness Conference (opinion piece), 168–169; *Pastoral Letter on Catholic Doctrine and Practice* (Curtiss) reprint, 160

Speaking of Faith (radio program), 237

Spirit, mediators, 8

St. Catherine of Sienna, CALL Patron Saint selection, 50–51

St. John the Apostle parish, bulletin, 60–61

St. Teresa Parish, Hennessey contract, 67–68

Stammer, Larry B., 176

Standpoint theory, 270–271

Steichen, Donna, 101
Call to Holiness appearance, 164; CTA conspiracy comments, 167

Stenftenagel, Jan, 20, 135

Stevens, Betty, 92

Stork, Joseph J., 141

Structure, duality (Giddens), 8

Subsidiarity
preference, 194–197; principle, 195

Sullivan, John, 30

Sullivan, Pat, 175
archdiocesan perspective, 268; extra-synodal legislation perspective, 145–146

Supreme Tribunal of the Apostolic Signatura, competence (absence), 225

Survivors Network of those Abused by Priests (SNAP), 253

T

Tabor, Pam, 267

Tafoya, Arthur (extra-synodal legislation comment), 143

Teens Encounter Christ (TEC)
program, initiation (attempt), 70–71; retreat, involvement, 14–15

Thavis, John, 176, 180

Thorburn, Timothy, 134, 135, 181
CTAN student report, 120; excommunication comments, 208–209; extra-synodal legislation: medicinal penalty, Canon Law (ambiguity), 130; publication, 127–128; letter, impact, 120–121; Mahoney State Park student reports, 202; student observers, McShane letter, 123: Thorburn response, 123–124; *Weekend Edition* (NPR)

appearance, 204

Traditionalism (Catholics type), 5–6

Transubstantiation, concept (difficulty), 13–14

U

Ungodly Rage: The Hidden Face of Catholic Feminism (Steichen), 101
Ruether response, 101

United States bishops, CALL documentation, 66–78

United States Conference of Catholic Bishops (USCCB), 52
CTA discussion, 139; Dolan election, 4; feedback sheets, response, 114; justice, dialogue initiative, 114; sex abuse audits, Bruskewitz nonparticipation, 249–254; sex abuse/minors issue, 249

University of Minnesota, Newman Center (classes), 31–32

University of Nebraska Lincoln (UNL)
faculty worship, prohibition, 75; seminary training, problems, 77; worship, student refusal, 72–73

Unsworth, Timothy, 177

Untener, Kenneth (extra-synodal legislation comment), 144

U.S. bishops, legislation response, 142–144

U.S. Catholic editorial, 40

V

Vasa, Robert, 56
"Bearing Witness," 287–288; CTAN communication, 198–199; Diocesan Tribunal, chair, 195; diocese, polarization, 287; Director of the Installed Lector Program, 38–39; dissenting opinion perspective (Casler interview), 129–130; loyalty oath, 286–287; McShane, communication, 46

Vatican
ambassador the United States, McShane

communication, 186; Council, Haley examination, 32; Crowley invitation, 240; CTA discussion, 139; CTAN appeal: advantage, 196; avoidance, 199–200; winning, chances, 226; CTAN contact, requirement, 222; direct CTAN appeal, 196; officials, Catholic News Service interview, 150

Vatican I (First Vatican Council), reforms (impact), 13

Vatican II (Second Vatican Council) Bruskewitz/CALL discussion, possibility, 98–99; documents, Diocesan Council of Catholic Women study, 31; Gaudium et Specs, 165–166; ideas, engagement, 30–33; Kelliher (priest, role), 25; pastor acceptance, 272; personal spiritual growth, 30–31; reforms, impact, 13; Seiker examination, 33; Veritatis Splendor, 191

Vitzhum, Edward F. (CCD funding), 68–69

Voboril, Mary, 178

Voices of Nebraska Catholics (newsletter), 169, 238

W

Walkowiak, Diane (authority question), 43

Walkowski, Diane, 55

Walsh, Tom, 220

Wanderer article (Gagnon quote), 165; Forum, Bruskewitz speech, 219; Moen interview, 167

Weakland, Rembert, 39–40 Bruskewitz, differences, 268; letter, 211

Weaver, Mary Jo, 20 *Being Right,* 3–4

Weavings, creation, 118

Weber, Rocky C., 240–241

Weekend Edition (NPR), Thorburn comments, 204

Weigert, Kathleen Maas, 20, 135

Welch, Richard, 180 Human Life International report, 164–165

Whalen, William J., 20, 135

Williams, Andrea S., 20, 135

Wilson, Charles M., 174, 175 Bruskewitz analysis, 140; extra-synodal legislation comment, 145

Winner, Frank, 167

Wirpsa, Leslie, 53, 135, 174, 175, 177, 178 Catholic divide article, 140

Wittberg, Patricia, 20, 135

Wittenauer, Cheryl, 176

Wojtyla, Karol, 265

Women discrimination, 38–39; emotional support roles, limitation, 44; ordained priests, Ratzinger perspective, 166–167; ordination: Bruskewitz perspective, 106; Catholic support, 129; social leadership, 44; speakers, attacks, 239–246

Women in the Priesthood? (Hauke), 100–101

Wood, Julia, 270–271

Word of God, reading (role), 36–37, 40

Z

Zahrt, Robert, 55

Zavoral, Nolan, 136

Zeleny, Jeff, 175, 177, 178

Zirkel, Don, 54

Zorn, Theodore E., 21

Zuerlein, Damian, 269